INDIA
ON OUR MINDS

INDIA
ON OUR MINDS

Foreword by Goh Chok Tong

Essays by Tharman Shanmugaratnam and
50 Singaporean Friends of India

Editors

Tommy Koh
Ambassador-at-Large, Singapore

Hernaikh Singh
Institute of South Asian Studies,
National University of Singapore

World Scientific

NEW JERSEY • LONDON • SINGAPORE • BEIJING • SHANGHAI • HONG KONG • TAIPEI • CHENNAI • TOKYO

Published by

World Scientific Publishing Co. Pte. Ltd.
5 Toh Tuck Link, Singapore 596224
USA office: 27 Warren Street, Suite 401-402, Hackensack, NJ 07601
UK office: 57 Shelton Street, Covent Garden, London WC2H 9HE

Library of Congress Cataloging-in-Publication Data
Names: Shanmugaratnam, Tharman, author | Koh, Tommy T. B. (Tommy Thong Bee), 1937– editor. | Singh, Hernaikh, editor. | Goh, Chok Tong, 1941– writer of foreword.
Title: India on our minds / foreword by Goh Chok Tong ; essays by Tharman Shanmugaratnam and 50 Singaporean friends of India ; editors Tommy Koh, Hernaikh Singh.
Description: New Jersey : World Scientific, [2020] | Includes index.
Identifiers: LCCN 2020037905 | ISBN 9789811224515 (hardcover) | ISBN 9789811224904 (paperback) | ISBN 9789811224522 (ebook) | ISBN 9789811224539 (ebook)
Subjects: LCSH: India--Foreign public opinion, Singaporean. | India--Relations--Singapore. | Singapore--Relations--India. | ASEAN.
Classification: LCC DS404 .S48 2020 | DDC 303.48/25405957--dc23
LC record available at https://lccn.loc.gov/2020037905

British Library Cataloguing-in-Publication Data
A catalogue record for this book is available from the British Library.

For any available supplementary material, please visit
https://www.worldscientific.com/worldscibooks/10.1142/11944#t=suppl

Printed in Singapore

Contents

Section II
Thinking About The Present

Foreword

India is very much on Singapore's mind. Our trading and cultural links go back centuries. Indian merchants were among the first to develop commercial ties with Singapore and Southeast Asia. Singapore's name is of Sanskrit origin. After independence, India was instrumental in helping Singapore gain entry into the Non-Aligned Movement (NAM). Our strategic priorities diverged during the Cold War but began to converge once again with Prime Minister P V Narasimha Rao's 'Look East' policy of economic reform and liberalisation in the early 1990s.

Today, Singapore's ties with India are strong, substantive and broad-based. We contribute to each other's prosperity. In 2015, to mark the 50th anniversary of diplomatic relations, Prime Minister Narendra Modi and Prime Minister Lee Hsien Loong signed the India-Singapore Strategic Partnership to strengthen our relations in many areas, such as defence, trade and culture. Our economic relations are anchored by the India-Singapore Comprehensive Economic Cooperation Agreement. Since signing it in 2005, bilateral trade in goods has doubled from S$11.9 billion in 2004 to S$26.4 billion in 2018. Singapore has S$57 billion of investments in India, while India has a stock of S$27 billion of investments in Singapore. With many flights each week connecting Singapore to multiple Indian cities, more than 1.4 million Indian tourists visited Singapore in 2018.

When I was Prime Minister, India beckoned. Singapore began to forge a long-term strategic alliance with India based on the complementarity of our strengths. We supported the strengthening of India's ties with the Association of Southeast Asian Nations and its entry into the East Asia Summit.

All this began after I first met Prime Minister Rao at the 10th Summit Conference of the NAM in Jakarta in 1992. Later, he invited me to visit India as Chief Guest on its Republic Day in 1994. I also built up a close relationship with Finance Minister Manmohan Singh who later became Prime Minister. I have the greatest of respect for him.

The global community shunned India in the 1990s after its 1991 economic crisis and the subsequent International Monetary Fund bailout. Even so, I was convinced that India would emerge as an economic power. I "infected" Singapore with a "mild India fever". The fever did not become full blown but I never lost faith in India. I continue to visit India regularly to engage its leaders, including current Prime Minister Modi who I first met in 2006 when he was Chief Minister of Gujarat.

India has immense economic potential. It has a deep pool of intellectual talent and daring entrepreneurs. Its many world-class companies have strong technological capabilities. Its young population, with the right vocational education and skills training, will be another tremendous asset. Through its 'Make in India' initiative, India is poised to take the next economic leap to become a global manufacturer. To achieve these goals, India will need to stay the course on its path of economic reform and stay connected to the rest of the world through global and regional trade agreements. Additionally, India can do more to enhance its transport connectivity with the rest of the world. It can be a global aviation hub, in addition to being a major tourist destination.

India should play a more active role in making this the Asian century. Asia can close our developmental gap with the West. Our fundamentals remain robust. However, one key risk to the Asian century is the ongoing strategic rivalry between the United States (US) and China. We must try to head off an ugly confrontation and advocate strategic co-operation.

India can exercise a moderating influence. It does not suffer the historical legacy and trust deficit that exists amongst the East Asian countries. Its democracy makes it ideologically closer to the US and the West than to China. It is not a strategic rival of China, at least not yet. India can be part of the "Voice of Moderation" which I have been advocating. This Voice is not a bloc or a new grouping but simply the concerted voice of concerned countries, leaders, institutions, media, business and people who want to avert a catastrophic clash between the US and China. Only by speaking in unison will the global powers take heed of the "Voice of Moderation".

The "Voice of Moderation" should be global but with a strong Asian accent. India's participation will give it weight. India should share its vision of its role in the region so that we can build up mutual trust and forge a common cause for peace and prosperity. With this common cause, Asia can chart its own way forward rather than simply respond to external forces and trends. There is much that we can do together to ensure a bright future for our peoples.

I am pleased that this book is being published to explain India's significance to Singapore and to the world. Full credit goes to the book's editors, Ambassador-at-Large Tommy Koh and Hernaikh Singh from the Institute of South Asian Studies, for this collection of essays by Singaporean thought leaders on a wide range of substantive issues on India and India-Singapore relations.

I hope readers of this book gain new insights into India's accomplishments and its future.

Goh Chok Tong
Emeritus Senior Minister
Singapore

Preface

We owe this book to Mr Chandrajit Banerjee. He is the Director General of the Confederation of Indian Industry. He visited Singapore in 2019. During that visit, he called on Professor Tommy Koh. At the end of the call, he requested Professor Koh to write a book on India. The latter responded that instead of writing a book on India, he would consider editing one. We would like to thank Ambassador Gopinath Pillai, Chairman of the Institute of South Asian Studies in the National University of Singapore, for his encouragement.

India is a very important country. It is the second most-populous nation and the largest democracy in the world. It is a country of continental size. It is the fifth largest economy in the world. It has an ancient and rich civilisation. It is the birthplace of four of the world's major religions — Hinduism, Buddhism, Jainism and Sikhism.

India has been in contact with Southeast Asia for over a thousand years. We share similar traditions, customs and cultures, dressing styles, languages and even cuisines. On the whole, India's interactions with our region had been peaceful and benign. India is a strategic partner of the Association of Southeast Asian Nations (ASEAN).

Singapore's connections with India are both deep and broad. At one time, the British ruled Singapore from Bengal. Several laws of Singapore were transplanted from British India. The British also brought Indians to work in Singapore. At the same time, Indian traders travelled to the island state in search of better business opportunities. In more recent times, Indian professionals have also joined the employment ranks in Singapore. As a result, ethnic Indians make up a significant part of Singapore's population. An Indian language, Tamil, is one of Singapore's official languages. There are extensive people-to-people ties between the two countries.

An Indian leader and a Singapore leader brought about a renaissance in the relationship between the two countries. They are India's former Prime Minister, Mr P V Narasimha Rao, and Singapore's second Prime Minister, Mr Goh Chok Tong. Mr Rao convinced Mr Goh that India had made a paradigm shift in favour of opening up its economy. Mr Goh believed him and responded by igniting a "mild India fever". He urged Singapore to engage India and to trade more with and invest more in India. As a result, there exists between the two countries, a very warm, substantive and trustful relationship. Mr Goh was India's champion in ASEAN. He helped Mr Rao to actualise his 'Look East' policy.

Many Singaporeans, however, do not understand India. They find India confusing. The purpose of our book is to throw light on this fascinating and complex country. We are very grateful to the 51 Singaporeans who have answered our call and written lucid essays on their knowledge about India, their experiences with India, their understanding of India and their hopes for India. We are particularly grateful to Mr Goh for his wonderful foreword and Senior Minister Tharman Shanmugaratnam for his illuminating essay.

We hope that the book will be of interest to Singaporeans who are interested in India and Indians who are interested in Singapore.

Finally, we would like to thank our publisher, World Scientific Publishing, our editor, Kim Tan and Jimmy Low, the designer of the book.

Tommy Koh
Hernaikh Singh

Section I

THINKING ABOUT THE PAST

1

India's Early Trade with Singapore and Southeast Asia

A. Mani

Introduction

The mercantile ambitions of the British East India Company (EIC) for trade expansion from India to China and Southeast Asia led to the acquisition of a new port on the island of Singapore. This essay provides a commentary on India's early trade with Singapore and Southeast Asia in the early 19th century. The discussion is limited to the period from 1818 to 1867. It is to be noted that in the years between 1818 and 1867, Singapore's position underwent a swift political transition due to a number of events. In 1826, as part of the Straits Settlements, Singapore became the Fourth Presidency of British India; in 1832, it became the centre of the Straits Settlements; 1833 marked the end of the EIC's monopoly of the China trade, and the abolition of slavery and forced transportation of convicts; in 1841, Hong Kong came under the British rule; 1842 saw the signing of the first of the unequal treaties — the Treaty of Nanking; in 1857, the Indian rebellion took place; and in 1867, the Straits Settlements become a Crown Colony.

Trade and Shipping

During the 18th century, Britain passed several parliamentary acts to protect British textile manufacturers from competition from Indian textiles. The EIC suffered as a result of the removal of its monopoly over most exports from India to Britain. As a company dedicated to realising profits for shareholders, tea from China had become the most important product in London. However, having fewer products which China needed, the EIC had to pay for tea in specie. As specie trading was dependent on precious metals, the EIC found a saviour in opium which was grown largely in the Bengal Presidency. As the EIC still held the monopoly on opium cultivation and manufacturing in India, China was considered a vast market despite the Chinese government forbidding its importation. Smuggled opium paid for the China tea and brought cash benefits to the EIC.

In the discussion of early trade of Singapore, one must bear in mind the shortcomings of trade statistics. Trade figures understated the actual value of the commerce of the port. The port was more prosperous than was shown in the returns. Trade returns refer only to visible trade. Data for invisible trade simply do not exist. The official explanation was that a large portion of the imports was consumed by the island's population. Export returns were generally more inaccurate and understated than import returns. This arose principally from the fact that the square-rigged vessels and Asian ships engaged in the distributing trade, especially in Southeast Asia, were often not included in the statistics. Early trade statistics also suffered from the varied currencies used to indicate trade. Four currencies were used for pricing commodities, namely, Sicca Rupee, Company Rupee, Spanish Dollar (Sp$) and the Pound Sterling.

In the first two and a half years of the British Settlement of Singapore, 2,889 vessels anchored at Singapore. Seventy percent of these ships were commanded by non-European captains. Opium was the most lucrative commodity, followed by Indian piece goods, specie, European goods and tin. Over the 1820s, Singapore became a vital point connecting India, Canton and the ports across Southeast Asia.

In 1822, the Singapore port hosted 1,756 vessels. Among these, 63 square-rigged vessels arrived from India. These were vessels that crossed the Indian Ocean instead of navigating along coastal seas. The rest of the total 219 square-rigged vessels included those from Malacca and Penang (49), China (31), Manila (3) Siam (6), Cochin-China (1), Borneo (6), Bencoolen and coastal Sumatra (4) and the other Eastern ports (21). It is evident that the Singapore port brought British India's trade closer to Southeast Asia and China as indicated by the number of native vessels visiting Singapore port which totalled 1,537. Of these, 362 were from Penang and Malacca; 5 from China; 31 from Siam; 9 from Cochin-China; 94 from Borneo; 45 from Java; 217 from Bencoolen and the coast of Sumatra; and 774 from the other Eastern ports. Singapore became an entrepôt for goods from India, Southeast Asia and China.

In 1822, the key imports included opium (359 chests) valued at Sp$684,800; specie valued at Sp$452,044 and Indian piece goods valued at Sp$498,727. The value of total imports was Sp$3,680,206. Thus, India's goods were significant import items in early Singapore. The main exports in 1822 included opium (339 chests) valued at Sp$593,018; specie valued at Sp$424,125; and Indian piece goods (7,601 corges) valued at Sp$365,323. The value of total exports was Sp$3,172,332. The EIC used India's goods to advance its mercantile profits.

The EIC was determined to protect and expand the opium trade which earned Calcutta between half a million and one million pound sterling annually. While two-thirds of the company's opium went to China, about 1,500 chests went to the Southeast Asian Archipelago earning merchants a profit of 30 to 40 percent. The EIC enabled Chinese and native traders to carry opium throughout Southeast Asia. As each chest of opium contained 40 balls of opium, countless small traders buying a few balls became a marketing strategy. These small balls of opium were exchanged for gold or specie.

In the early 19th century, China tea and Bengal opium underwent transformations that affected India's trade with Singapore. Firstly, the EIC attempted to replace its dependence on China tea by attempting to cultivate tea in British India. With the help of hired Chinese tea cultivators, the first batch of Assam tea arrived in London in November 1838. Assam tea and the Assam region became a hot topic of discussion in the British trade process in 1839. Secondly, the introduction of Malwa opium from western India into the Chinese market posed a challenge for the EIC as it could no longer hope to be the exclusive supplier of Indian opium. Private Indian and European traders pioneered the export of Malwa opium to China. The EIC was unable to attain success in the opium trade due to the rampant smuggling of the drug through the Gujarat coast. Thirdly, the abolition of the EIC's monopoly of trade with China led to an increase in the number of private traders operating in the South China Sea from 1834 onwards. Most of these private traders were attracted to the lucrative opium smuggling enterprise centred on Canton. Among the private British firms in China engaged in opium smuggling, the two most prominent were Jardine & Matheson and Dent & Co. By the 1820s, a substantial portion of the drug sent out from Calcutta and Bombay was consigned to them. Of the two, Jardine & Matheson, the bigger of the two firms, pushed its business more aggressively.

After the early years, the opium trade of Singapore with China, however, became insignificant when compared with that of direct shipping from India. Trade figures on the import of opium into China from Singapore and India showed a widening gap in the periods between 1836 and 1866. China's import of Bengal and Malwa opium from Singapore was 418 chests in 1835–36. It increased to 3,796 chests in 1840–42 but declined to 907 chests in 1865–66. It can be said that the rest of the opium exports from Singapore went to Southeast Asia. However, direct opium imports by China from India increased significantly from 30,202 chests in 1835–36 to 76,863 chests by 1856–57.

In the days before the advent of the opium clippers, the passage up the China Sea by the Eastern passage during the northeast monsoon involved great difficulty and delay. Opium merchants, therefore, preferred keeping the stocks of opium and storing them in Singapore.

With the advent of opium clippers, Singapore became even more unimportant as a stopping place except for provisions and repairs. In 1832, the clipper, Red Rover, the first vessel designed specially to travel on the China Sea against the strength of the northeast monsoon, made a stop at the Singapore port. Singapore, however, still served as a useful intermediate station for the opium country ships. Despite the introduction of the clippers, opium trade from Singapore to Southeast Asia increased. Opium export steadily increased from 1,284 chests in 1836 to 3,196 chests in 1846 and 4,689 chests in 1856 before tapering off to 3,081 chests in 1866.

India's share of shipping activities at the Singapore harbour is another indicator of trade between India and Singapore. Data on the proportion of the shipping of various countries in the Singapore harbour between 1829–30 and 1865–66 provide valuable insights into India's trade with Singapore. The three major participants who contributed to the shipping activities at the Singapore port in 1829–30 were India (24.3 percent), the Malay Archipelago (34.5 percent) and China (23.5 percent). They jointly contributed to 82.3 percent of the total shipping activities at the harbour.

India's shipping activities formed a quarter of the total shipping activities at the harbour until 1842–43. However, its activities began to decline steadily and were reduced to 11 percent of the total shipping activities at the harbour in the 1840s and beyond. China and Southeast Asia steadily experienced increasing shipping activities at the Singapore port. By 1853–54, India's proportion was 13.6 percent, while Southeast Asia and China accounted for 35.1 percent and 21.1 percent of these activities respectively. The three regions, however, jointly contributed to 70.8 percent of the shipping activities during this period.

These three regions continued to dominate the shipping activities at the Singapore harbour till the opening of the Suez Canal in 1869. The opening of the Suez Canal and the size of the ships reduced the triumvirate regions' share to 69.8 percent and 67.8 percent in 1854 and 1866 respectively. As India's goods, especially opium, could be shipped directly to China without being transferred through Singapore, India's shipping activities declined steadily. In addition, the Indian Rebellion and Britain's direct rule replacing the EIC changed India's position of India's trade with Singapore and Southeast Asia.

Conclusion

Beginning with the Bengal Presidency, British India played an important role in the mercantile development of Singapore. The EIC depended on China tea as an early commodity to make huge profits by exporting it to London. Having nothing of value to sell to China, the EIC turned to promoting opium despite its import ban by China. Its early commodities for trade with China and Southeast Asia were Indian goods, namely, Indian textile piece goods, raw sugar, raw silk and opium. The use of specie (especially silver) for trade could not be sustained for long. Opium became a major item of trade for the EIC with Canton and Southeast Asia. As a smuggled commodity into China via Hong Kong and distributed widely in Southeast Asia, opium provided the much-needed income for the operation of the early Singapore establishment from Calcutta. The EIC was able to establish the trade link between India, Southeast Asia and China via Singapore. The advent of steam ships and the opening of the Suez Canal changed the early trade flows among India, Singapore and Southeast Asia.

2

Red Ambassador, *Parathas* and Other Joys

Eirliani Abdul Rahman

The India in my mind's eye, writing now during the COVID-19 pandemic, seems so far away, bereft of its tumultuous smells, colours and sounds. Now and then, a picture pops up on a friend's timeline on Facebook that reminds me of what I miss: a pink stuccoed *haveli* (mansion), a fierce chicken *korma* (a cream/yoghurt-based Indian dish) scooped up with homemade *naan* (flat leavened bread), elaborate *henna* (reddish-brown dye) patterns on a bride's fair hands, a peacock — its feathers glinting emerald green — strutting the grounds of some long-forgotten fort.

I served as Political Counsellor at the Singapore High Commission in New Delhi from December 2011 to December 2014, and then took a sabbatical for a year to work with the Nobel laureate Kailash Satyarthi, before resigning from the Singapore Foreign Service in December 2015.

I had chosen India as my posting as it was an important one for my country, and also because I wanted to be closer to my parents. I had spent a good 10 years of my life in Europe, first in England and Moscow for my studies, and then in Berlin for my first posting with the Singapore Foreign Service as First Secretary (Political).

India, if anything, is a study in contrasts.

This was where I bought my first car, an Ambassador, whose production has since been discontinued by Hindustan Motors. I had it customised and painted fire engine red and the seats reupholstered in leather. With my blue diplomatic licence plate, my car was hard to miss. I was told that there were only three of us with such a car in the capital: the other two being the German Ambassador and the principal of the French school. I would often return to it after a shopping trip seeing tourists and locals taking photographs of my car, much to the bemusement of my driver.

I had trained my driver well. He would help me with my errands. However, I was wary and would sometimes feel ashamed at the thought that if he knew how much my friends and I would spend on a meal in a five-star hotel. In a city where one could purchase a *samosa* (fried or baked pastry) for ₹7 (about S$0.13) and hot milky *chai* (tea) for even less, we could easily spend ₹2,600 (S$48.60) each on a buffet lunch at the hotel.

Right next to the Singapore High Commission's compound in Chanakyapuri, several squatters had moved onto a vacant plot of land. It was by no means the worst slum that I had seen but it made me more cognisant of the poverty that surrounded me. I would be awakened each morning by the crowing of a rooster from the slum. Children would often play in the streets, their laughter punctuating the evening air, their slippers creating dust where their feet fell.

India changed me. This was where the Gini coefficient was no longer some abstract theory. On one occasion, we had a visiting delegation from Singapore. While on the bus, each delegate was presented with a lavish breakfast pack purchased from a hotel as we needed to hit the road early in the morning. After they had finished their breakfast, I took to the microphone on the bus and requested that they leave behind on the bus any food or drinks that they did not plan to consume so that my colleagues could give them to the slum dwellers next to the High Commission's compound.

However, this wasn't about charity or poverty pornography. There is much more to India than that.

When I get on a video conference call with my friends during this current lockdown, I am struck by their resilience and derring-do. Indians have a term for their creative problem-solving skills: *jugaad* in Hindi, which loosely translates to having a 'flexible and innovative approach to solving a problem by using limited resources'. I have not seen a calmer, more creative lot when the situation warrants it. When COVID-19 struck India, friends, who were previously involved in children rights or advocated for LGBTQI (Lesbian, Gay, Bisexual, Transgender, Queer and Intersex) folks, started food distribution efforts to help daily wage labourers, and migrant workers and their children in Delhi, Mumbai and further afield. Those whose families own factories switched to making personal protective equipment such as medical grade face masks. I observed the numerous messages on WhatsApp in the early weeks of April 2020 as my friends in India tried to figure out what was lacking and what was needed on the ground.

Indians are generous to a fault and they make fiercely loyal friends. They do not take 'no' for an answer. They will persist until you relent, succumbing to their very many calls and text messages. They will constantly beckon you home and pamper you with their home-cooked meals. I was startled, at first, by their directness and confidence in pointing out the flaws in an argument. Indians just love a rigorous intellectual debate; I was never in want of good company.

At times, it was difficult being a female diplomat in a patriarchal society. When we met with older Indian bureaucrats and politicians, they tended to look to my male colleagues for the answers. At one National Day reception hosted by the Singapore High Commission in New Delhi, as I stood at the head of the receiving line to greet the guests, many of the Indian guests assumed that I was the spouse of a male colleague standing next to me. However, being a female diplomat in New Delhi at the time also worked to my advantage, as there were fewer of us, compared to my male peers. I suppose it was easier for people to remember me.

Having a Muslim name was never an issue for me in India. Like anywhere in the world, in the social milieu I moved in, then as now, one's commonality with others often came to the forefront more than one's differences. The India I know is all-embracing. Hindus and Muslims alike flock to the *dargah* (shrines) of the Sufi saints, listening to the *qawwali* (Sufi devotional music). In intellectual circles, Faiz Ahmed Faiz is a beloved poet. The February 2020 riots in New Delhi were, I hope, an aberration.

Our memories are, by necessity, a selective, fickle thing. In his book, *Midnight's Children*, Salman Rushdie spoke thus of 'memory's truth':

> It selects, eliminates, alters, exaggerates, minimizes, glorifies, and vilifies also; but in the end it creates its own reality, its heterogeneous but usually coherent version of events; and no sane human being ever trusts someone else's version more than his own.

What are my favourite memories of India? Well, these would be wandering through the ancient alleyways of Old Delhi in search of the famous Gali Paranthe Wali, a narrow street in Chandni Chowk, for the aroma and taste of hot curry mopped up with freshly made *parathas* (flatbread); picnicking with friends on the lush grounds of the Lodi Gardens and exploring the Mughal-era tombs; bird watching in the jungles of Rajasthan and looking out for tigers, slothful in the summer heat, in Ranthambore National Park; sharing food on the long train journeys in the second-class cabins en route to rock climbing outdoors in the states of Uttarakhand and Madhya Pradesh; and watching the mango leaves outside my balcony drip in the monsoon rain.

India, you are intoxicating, chaotic, beautiful and generous. India, you are missed.

3

The Global Plot behind the 1915 Singapore Sepoy Mutiny

Umej Bhatia

In the summer of 1914, India shone as the jewel in the crown of the British Empire. The diamond-shaped island of Singapore glistened as a strategic pendant on the British-controlled chain of trade connecting India to China. Mighty Britannia ruled not only the waves, but also controlled crucial infrastructure under the seas, connecting its far-flung empire in a form of telegraphic imperialism. With steamers from 50 shipping lines calling at its port, Singapore served as a key node in this global network of trans-imperial submarine telegraph cables and shipping routes.

As the world's seventh busiest port straddling the approaches to a sea, a pair of oceans and a trio of straits, Singapore's land-based defence focused on protecting its world-class harbour. In the shadow of the First World War, the city-settlement's military garrison included an all-white British infantry battalion and an Indian one led by Hindustani speaking white officers. Known as sepoys, the Indian soldiers of the island's 5th Native Light Infantry were stationed at Alexandra Barracks near the harbour. The all-white battalion at Tanglin Barracks guarded the European settlement and town centre. Primarily Muslims from

Eastern Punjab (today's Haryana), Delhi and its surroundings, half the sepoy battalion was ethnic Pathan and the other half Ranghar (Muslim Rajputs). Race and religion aside, the 5th was known for having stayed loyal to the British during the 1857 Indian Rebellion.

The 1857 rebellion was traumatic for the British. The uprising by Hindus and Muslims began with a mutiny of sepoys in the army of the British East India Company near Delhi. With 6,000 British soldiers and civilians killed and nearly one million Indian casualties, 1857 shook the foundations of Britain's autocratic rule in India. Indian nationalists framed the revolt as a fight for freedom — labelling it *1857 Ka Swatantrya Sama* (The 1857 Indian War of Independence). This was the title of a 1907 book by a 24-year-old Indian revolutionary named Vinayak Damodar Savarkar. Secretly researching his book in the British Library in London, Savarkar published his historical exposé on the revolt's 50th anniversary. His 1857 history would help to light the fire of the *Ghadar*, leading to an abortive pan-Indian rebellion in 1915 that spilled into Singapore.

Shipped from Calcutta to Singapore in April 1914 for their first overseas post, the 800 sepoys of the 5th had little clue of the troubles ahead. The drama that followed was a product of British ineptitude, European geopolitics, Pan-Islamism, Asian maritime connectivity and a shadowy network of expatriate Indians supporting the mutiny movement in North America. The glue that held the 5th together despite clashing loyalties of race, religion and regiment would come unstuck in the coming global conflict.

After the war's outbreak in August 1914, Singapore's all-white infantry battalion was sent to fight in France, replaced by a mixed battalion of Sikh and Punjabi Muslim sepoys of the Malay States Guides regiment from Taiping in Perak. The Guides operated as a military force for the internal defence of the Federated Malay States. Arriving in Singapore, the Guides' Punjabi-speaking sepoys joined the Hindustani-speaking sepoys of the 5th. The sepoys of both battalions came from contiguous areas of the Punjab and Haryana. They had the opportunity to share notes and compare terms of service but were separated from Singapore's disciplined 200-strong Sikh Police Contingent.

Although the sepoys were ring-fenced from the Sikh police, the island-settlement's inter-connectedness as a key node for trade and transport proved a vulnerability. The sepoys were thus easily exposed to agents of influence and political viruses passing through the port. With war on the Western front transformed into a global conflict, the British battled a foe in Europe and one in Asia. As the Ottoman Turks allied with Imperial Germany, the British faced a Muslim enemy state with the power to declare holy war and exploit a major weakness of British India. Muslim sepoys recognised the Ottoman Sultan as the Caliph of Islam, spiritual head of all Sunni Muslims. The Germans persuaded the Ottomans to issue a series of *fatwa* (religious opinions) to turn Indian Muslims against the British Empire. Responding with *fatwa* from loyalist Indian clerics, the British and German/Ottoman's 'rival *jihads*' soon became entangled in the gathering force of a pan-Indian mutiny movement.

To evade British secret intelligence, Indian nationalists planted overseas bases across Europe. Connections enabled by open borders allowed them to foment sedition worldwide. Migrating to North America for a better life, Punjabi farmers and mill workers were frustrated by race laws and casual racism. The disaffected migrant workers soon formed an alliance with exiled Hindu radicals and Bengali students that crossed lines of class and race. In the then global revolutionary hub of San Francisco, the Indian diaspora established the headquarters of its movement, officially known as the Hindustan Association of the Pacific Coast. In 1913, the Indians published a revolutionary newspaper in San Francisco called *Ghadar.* Calling on Indians to unite, rise and throw the British out of India, *Ghadar* meant mutiny or revolt. Printed in four Indian languages, the newspaper was inspired by Savarkar's book on the 1857 mutiny and covered episodes of racism and repression in British India. As its readership expanded, *Ghadar* became synonymous with the militant movement it fostered — the *Ghadar.*

Ghadar's founding editor was a talented but mercurial revolutionary named Har Dayal. For a brief time just before the First World War, the Delhi-born Punjabi became the movement's main ideologue in North America. Influenced by Savarkar, Har Dayal abandoned his prestigious civil service scholarship at Oxford University to oppose British rule. Hunted by imperial police, Har Dayal sought refuge in the United States where he roused expatriate Indian workers and students with his revolutionary speeches. Har Dayal was actively encouraged by German agents who backed the mutiny movement to subvert the British.

Racism and the rules against non-white immigration to dominions of the British Empire remained a major sticking point for the Indians in North America. White-ruled outposts erected subtle barriers to entry by brown-skinned British subjects. Matters came to a head in 1914 with the incident of the Komagata Maru, a Japanese passenger steamer chartered by Singapore Sikh businessman Gurdit Singh. Imbibing revolutionary ideas from *Ghadar*, Gurdit launched a protest voyage to challenge the colour bar put up by white Canadian nationalists had erected with imperial connivance. His enterprise attracted migrants, revolutionaries and ex-sepoys battling for equal rights. Bound for Canada via Singapore and several East Asian ports, the ship was denied entry to Vancouver. Chased away by a Canadian warship, the Komagata Maru was forced back to India where several passengers were killed in an encounter with British security forces near Calcutta. The ship's fate became a rallying cry for *Ghadar* propagandists.

In the opening months of the First World War, a stretched British Empire's vulnerability to seaborne attacks also emboldened the revolutionaries. It took a single German naval cruiser to terrorise allied shipping across the Indian Ocean. Known as the SMS Emden, the commerce raider bottled up Singapore's western approaches and created panic by shelling Madras port and carrying out a daring raid on Penang harbour. The German lone wolf also targetted isolated island relay stations in Britain's global 'All Red' telegraph cable network. British shipping and imperial prestige suffered several blows before the Emden was finally sunk in November 1914. Some of its captured crew were then interned in Singapore, where the sailors plotted further damage on British interests by swaying the loyalties of their sepoy guards. The sepoys formed Singapore's single largest armed force. The Komagata Maru incident and the exploits of the Emden played heavily on their minds.

As perceptions of German naval superiority and British weakness began to take shape, Indian revolutionaries in America prepared to strike while Britain was bogged down in Europe. Under the flag of revolt, the *Ghadar* revolutionaries devised a plan with three parts. One, rouse politically conscious Indians in North America and Asian port cities on the Pacific-Indian Ocean steamer route. Two, ship these men in insurgent cells back to the Punjab in India. Three, trigger sepoy mutinies in the Empire's overseas garrisons and India. Properly executed, the plan would produce a general uprising in the homeland to topple the Raj and secure India's independence. As Savarkar envisioned it and Har Dayal sold it, the immediate goal was a second and successful revolt, 60 years after the 1857 mutiny.

Steamers operated by Japanese-owned shipping lines unloaded revolutionaries in transit ports like Singapore, Penang, Manila, Rangoon and other outposts. Returning to India via these ports, the *Ghadar* party conspirators encouraged sepoys in garrisons of the Eastern Empire to mutiny. At the same time, Pan-Islamist supporters and German agents coordinated stealthily across bases in Southeast Asia via trade and shipping routes and the regional consular network to turn Indian Muslim sepoys. Stoked by appeals to faith and freedom, some of the sepoys decided to make a fateful choice — to embrace a cocktail of *jihad* and *Ghadar* mutiny.

First, the Sikh and Muslim sepoys of the Malay States Guides infantry refused to be deployed overseas. Packed off back in disgrace to their Perak headquarters, the near-mutinous Guides took some pride in standing up for their rights. Only a single section of apparently loyal Guides artillery remained in Singapore, along with the sepoys of the 5th. They were clearly affected by the actions of the Guides infantry and they were resentful about pulling double duty. The revolutionary intriguers, encouraged by their success, latched on to pre-existing grievances in the 5th. Morale in the ranks plummeted over the high cost of living, the additional mobilisation duties and sepoy factionalism in the bubble of barracks life. The volatile chemistry of uncertainty, fear and powerlessness was stirred by spies, propagandists and revolutionaries. As the 5th's sepoys prepared to redeploy from Singapore, uncertainty over their destination deepened tensions to breaking point. Under the pressure of these various forces, half the battalion of Ranghars rose up in mutiny on the eve of their transfer from Singapore to Hong Kong. The other half, the Pathans, mostly stayed loyal. Notably, a small number of Pathan officers held their half of the battalion together.

It was a Ranghar sepoy, Ismail Khan, who fired the first shot that signalled the start of the mutiny on 15 February 1915. Amidst the fire-crackers of Chinese New Year celebrations, the mutineers at Alexandra Barracks seized the ammunition store, killed British officers they encountered and made for the Guides' artillery camp to enlist its Sikhs. They then dispersed to several parts of the island, freed German prisoners of war in Tanglin Barracks, shot other British officers and civilians in town and waited for a rumoured German warship that never turned up. Altogether, the mutineers took 44 lives on the island, including British officers and enlisted men, a few Malay and Chinese civilians as well as members of the Johor Military Force (JMF).

After the initial surprise, British reinforcements from Rangoon, allied forces of Russian, French and Japanese marines, the JMF and local volunteers tracked down and killed over 50 mutineers. Two hundred sepoys were court-martialled with 47 sentenced to death. Several rounds of executions were conducted in public along the wall of Outram Prison. The British convened a Committee of Inquiry to examine the causes of the mutiny but then embargoed the final report for 50 years to cover up potential damage to imperial prestige. The myth of British invincibility was punctured as it took about 48 hours to regain the initiative, a week to establish full control of the situation and nearly two months to round up and deal with all the mutineers.

The Singapore mutiny pre-empted the larger planned revolt in India by a week. With far better intelligence in India and slipshod organisation by the Indian revolutionaries from America, the British quickly quashed the mutiny in the Punjab. Locally driven, but also part of the string of planned uprisings in India, the 1915 mutiny in Singapore signalled that all was not well with the entropic British Empire, an overlooked precursor to the eventual, hard-won success of the Indian freedom movement.

4

A Novelist's Understanding of India

Meira Chand

If I had not been obliged to settle in India in the 1970s, I may never have become a novelist. Instead, the experiences of living there became a turning point in my life. I have a complicated relationship with India. It is my father's country, land of my paternal ancestors; yet, I did not come face to face with India until I was in my early thirties. Then, the emotional effect of the country upon me and the ambivalent nature of my own feelings towards it forced me to confront, as I had not done before, both my connection to the place and the impact of it upon me. The only way I could explore this concern was through the act of writing.

The writer writes to pin down experience, and experience is processed through the senses. There can be few places where the senses and emotions are both assaulted and seduced simultaneously, as they are in India. There is nothing bland in India. Little of life is hidden away as it is in the more technologically-advanced nations of the Western world. The cycle of life and the battle to survive it — birth and death, poverty and wealth, human darkness and the light of transcendence — can all be openly observed on any Indian pavement. This close and daily ringside view of Indian life had a profound effect upon me and my writing.

All literature, in one abstract sense or another, is about the impoverishment of human existence. What tears apart the emotions for anyone fresh to India is the sight of constant abject physical poverty. Whatever may be said of India's phenomenal growth in modern times, the fact still remains that too many people spend their lives hungry and the country still has the highest child malnutrition rate in the world. Sights of human misery assail one everywhere, even in the midst of splendour. As painful as these sights are to absorb, the Indian attitude towards such wretchedness is equally distressing. Social belief in the caste system and religious belief in *karma* allow such human deprivation to actively prevail. They allow the business tycoon to step out of his gleaming mansion each morning and step into his gleaming car, ignoring the filthy hutments on the land beside his home, and to mercilessly shoo away the crippled beggar pleading for alms with which to buy food, or the child with an amputated limb, or the disabled leper in a cart pushed by another leper. Inescapably surrounded by suffering about which they can do little, people can become conditioned to the sight, and in the end chose not to see.

Appalled as I was by the human misery I must witness, I was equally entranced by the deep magnificence of Indian life. The colour and emotional warmth of the land, the horror and pathos, the magic beauty of dusk and dawn, the smell of jasmine and the sound of prayer bells and the sensuality that pervades even the darkest corner of Indian life, all did its work upon me. I wrote a great many short stories about India in the years I lived there. At some deep emotional level, I felt complete for the first time within myself, outsider though I was in my father's country.

As I wrote, I also read novels by Indian authors that were written in English, the only language in which I can read and write. My linguistic limitations meant I could not experience the writing of any regional community directly but must rely on English translations. English, however, is curiously the language of choice for many Indian authors, who could also write in their own regional tongues if they wished to but chose instead to write in the language of their colonial masters. Filtered to me through my father's experiences, and born as I was in England, the heart of the Empire, the shadow of colonialism has shaped my whole life, and my cultural duality has created deep issues of identity for me. It was, therefore, interesting to find that India itself, in its own way, was fractured by issues that were familiar to me.

The 'civilising' Christian missions of early 19th century British colonial India brought both the Book, initially in the form of the Bible, and the English language to the country. In his essay, *Signs Taken for Wonders*, the academic and critic, Homi Bhabha, asserts that the discovery of the Book allowed a practice of history and narrative to begin in India, even as it established a mode of civil authority and order, and a measure of mimesis. Yet, the establishment of the Word in the wilds of India also began a process of displacement, distortion and dislocation that in the India of today has created a strange crisis of identity. This predicament is clearly on view in the area of Indian English literature.

The rise of the Indian novel in English coincided with the emergence of Indian nationalism and the heightened sense of dislocation this nationalism aroused in the country. Already, in early Indian English literature, the emerging shape of a distinct hybridity can be seen. Early Indian novels in English anticipated the identity of India as an independent nation-state, but novelists like Raja Rao, Mulk Raj Anand and R K Narayan were aware of the contradiction of expressing an Indian identity in English, and of appropriating the English language to create an Indian idiom. In the Foreword to his novel, *Kanthapura*, Rao crystallises this dilemma when he says: "We cannot write like the English. We should not. We can only write as Indians." Bhabha, however, sees the positive effect of colonial rule in the production of such hybridisation. Salman Rushdie has also pointed out the unifying effect of the English language upon a divided and sectarian India, and how it allows two Indians, who otherwise might have no common language in which to communicate, to talk to each other in a tongue neither party hates.

Bhabha also points out that colonial rule did not repress native traditions or indeed the Indian religion. As hard as early Christian missionaries tried, little headway could be made in converting the 'heathen' against the overwhelming and all-encompassing influence of Hinduism. Since time immemorial, religion has guided the soul of India.

The early Sanskrit writings of the Vedas are as alive today as they were in the past, and still mirror India to itself. God somehow seems more present and available in India than almost anywhere else in the world. India's two great literary epics, the *Ramayana* and the *Mahabharata*, are more than mere classics of literature. They are grounded in an Indian spiritual view of life, family system and societal structure. The culture and traditions that shape both these great works are still valid in modern India.

Every day I lived in India, religion seemed to surreptitiously permeate each hour, from the strains of devotional songs played on a transistor radio by a roadside hawker, prayer bells at dawn and conch shells blown at dusk in the nearby temple, the smell of incense, the naked ash smeared aesthetic meditating on the river bank, the chanting of prayers before pink-cheeked idols and the ubiquitous religious calendars in every household and shop. In worship and ritual, through birth, marriage and death, in the workplace and the social system and in immovable caste attitudes, religion has always been the life force of India, and remains so today. Not surprisingly, it is a strong and eternal strand in much of Indian literature from Rabindranath Tagore and Raja Rao, to Arundhati Roy and her contemporaries today. When I came to write my own fiction about India, religion and its steerage of every Indian life was impossible to ignore. Human darkness and our collective search for the light of transcendence, permeated in one way or another everything I wrote.

The busy and mundane forces of life collude to hide from us our spiritual essence and the mystery of our lives. It is the task of literature to investigate and lay bare before us both the poetry and paucity of our existence. More than 30 years after I lived in India, the residue of that land continues to hum within me. After leaving the country, I wrote two novels about it that drew heavily on my experiences there and I have no doubt that I will turn to it again to provide new work. India, like nowhere else, has an ability to unveil and integrate into consciousness the source of all that is eternal in our lives. The novelist can ask for no greater inspiration.

5

A Journey No Longer at Sea... Singapore's Tamil Narrative

Nalina Gopal and Arun Mahizhnan

In the thick web of connections between India and Singapore, the strand that speaks most eloquently and enduringly of this umbilical relationship is the Tamil connection. Singapore is home to a Tamil community that originated in south India and northern Sri Lanka conducted out of it primarily by the colonial enterprise. Today, Tamils number about five percent of the littoral city-state's population and nearly 55 percent of the Indians. However, the movement of Tamils to this part of the world under the colonial rubric is but a more recent repeat of crossings undertaken in centuries past by voyaging mercantiles and others. This essay focuses on the long journey of Singapore's Tamil diasporas from sojourners to settlers.

Reconsidering 200 Years and Beyond

The narrative of Singapore's Tamils has long remained shrouded in mystery and amidst erroneous stereotypes. Tamil connections with Singapore are inextricably intertwined with that of the region in the pre-modern era. In light of recent interpretations of archaeological evidence found on the island, principally in the form of the Singapore Stone, scholars such as Iain Sinclair estimate that Singapore's Tamil-Chola connections date back to the 11th–13th centuries CE in the aftermath of Rajendra Chola I's naval expedition against Kedah in the Malay peninsula in 1025 CE. In addition, the well-known literary treasure, *Sejarah Melayu*, annals of the ancient Malay world, offers us one of the earliest references to people of the Tamil country when it cites the term *keling* or *kling* in the context of Singapore. It makes reference to a proud genealogy of the Kings of Singapura tracing back to a kingdom of glory that had long-established commercial, political and even marital alliances with the Malay Archipelago. However, this glorious connection stands long forgotten, with modern, colonial narratives of convicts and indentured labour overshadowing all other aspects of Tamil history in Singapore (and then Malaya). Could this be because of the abject neglect of Tamils in preserving a written record of their own history? Or could this have been a case of doers versus dreamers wherein the everyday was engulfed in mystery while the extraordinary found common expression?

Who were the first Tamils to arrive? Ever since the establishment of Singapore as a British trading post in 1819, Tamils have made their presence felt on the island. Accompanying Stamford Raffles to Singapore in 1819 was Naraina Pillai, a Tamil merchant from Penang. Dubbed a native of the Coromandel Coast in the correspondences of William Farquhar, then Resident and Commandant of Singapore (1819–1823), Pillai is the earliest Tamil arrival recorded. Pillai's crucial role in establishing the Sri Mariamman Temple (now in Singapore's Chinatown heritage district) ensured the preservation of his name in collective memory and history. Pillai was but an archetypal member of the trade diasporas circulating among the British settlements in the Straits. Sangra Chitty (or Sangara Chitty), a Hindu native of Malacca, and Vaiyapoori, a merchant in trade with the East India Company (EIC), were influential Hindu traders of note as early as 1822. Chulia or south Indian Muslim merchants from the Coromandel (Cholamandalam) region had long controlled seaborne commerce and were in trade with the EIC in the Straits. Mahomud Hussein, Ismail Lebbai (also known as Tamby Ismail) and Sheikh Mahomet were prominent merchants in Singapore in the first half of the 19th century. These are names preserved in mundane administrative colonial documents — the Straits Settlements Records — beyond which their stories have not been chronicled in elaboration. Abdullah bin Abdul Kadir, better known as Munshi Abdullah, is widely considered as the father of Malay literature. Yet, in his own autobiography, he traces his Tamil genealogy (his father from Nagore was of part Yemeni and part Tamil descent). He arrived in Singapore from Malacca in mid-1819 and served as a scribe and interpreter for Raffles, and has authored some of colonial Singapore's earliest accounts. These early sojourners personify the system of circulation of trade diasporas in place in the region.

However, were there only Tamil transients in the first half of the 19th century? Or were there settlers too? Paucity of space has limited us to two exemplaries — Seetharama Pillay and Sangoo Thevar. In the tale of Pillay and his descendants lie relatively unknown patterns of migration and glimpses of early Tamil women settlers. Pillay and his son-in-law, Kotaiya Kounder, natives of Erode, India, arrived in Singapore in 1837. One version of the family's oral account notes that they arrived after having been incarcerated at the Andaman & Nicobar Islands. Kounder established himself as a stone mason in the construction industry while Pillay ran a successful dairy farm which, as a line of work, his grandson, Koona Vayloo Pillay, later undertook. Koona Vayloo's wife, Alamayloo Sabapathy Pillay, moved from Mauritius to Singapore with her father Sabapathy Pillai in the second half of the 19th century. Eight generations of this family have now lived in Singapore. Thevar, on the other hand, arrived in Singapore in the 1850s with his wife, Valleyammal. They came from Mannargudi in Thanjavur district, the heart of the Indian migrant belt that moved to Singapore. Thevar was also an anomaly in occupational profile — he entered the transportation business and supplied horse carriages to the public. Seven generations of his family have now lived in Singapore. Furthermore, a uniquely Singaporean Tamil identity punctuated with local influences had taken shape, complete with inter-racial, inter-ethnic relationships that typify a cosmopolitan society, over several generations in these instances.

In spite of such exemplary narratives, a preponderance of the Tamil labour narrative has persisted. This could be because of sheer numbers — many Tamils arrived as a result of assisted and involuntary migration of Indian labour between 1867 and 1941 from the Madras Presidency which was then the designated official source for procuring labour. Furthermore, Singapore served as a penal colony from 1825 to 1860. The contribution of these prisoners is often understood as that of physical labour in the construction of 19th century buildings but their expertise in the use of traditional techniques such as the making of bricks or the application of Madras chunam (lime plaster) in the making of these architectural landmarks should also be remembered. Could the focus on Tamil labour migration also be because of the application of a contemporary lens influenced by the continued employment of low-wage Tamil labour in Singapore's economy?

Land of their Adoption...

World War II was an epoch of disruption and turbulence. The Tamil experience of the war in Singapore encompassed refugees who returned to the Subcontinent to escape the trauma of the war; it included those who were recruited for the Death Railway; those who volunteered to join the Indian National Army in pursuit of an anti-colonialist agenda of Indian independence; and those who just struggled to make ends meet to survive the turbulent times of the Japanese Occupation.

The post-war period saw a subtle shift in the profile of the Tamils in Singapore. The stoppage of labour immigration prior to the Japanese Occupation led to a decline in the proportion of labour, which until then had formed the bulk of the movement of Tamils to Singapore and Malaya. Combined with the ideas of anti-colonialism, nationalism and sub-ethnic nationalism flowing from the Subcontinent, dreams of a better future also saw a spurt in efforts towards education, social mobility and modernisation.

In the post-war period, the umbilical cord between India and Singapore began to atrophy. By this period, a significant number of Tamils were Singapore-born, displaying the strong influence of local culture and social practice. In fact, till the 1950s, many Tamils were in the mode of the sojourner, retaining emotional ties with the homeland or '*ur*'. Perhaps the most significant impact on Tamil identity here was made by the Dravidian movement in Tamil Nadu. Many of the roots of a collective Tamil identity, societal reform and progress in Singapore and Malaya could be traced to this one movement. However, with the pan-Malayan independence movement gaining traction, actual contact with the mother country steadily declined. Tamils were encouraged by the likes of G Sarangapany, pre-eminent leader of the Tamil community then, to become Singapore citizens to contribute to local society amidst a climate of economic growth, meritocracy and equal opportunity.

Choice and Conviction, not Ancestry...

With Singapore's independence in 1965 and exhortations from the government to all ethnic groups to adopt a common Singaporean identity, many Tamils adopted Singapore as home and became Singaporeans, deprecating their ethnic identity to a large extent. One of the founding fathers of independent Singapore and its first Foreign Minister, S Rajaratnam, famously noted: "Being Singaporean is a matter not of ancestry, but of choice and conviction." He argued that remembering ancestral heritage would lead to building ghettoes in the minds of the community. Adding to the political and emotional disengagement with India, physical presence began to shrink too as new ordinances limited immigration to only those who could contribute to Singapore's economic development. However, history has its own designs. As Singapore rose rapidly in the economic ladder and became a global hub, from the 1980s onwards, foreign labour and foreign investment on a large scale was urgently needed. India, as a major economic power, was reconnected.

In recent decades, a significant influx of new migrants from India has complicated an already complex ethnic, linguistic and religious diversity, creating challenges of social cohesion, ethnic integration and religious harmony.

Despite early attempts to create a monolithic Singaporean identity devoid of ethnic overtones, the government realised and then incorporated the ineluctable nature of ethnicity. It allowed for the double-barrelled identity of Chinese-Singaporean, Malay-Singaporean, Indian-Singaporean and so on. Sub-ethnic groups consequently formed their own identities such as Tamil-Singaporeans, Malayali-Singaporeans, Telugu-Singaporeans, etc. These sub-ethnic identities have, once again, woven the web of connections between India and Singapore. All of them, though to varying degrees, look to India for their information, education and inspiration in cultural, linguistic and religious matters. Though unambiguously Singaporean nationals, they are culturally Indians to a significant degree.

However, cultural connections are not a 'plug and play' option for people to switch on or turn off their preferences. It takes conscientious and consistent effort to cultivate and maintain cultural attributes. In Singapore, a big struggle for the Tamils is to maintain their cultural and linguistic practices against inexorable erosion caused by Westernisation and English language dominance. They are, of course, not alone: the Chinese, Malays, Eurasians and others face similar fates.

This is where the Indian connection is, once again, proving to be a boon and a bane, as it always was. The influx of Indians in recent times has greatly enhanced the cultural scene in Singapore and the Tamil literary landscape is propped up by recent arrivals. They are the lifeblood of literary production in Singapore. Indeed, in many other walks of life, beyond culture and language, these benefits are manifest too. On the other hand, the congenital caste and class divisions that pervade their homeland are being re-injected into a community that fought long and hard to minimise, if not eradicate, those viruses.

Perhaps it is no longer a question *if* India will have any influence on Singapore's Tamils and Indians in general. More than 1,000 years ago, India and Southeast Asia, including Singapore, had an extensive and largely salubrious relationship. Contrary to some assumptions, that relationship was built on mutual benefit and respect and mostly on peaceable terms, in sharp contrast to the colonial experience with the Europeans. Indian soft power was at its best at its height. It exercised its immense power gently and wisely against foreign races and cultures. Indian-Singaporeans are not quite the aliens of the past but different and distinct nevertheless. Just as Singapore Chinese are not the Chinese of China, Singapore Indians are not the Indians of India. However, we are now in somewhat similar circumstances as in the millennia past where a tiny island nation is dancing with a giant and trying not to step on its toes but neither can it afford to be crushed by missteps of the giant. It is such a delicate dance.

6

Gujarati Shia Muslims of Singapore

Mustafa Izzuddin

A Case of Migration

For more than a century, Gujarati Muslims have defied their small size by punching above their weight in their contributions to Singapore. The pioneering Gujarati Muslim diaspora took shape in Singapore following its migration from India between the 1850s and 1920s. The Singapore Gujarati Muslims are distinguished between Sunnis and Shias, the latter being three doctrinally-different Shia communities: the Dawoodi Bohras, Ithna Asharis and Ismailis.

Gujarati Shias hail from different parts of Gujarat, including its periphery in Western India. Bohras came mainly from Surat and Dahod while Ithna Asharis and Ismailis (also termed Khojas) were from Kutch district and Kathiawar peninsula. Internal migration by the Gujarati Shias also led them to Gujarat-bordering states of Rajasthan, Maharashtra and Madhya Pradesh, further a field to West Bengal and southwards to Telangana, Karnataka and Tamil Nadu. While the early migration took off from Gujarat and its periphery, internal migrations also led to an outward movement from other parts of India to Singapore and Southeast Asia.

Each individual story of a Gujarati Muslim, and as a collective, is intricately interwoven into and enriches the modern history of Singapore with their manifold and multifarious contributions. Today, there are about 3,000 Gujarati Muslims in Singapore, with Gujarati Shias making up half of them.

Economic Contributions

The early Gujarati Shias were merchants inspired by 'vohra' or 'vohora', which in Gujarati, means 'to trade'. They were in import-export trade of all kinds of goods and commodities and real estate investments. The firms, which were mainly family-owned, acted as middlemen to capitalise on Singapore's free port and geographical location along the Silk Road, taking full advantage of the Indian Ocean, including the Bay of Bengal. They also used Singapore as a hub to trade with the rest of Southeast Asia. Their early business presence was mainly at Malacca Street, Market Street, Arab Street and Orchard Road. They were described as Bombay merchants, as Gujarat was then part of the Bombay state before it dissolved to Maharashtra and Gujarat.

While some old firms have wound up, others have continued through acumen, innovation and technology. It was also common practice for past employees of the firms to establish their own family firms and, thereafter, compete with their former employers. Newer firms have also propped up, focusing instead on the profitable trade of the digitised age. Many Gujarati Shias have also become working professionals, chiefly among younger generations and the expatriate population.

Gujarati Shias were pivotal in setting up associations to pool the resources of Indian businesses in Singapore and enhance their clout vis-à-vis the colonial and post-colonial governments and other business communities, including the Chinese. For example, Gujarati Shias helped set up the Indian Merchants Association (IMA) in 1924 and spearheaded it at various times. Thereafter, the IMA underwent several phases of change before eventually becoming the Singapore Indian Chamber of Commerce and Industry (SICCI) in 1991. Gujarati Shias played important leadership roles to make the chamber a business pacesetter and interlocutor between Singapore and India, and remain active members of SICCI today.

Philanthropy and Community Service

Gujarati Shias were active financial contributors to British colonial and Japanese funds when Singapore was under occupation, being known as the Syonan Gujarati Indians. During the Japanese Occupation, Gujarati Shia merchants like Abdeali Motiwalla were involved in the Indian Independence League. Abdeali donated $20,000 (likely Malayan Dollar) to Subhas Chandra Bose for the Indian National Army but more to protect his own business. Gujarati Shias have also provided voluntary leadership in community service as Malay/Muslim leaders, Rotarians, Lions, Freemasons, and in grassroots committees and national bodies.

Inspired by the Aga Khan Development Network or Ismaili Civic, Ismailis have been donating to various causes in Singapore. For example, Ismailis disbursed S$5,000 in 1981 through the Quaid-i-Azam Memorial Fund named after Pakistan's founder, Muhammad Ali Jinnah who was born an Ismaili. During the visit of Aga Khan, who is hereditary Imam and leader of the Ismailis, to Singapore in the 1980s, S$500,000 was donated to Yayasan Mendaki. Later, Aziz Merchant and his wife Reshma donated a long-term scholarship to it.

Guided by their spiritual leader Dai-al-Mutlaq, Dawoodi Bohras have made donations through the Singapore Dawoodi Bohra Muslim Association from 1965 to 1979. When the 52nd Dai visited Singapore in 1979, Bohras donated S$10,000 to the Islamic Religious Council of Singapore (MUIS) and S$10,000 to Jamiyah. When the 53rd Dai visited Singapore in 2018, the Bohras donated to the President's Challenge. The Yahyabhai Abdulhussain Lukmanji Saif Charity Trust has helped with education and medical expenses of the needy. Another is Abdul Tyeb Esmailji Maskati, the first Bohra firm to venture into Indochina. Basrai Brothers, a Bohra stationery firm along Chulia Street, was cited by Singapore's first Prime Minister Lee Kuan Yew in his memoirs, as it had an indirect hand in bringing him closer to his future wife in the 1940s.

The most notable Ithna Ashari philanthropist was Rajabali Jumabhoy who created a charitable foundation that has contributed to innumerable causes. His son, Ameerali Jumabhoy, has followed his father's footsteps. The Jumabhoys have also contributed to the development of the arts and theatre in Singapore, received Rabindranath Tagore during his visit to Singapore in 1927 and were responsible in building the Mahatma Gandhi Memorial in Singapore in 1950.

As successful Muslim businessmen, the Gujaratis were roped in by the British to safeguard Islamic affairs in Singapore. The wealthier the Gujaratis, the more influential they were on Muslim matters, either through voluntary leadership or financial contributions. Examples include the Moslem Association, Muslim Students' Aid Fund, Mohammedan Advisory Board and Muslim Advisory Board. Mohamed Javad Namazie, a non-Gujarati Shia lawyer close to Gujarati Shias, played a pivotal role in drafting the Administration of Muslim Law Act which was passed in parliament in 1966, leading to the setting up of MUIS which coordinates and oversees Muslim matters in Singapore.

Being affluent, Gujarati Shias have purchased vast amounts of land and properties since the 19th century. The Jumabhoys of Scotts Holdings and the Bohras with land in Serangoon Road and Hill Street are cases in point. Over time, the land and properties of Gujarati Shias have reduced exponentially due to family feuds or being taken over by the government. However, the purchasing power of Gujarati Shias have helped them to still build places of worship and preserved them for the benefit of their communities.

In Singapore, the only Shia mosque and one of two Gujarati mosques (the other being Angullia mosque) is Masjid Burhani along Hill Street, first built in 1897 by the Bohras through Abdoolkayom

Moola Essabhoy. The place of worship for Ithna Asharis, described as Imambara, was housed in properties owned by the Jumabhoys at Lim Ah Woo Road. Due to an increase in the congregation size due to an influx of Malays transitioning from Sunnism to Shiism, the place of worship moved to Ahlulbayt Centre in Geylang. The place of worship for Ismailis, called a Jamatkhana, was at a residence in East Coast Road before it moved into a building in Geylang. For Ithna Asharis and Ismailis, the place of worship is modelled as a sociocultural centre through which private religious events take place. Masjid Burhani is overseen by a mosque management board, in coordination with MUIS, while the centres of the Ithna Asharis and Ismailis are managed by the Jaafari Muslim Association and local Ismailis as part of the Far East Ismaili Council respectively.

In political service, the highest position was held by Jumabhoy Mohamed Jumabhoy as Minister for Commerce and Industry in the pre-1965 Singapore Legislative Assembly. He was also elected a city councillor, along with Hasan Ali Jivabhai, while Rajabali Jumabhoy served on the pre-1965 Singapore Legislative Council and was a municipal commissioner. In diplomacy, Haider Sithawalla and Shabbir Hassanbhai served as non-resident ambassadors for Singapore. Hussein Hasanally Abdoolcader, whose father was an early Bohra pioneer in Singapore before moving to Penang, was the first Indian in Malaya to receive a knighthood in 1948. Rajabali Jumabhoy, Abdeali Nomanbhoy and Fidahusein Mohamedali Nakhoda were the first Gujarati Shias to be conferred the Justice of Peace in the 1930s and, in recent times, Izzuddin Taherally and Ameerali Abdeali.

Gujarati Shia women have also been active in Singapore Council of Women's Organisations, Singapore Muslim Women's Association, Kamala Club, and Inner Wheel Club. They included Rosy Nakhooda, Amina Jumabhoy, Nisha Jumabhoy, Sakina Abidally Abdulhusain Kagda, Roshan Moledina and Salma Moiz. Zareena Nazeemali Bana was the first female to be elected to the Indian Chamber of Commerce in 1984, Yasmin Yahyabhai Saif was the first Indian to win the Miss Singapore pageant in 1968 and Amina Hatim Degani was the first Gujarati to receive the Commonwealth Scholarship in 1960.

Sports Diplomacy and Cultural Heritage

Gujarati Shias have been avid sportsmen in cricket, hockey, equestrian and tennis. The Jumabhoys, Nomanbhoys, Sithawallas and Motiwallas are prominent illustrations. Rajabali Jumabhoy helped establish the sports-centric Indian Association in 1923, Haider Sithawalla became the second non-European and first Gujarati President of Singapore Cricket Club and later Zoher Motiwalla was its Deputy President. Ameerali Jumabhoy is a long-serving patron of Singapore Polo Club.

Gujarati Shias boast a rich cultural heritage that is influenced by their ethnicity, religion and geography. Some households prefer Gujarati cuisine while others fusion food, influenced by Malay, Chinese or Arab cultures. As Muslims, they do not eat pork but love meat, namely, mutton and chicken. Sweets are also synonymous with the taste buds of Gujarati Shias.

The Bohras, Ithna Asharis and Ismailis are able to speak some variant of Gujarati. For Bohras, it is known as Lisan-al-Dawat, a mix of words from Arabic, Urdu and Gujarati and written on a Perso-Arabic script. Pre-1990s, Gujarati Shias took mainly Malay as second language in schools, with some taking Mandarin. Post-1990s, when there were more offerings, they began to choose Hindi, Urdu or Gujarati as their second language. Educational standards are also high, with Aberdeen Tyebally becoming the first Gujarati to receive the President's Scholarship in 1967.

The attires of the Bohras, Ithna Asharis and Ismailis are similar to Indian fashion. For the ladies, saris, Punjabi suits, ghagra orhni (dress with shawl-like scarf) are prevalent, although for conservative Ithna Asharis, a chador, and Bohras, a ridah (coloured two-piece attire top to bottom). Wearing a headscarf for women is dependent on whether they are more religious or secular. The attire for men is usually shalwar kameez or kurta. For Bohras, it is a three-piece attire called saya-kurta-izar alongside a white and gold cap (topi). Marriages have been endogamous but in recent times, there has been a slight increase in exogamous marriages.

Enriching Singapore

Gujarati Muslims are an integral diasporic piece in the multicultural mosaic and social fabric of Singapore. As a heterogeneous minority, the secular framework in Singapore is critical for the survival of Gujarati Muslims, not least the Shias which are lesser in number than the Sunnis in Singapore. The faith of Gujarati Shias is private but their contributions are public. As Sunnis and Shias are recognised by MUIS as Muslims, Sunni-Shia conflict is not discernible in Singapore.

Gujarati Shias have close interconnections with one another through business, culture and language. They are outward-looking and have built bridges with Sunni Muslims and other communities in Singapore society — interfaith dialogue and intercultural engagement being central to their thinking. Their intra- and inter-networks are critical to their existence and identity preservation as Gujarati Muslims and good citizens of Singapore whilst also keeping a familial and business link to India. Despite being a minority within a minority in Singapore, Gujarati Shias have demonstrated a tenacious capacity to stick together as a closely-knit heterogeneous and enterprising community. The onus is on the younger generation to take on the mantle of leadership to continue the good work of its forefathers, and thus, write the future script of Gujarati Shia Muslims in Singapore.

7

In Search of India's Indic Past

K. Kesavapany

> I see India everywhere but find it nowhere.
>
> — Rabindranath Tagore

On 14 July 1927, Asia's first Nobel laureate sailed from Madras and arrived in Singapore five days later. The purpose of his four-month journey, which also took him to Thailand, Malaysia and Indonesia, was to raise funds for Santinikiten, an ashram and educational institution, situated 165 kilometres from Calcutta.

Tagore's own interest, as described by Professor Suniti Kumar Chatterji, who accompanied him on the trip, was "to see for himself how India had made Javadwip [Java but here covering the entire East Indies and Straits region] its own and to understand something of the culture of Javadwip." The tour was also notable for the 18 poems that Tagore wrote of the inter-connection between his native country and the foreign lands he visited. Tagore observed that Buddhist doctrines had deserted their original homes in India to find a home for their "living images" in the green and vital heart of Siam — like a river that arose to flow from Siam: a holy Ganga of the spirit, superior to the actual Ganga confined to the sub-continent.

On the ship from Singapore to Java, Tagore composed the following poem:

> You and I were united in this place, who knows how many ages ago
> Our languages were linked as were our hearts
> When the conch shell was blowing in the temple beside the Ganga, your words mingled with the sound.
> Vishnu and Durga spoke in my ear "We want to be worshipped on the unknown shore".
> The *Mandakini* stretched out its hand to the eastern shore and said, "Let us go there".

Tagore's poems and interpretative essays by scholars like Emeritus Professor Sukanta Chaudhari stirred a desire in me to pursue this ancient and historical connection between India and Southeast Asia. Fortunately, my diplomatic career and later my entry into the academic world made this possible.

The first opportunity came with my posting to Jakarta, Indonesia, in 1973. The posting was at short notice. As such, I did not have the luxury of time to read up on the country of posting. All I knew about Indonesia was that it was the largest country in Southeast Asia and had the most number of Muslims, with Bahasa Indonesia as the *lingua franca*. It, therefore, came as a surprise when accompanying Singapore's Ambassador Lee Khoon Choy to Merdeka Palace for a call on President Suharto, I saw a large sculpture of a chariot on which Lord Krishna was giving advice to Arjuna on the battlefield of Kurukshetra.

As a Hindu, I immediately recognised the sculpture as an enactment of '*Gita Upadesam*', the immortal message enshrined in the holy book of the Bhagavad Gita. I expressed my surprise to Ambassador Lee that the most iconic symbol of Hinduism should be so prominently located and that too in front of the Presidential Palace. With his inscrutable smile, Ambassador Lee said: "You have a lot to learn!" Indeed, I had much to learn and that too from the Ambassador himself. A multi-talented person, he was steeped in culture and mysticism. His practice of the

Javanese spiritual creed of *kebatinan* (mysticism) brought him close to the Indonesian ruling elite, including President Suharto and General Sujono Humardhani. Slowly, I came to learn about the layers of socio-cultural teachings and practices that made up the syncretic Indonesian society, which is well reflected in the state's motto, '*Bhinnaka Tungall Ika*' (Unity in Diversity).

My immersion into Indic culture in the country was through an unplanned journey across Java. One day, a few months after my arrival in Indonesia, while playing golf with a close Singaporean friend, Alvin Kwan, I proposed the idea of making a trip to Yogyakarta about 500 kilometres from Jakarta.

Over a period of two days, we passed through towns like Bogor and Semarang and several villages. We could see and feel the changes in culture and cuisine from West Java to Central Java and Solo. One thing, however, was constant: the language. While the people in the provinces spoke in their regional tongues, everyone spoke Bahasa Indonesia, which was laced with Sanskrit words. This unity through language was President Sukarno's enduring legacy to the nation.

After a two-day journey, we reached Yogyakarta, the capital of the province of Central Java. Together with the neighbouring town of Solo, Yogyakarta is acknowledged as the spiritual capital of the country. The following day, we toured Borobudur, reputed to be the largest Buddhist structure in the world. Standing at the bottom of this awesome structure, I was amazed that such an edifice, so far from Lumbini — Lord Buddha's birthplace — should find a home in this eastern corner of the world. This was indeed a vivid example of India's Indic reach.

After Borobudur, we toured Prambanan, a Hindu temple complex situated about 40 kilometres away. Again, a feeling of pride that Indic influence had spread so far from the source, welled in me. It is in this vicinity that the Ramayana festival is staged every year, with the full moon as the background. I wonder whether anything similar exists in the country of origin.

As we prepared for our return journey to Jakarta, our guide suggested that we also visit a complex of temple ruins in the Dieng Plateau. Intrigued, we allowed ourselves to be persuaded. Off the beaten track, about 112 kilometres from Yogyakarta, we travelled on a hilly and winding road. After three hours, we reached the top of the plateau. We went on a tour of the ruins of the four temples dedicated to Hindu deities. One of them was of particular interest to me as it was a shrine dedicated to Lord Brahma. Rarely have I come across a shrine dedicated to this particular deity, even in India. Again, I asked myself who were these worshippers and what had inspired them to build these shrines in such a remote place. Maybe it was *really* not such a remote place!

Bali, the citadel of Hinduism, beckoned us but we had to postpone that pleasure for another day. And that day was not long in coming. Both official and private visits took me to what is described as the Isle of the Gods on several occasions. Tagore's descriptions in several of his poems of his own voyage to Bali had prepared me well for the experience. One particular account, as pointed out by Professor Chatterji, writes of a king, Karen Asam, in Bali who suddenly pointed to the landscape and began uttering Sanskrit words for natural features and the names of India's rivers — Ganga, Yamuna, Narmada, Godavari, Kaveri and Saraswathi. Professor Chatterji explained: "The man did not know Sanskrit nor had he been to India but the traditions of his own island had preserved the mental landscape of a total culture embracing the whole of South and Southeast Asia."

Although Hindu in name and spirit, the Hinduism of Bali I encountered was different from that of India. The following were just two of the differences that caught my attention:

1) Although the names of the deities are the same, for example, Rama, Lakshmana, etc., their facial features and dressings are completely different.
2) Meat is used in some of the prayer rituals in Bali. However, this practice is uncommon in such rituals in Hindu temples in India.

The above points serve to illustrate that while Hinduism came to Bali from India, it was transformed and adapted to suit local norms and conditions.

My appointment as Director-General of ASEAN-Singapore provided further opportunities to me to explore the links between India and Southeast Asia. On working visits to Thailand, Cambodia and Myanmar, I came across manifestations of Hindu-Buddhist culture in these countries — Angkor Wat, Shewdegon and the countless Stupas in Pagan are just a few that come to mind. Just like the horse and chariot sculpture in Jakarta, the 'Churning of the Ocean' in Bangkok's Suvarnabhumi International Airport is a modern day representation of ancient epics.

It was, however, when I moved to the academic world that I was able to pursue, in earnest, my life-long interest in India's Indic past. This came about as a result of a call on me by Professor Lily Kong and Professor Tan Tai Yong (at the National University of Singapore then) at the then Institute of Southeast Asian Studies (ISEAS). The purpose of their call was to enquire if ISEAS would be interested in setting up a Buddhist Studies programme. This query coincided with my own interest in expanding the Institute's research scope to include the ancient and historical past of the region. It became apparent that, without an understanding of the past, present and future trends cannot be adequately explained.

Fortunately for me, I had, as Chairman of the Institute, the celebrated historian, Professor Wang Gungwu. He readily saw the merit of the proposal. However, then Minister for Foreign Affairs George Yeo felt that the research agenda should have a wider coverage and should include studies on the connectivity between India and Southeast Asia. Accordingly, the Buddhist Studies Centre was re-named the Nalanda-Sriwijaya Centre (NSC) with Dr Tansen Sen, seconded from the City University of New York, as the Head.

The key objective of the Centre, in the words of Dr Sen, was "to understand the intricacies of inter-Asian intersections, focused on the role and contributions of Southeast Asian countries." The NSC was successful in reviving interest in the ancient links between India and

Southeast Asia, which had been dimmed by the fog of history and the 20 decades of colonialism and imperialism.

Among the notable conferences that the Centre organised were:

1) Interactions between South and Southeast Asia; Reflections on Cross Cultural Exchange; and
2) Nagapattinam to Suvarnadeepam; Reflections on the Chola Naval Expeditions in Southeast Asia.

Attended by over 200 local and international scholars, the conferences resulted in two landmark publications on the two themes.

I had often wondered why Singapore, alone among the Southeast Asian countries, did not have a dedicated place to study archaeology. The response I received was "What is there to dig in Singapore?" However, a seminal work by Professor Tan and Dr Kwa Chong Guan, resulting in a publication, *Seven Hundred Years: A History of Singapore*, served to underscore the fact that there was indeed a story to be told even before that period. I was, therefore, pleased to establish an archaeology unit as part of the NSC. As the Head of the unit, Professor John Miksic succinctly explained:

> It was a great opportunity to emphasise the ancient roots of Southeast Asian cultures, including arts forms and aesthetic values that they shared as well as local originality and links with China and India.

The unit has become recognised for its work in Singapore and the region.

Yet another focal point for the study of the region's cultural links with India was the setting up of the Indian Heritage Centre. Opened by Prime Minister Lee Hsien Loong on 7 May 2015, the Centre has evolved into a research centre and a tourist attraction. Ambassador Gopinath Pillai, as Chairman of the Content's Sub-committee, and I, as Deputy Chairman, worked with Dr Gauri Krishnan and her colleagues on the cultural aspects of the Centre.

The latest acknowledgment of India's link with Southeast Asia came in the form of an invitation from Indian Prime Minister Narendra Modi to the 10 Heads of States/Governments of the member states of the Association of Southeast Asian Nations to attend India's Republic Day parade on 26 January 2018. Curiously, the geographical contours of the 10 countries whose heads were invited to the inauguration were similar to that of the scope of study of the NSC.

History may be dimmed by the passage of time but never forgotten.

8

Joys and Sorrows of Investing in India

Sat Pal Khattar

Investing in India has its joys and sorrows. Every investment comes with its own business risks. The choice of partners with whom one invests is a paramount risk especially when one is a minority shareholder. The choice of the business to invest in also involves a risk. A change in laws or unexpected regulatory actions may also affect the investment. Similarly, unexpected economic changes may result in a sudden unfavourable economic environment. These may be unexpected and are due to no fault of the promoter or lead shareholder of the business. This essay looks at the joys and sorrows of investing in India not due to the above factors.

Radisson Hotel

We made an investment as a minority interest in a five-star hotel in Delhi near the Delhi International Airport. It was to be managed, upon completion, by Radisson Hotels. The original Indian promoter was a successful Delhi businessman. He got Unitech, an established company in Delhi in the real estate sector, to be his joint venture partner. It was finally approved as a hotel with a small wing approved for office use.

The Department of Civil Aviation (DCA), which controlled all airport activities, owned the land. It had a representative on the Board of Directors of the company building the hotel and office wing on a 30-year lease from the DCA. The hotel was being built when we came in as a minority investor. The company needed additional funds to complete the development. Neither partner wanted the other to put in more money and increase his shareholding at the other's expense. They decided to bring in a third shareholder. We took a 28-percent share in the venture. The fact that I was known to the other shareholder, Unitech, also helped.

The project was eventually completed. Both the office wing and the hotel were ready. Guests were invited for the opening and included ministers and other dignitaries. At the last moment, the Municipal Corporation of Delhi (MCD), the local authority, refused to approve the hotel's opening because it said the hotel was within a prohibited distance of the NH8 Highway. This new condition was prescribed by the local authority long after the DCA had approved the hotel's plan. The MCD, which had jurisdiction over planning approvals in Delhi, was adamant in not giving its approval, despite the DCA having earlier approved our plans. The new rule was not retrospective. We argued that it was inapplicable to us. However, our pleas fell on deaf ears.

In normal circumstances, such an enterprise would be financed by some debt. It would soon become insolvent if it was unable to generate revenue. In this case, the new hotel was fully completed, with staff recruited but it was not allowed to operate. Fortunately, the office wing had been let and tenants had moved in. The rentals generated some income. The hotel remained unopened. The owners made repeated appeals but all were unsuccessful.

Several senior leaders from India visiting Singapore were informed of this problem as a Singapore shareholder was involved. The Deputy Chairman of the Planning Commission of India and the Deputy Chairman of the MCD were also made aware of the problem. They assured a solution would be found. It never happened. About two years later, a senior Indian civil servant convened a meeting of the various heads of departments involved in the matter and insisted that the issue must be resolved. At last, we were given the approval to open the hotel. I dread to think of what would have happened if the income from the office wing was not coming in and if the lenders were less understanding. The whole enterprise would have folded up and a completed new hotel would have gone bankrupt. This is a terrible example of the risks of doing business in India.

This lamentable position could have caused financial havoc to a normal investor. Rules were applied retrospectively which is against the rule of law. There was also no coordination between the various agencies.

Tiger Balm

I have been a Director of Haw Par Brothers International Ltd for a long period. The Singapore listed company is the worldwide manufacturer of Tiger Balm products and owner of the brand. It decided to manufacture and sell its product in India. Before it could commence manufacturing operation, a small Indian enterprise, which had registered the same name and manufactured and sold its product as Tiger Balm, warned Haw Par that it would apply for a court injunction to prevent the latter from carrying out its plan. Intellectual property lawyers assured Haw Par that Indian jurisprudence recognised worldwide ownership and usage of international brands and it would be successful in resisting the injunction. However, when the matter came up for the first hearing in the High Court, we found ourselves at the losing end. An injunction was issued to restrain Haw Par from manufacturing or selling Tiger Balm in India. Fortunately, on appeal, the Divisional Court heard it quite expeditiously and overruled the Lower Court. As a result, Haw Par has been manufacturing and selling its world famous balm in India since.

Signature Towers and Gurgaon Tech Park

We invested in two other projects with Unitech. One was to build a first-class office tower in Gurgaon called Signature Towers. I insisted on using a Singapore architect to design the building and supervise its construction. There were many delays, which happen with most property developments in India. It was finally completed. Since its completion, the building has commanded good rentals because of its Singapore quality and finisher. That was a joy.

The second project was the Gurgaon Tech Park. A Singapore company, on whose board I sat (Parameswara Holdings), and another Singapore company, Thakrals, and my family company, were joint venture partners. The Indian partners were Unitech and the state government of Haryana. There were many problems. But with persistence, these were dealt with. After several years, the Singapore shareholders wanted to sell their shares in the project. We were told that it would take years for permissions to be obtained from the authorities. However, if they bought out the other shareholders, this could be done quickly. We took this route and exited the project by selling it to the Haryana government. We could have gotten a higher price if we had sold our shares in the open market. The exit resulted in a half-hearted joy.

HDFC Bank

One of our most successful investments in India was in HDFC Bank. After Prime Minister Indira Gandhi nationalised most of the large private sector banks in India, no new banking licenses were issued for many years. Then, under a new policy of opening up India, new banking licenses were issued under Prime Minister P V Narasimha Rao's watch. One of these was HDFC Bank which was sponsored by HDFC, a successful housing and property finance company. The sponsors of this new bank wanted DBS Bank in Singapore to take a 20-percent shareholding in their bank. DBS Bank was willing to do so but when it was told by the Indian authorities that it would not get a separate licence if it took up the 20-percent interest in HDFC Bank, DBS Bank backed out. The proposed shareholding was then offered to Natwest Bank in the United Kingdom (UK), which took it up. Natwest eventually sold its shares to Chase Capital Partners at a meaningful profit.

For my efforts in bringing DBS Bank to the table, even though it was unsuccessful, I was offered shares at par in HDFC Bank, which I took up. With such prestigious partners, I felt that this was a good investment. India's then Finance Minister, Dr Manmohan Singh, told me that this approval was given to me, as an established non-resident Indian, who would be able to raise deposits for the new bank. Dr Singh later became the Prime Minister. I promised him and the bank to raise deposits for the bank. I was faced with the challenge of getting people to put deposits in a new Indian bank with no track record. I decided to use my own resources to make the deposits. Fortunately, I had sold two properties which provided me with the means to do so. Later, when I sold some of these shares, I had to pay substantial Indian withholding taxes since the shareholder was a Singapore entity. I did not mind as I made a handsome profit on the sale of the shares. The tax on the sale of listed Indian equities was later abolished by India.

Later, HDFC Bank took over the Bank of Punjab. I was offered the opportunity to take some HDFC Bank shares which I did. It was a profitable investment again.

If I had kept all my HDFC Bank shares, I would not need to make any new investment in India or elsewhere. However, I have always regarded the surpluses as fortuitous and to which I have made no real contribution other than showing confidence in a new bank. It was a story of faith, persistence and, to some extent, luck. It was a joy to be involved in this investment.

Gateway Distriparks Ltd

A few of us in Singapore decided to build a container warehouse facility in India with a local Indian partner.

Ambassador Gopinath Pillai took on the mantle as Chairman of Gateway Distriparks Ltd. A Port of Singapore Authority (PSA) subsidiary offered to be one of the Singaporean shareholders, as was Parameswara Holdings, another Singapore company. The business of owning and managing bonded freight stations was until then a monopoly of CONCOR, an Indian government company and an affiliate of Indian Railways. The approvals took a very long time. Two Singapore shareholders, including the PSA subsidiary, quit. New Singapore shareholders, including the Thakral Group, were brought in. In 2004, Temasek took a 10-percent stake in Gateway but sold its shares and exited from the company in 2009.

These delays were mostly of a governmental nature. For instance, we were shown a piece of land to build on. We accepted. Several months later, we were told that the Indian government had decided to give the land to the Punjab government to build a container freight station, which was what we were intending to do. We were then shown another piece of land. It was partly underwater and required massive filling. We again agreed to accept the site.

Our company eventually became the largest and most successful container facility in the private sector in India. Later, we became a listed company. Several others in India entered the same business. However, none could measure up to us in efficiency or profits. We ran it on a professional basis — Singapore style. Eventually, we made a very successful exit by selling our shares in the market. After plenty of pains, we finally had a joyful exit.

Gateway had later expanded its area of logistics into railways, that is, the carrying and storing of containers by rail all over India, then a monopoly of CONCOR. The capital expenditure was large. A private equity firm, Blackstone, came in as a shareholder. Blackstone later sold its interest back to Gateway. The company also entered the storing and logistics of cold storage warehousing and transportation. Other investors in the fledging company, which Gateway took over, were Mitsubishi, an American mutual fund and some Indian shareholders.

Both these companies were pioneers in their respective fields in the private sector. However, as they were competing in areas which were, until then, government monopolies, it was not easy. CONCOR was not happy since what had hitherto been its monopoly was being challenged by an outsider. But there was little CONCUR could do to block it.

Conclusion

When one invests, some risks are inevitable. As investors, we accept that. However, when the risks are caused by administrative interference and often without legal basis, the frustrations are painful and financially threatening. In these and other instances, we have generally persisted. We have had some successes, plenty of frustrations, a fair amount of angst and lots of experience to match. These are an integral part of the joys and sorrows of investing in India.

9

Buddhist Links between India and Singapore/Southeast Asia

Gauri Parimoo Krishnan

Introduction

In understanding the Buddhist roots of Singapore, we have to consider archaeological findings, and trade and migration patterns, both of which point in the direction of China rather than India. However, the Indic civilisation's ancient Buddhist connection with Southeast Asia goes back to the beginning of the current era which is closely connected with trade and commerce in the Indian Ocean. With archaeological evidence in Malaysia, Indonesia, Thailand, Cambodia, Laos and Vietnam from the 6th–7th centuries, it is a clear indication of how Buddhism developed in a localised form intermingling with the local belief systems and manifested in their art and architecture. Both Therevada and Mahayana traditions took root followed by Vajrayana practices in certain periods and regions. The role of Buddhism in passing on the knowledge of the triple gem, Tripitaka texts, universal humanism and compassion is worth telling.

In Singapore, many of the early Buddhist Theravada and Mahayana religious practices and study of texts came from Sri Lanka, China, Thailand, Tibet and Myanmar. This can be seen through the major monasteries, temples and Buddhist colleges set up in the 19th and 20th centuries. The only Indian Buddhist meditation practice that came into Singapore is the Vipassana meditation practice popularised by S N Goenka at Igatpuri in the tradition of Sayagyi U Ba Khin. It has centres all over the world, including Singapore. The centre has teachers and practitioners engaged in this practice of mindfulness and training of the mind. It is one of the oldest methods of meditation as documented in *Satipatthana Sutta* attributed to a discourse given by the Buddha himself. It has deep roots in Singapore.

Buddhist Monuments in Southeast Asia with Indian Connection

While Hindu-Buddhist beliefs, practices and art seem to have travelled along the land route via Myanmar and the maritime trade route via Java, Sumatra, Malaysia, Thailand and Cambodia in different waves since the beginning of the current era or even earlier, archaeological and epigraphical evidences do not appear before the 5th century. Important Buddhist monuments, votive plaques and carved relief panels, with inscriptions in Sanskrit and Pali from the Srivijaya period, have brought to light the presence of Buddhist practice, recitation of Buddhist creed, and committing them to written form on votive plaques and stone carved inscriptions. Stone, terracotta and bronze images of the Buddha, produced in different styles found in Bujang Valley in Kedah, Malaysia, have highlighted how Buddhist iconography had been localised and images produced for meditation and worship by the local Buddhist communities. Yijing, a Buddhist monk from China in the 7th century, heading to India, had stopped over in Palembang to learn Sanskrit, before reaching Nalanda Mahavihara, a great university of diversity and high standard of education, foremost being Buddhist philosophy.

The Borobudur Stupa, near Jogjakarta in Central Java, was built around the 9th century by the Sailendras. Its grandiose vision evokes the kind of planning that must have gone into its conceptualisation. The entire programme of its architectural layout, sculptural decoration and relief narratives combined to illustrate its Mandala concept evolving from the physical to the spiritual realm. The artists, sculptors and architects of the Borobudur Stupa would have studied Mahayana Buddhist literature, Sanskrit and artistic aesthetics, all of which would have arrived from India but were assimilated and disseminated selectively. Other notable Buddhist monuments in Thailand of the Mon Dvaravati (6th–11th century) and Sukhothai period (13th–14th century), and in Cambodia of the Angkor Thom and the Bayon of the Jayavarman VII period (12th–13th century) reflect numerous Hindu-Buddhist beliefs, practices and art forms that were associated with the Indian subcontinent and later were adapted by the Mon, Khmer or Thai royal patrons.

In the absence of any Buddhist relics found on Singapore's soil, it is not certain if Singapore was active during the Srivijaya period but it certainly was during the Majapahit period in the 14th century, based on a cache of gold ornaments excavated on Bukit Larangan, Fort Canning Hill.

Buddha Relic in Singapore and Cultural Memorandum of Understanding between Singapore and India

One of the first major exhibitions organised by the National Heritage Board of Singapore and the Ministry of Culture of the Government of India was 'Alamkara: 5,000 Years of Indian Art' (1 July 1994 to 1 January 1995) hosted by the former National Museum on Stamford Road. It was the largest and the most comprehensive loan of high quality artefacts to have ever left India's shores from the National Museum in New Delhi. The many projects organised under the memorandum of understanding between the two governments since 1990s has enabled Singaporeans to gain a deeper appreciation of the richness of Indian heritage.

A key Buddhist artefact in this exhibition worth discussing here was a rare and historic first-ever loan of a real bone relic of Lord Buddha which was excavated in Piprawah in Uttar Pradesh — it was kept in a steatite relic casket that was uncovered in 1898. This site is close to the location of Gautama Buddha's *Parinirvana* in Kushinagara. The inscription on one of the caskets found, referring to the Shakyas who most likely built the Stupa refers to the historicity of Gautama Buddha. It was his instructions to erect a Stupa over his relic as well as the dedication by the descendants of his clan, the Shakyas. The relic drew an unprecedentedly large audience of about 165,000 visitors to the exhibition. The relic was placed on a pedestal with a circumambulatory platform that allowed visitors to observe and pay their respects to it. The same relic was also displayed a couple of years later for the Vesak Day celebration by the Buddhist Library in Geylang, Singapore. It drew an equally large crowd of devotees. The trend of venerating the relics became such a popular phenomenon that Singapore now boasts of a large temple dedicated to the Tooth Relic of the Buddha. It was established along South Bridge Road in the Chinatown area in 2002 and draws large numbers of visitors and devotees alike.

3rd East Asia Summit and Singapore and India Collaboration

The 3rd East Asia Summit (EAS) was hosted by Singapore in 2007. The summit endorsed the proposal to build a new Nalanda University near the site of the original university. The summit also established a Nalanda Mentor Group which included then Foreign Minister of Singapore George Yeo. I was fortunate to be part of the delegation of the late Minister of State for Foreign Affairs, Dr Balaji Sadasivan, to Bihar in 2006. The idea of a special exhibition on Nalanda and its legacy sprouted during this visit. It was developed and curated by me for the Asian Civilisations Museum (ACM) titled 'On the Nalanda Trail: Buddhism in India, China and Southeast Asia' (1 November 2007 to 23 March 2008). It was an iconic exhibition, summing up the many strands of Buddhism that converged and developed through and around the Nalanda Mahavihara and other Buddhist centres of learning along the land and maritime trade routes that became rich repositories of manuscripts and learning, art and architecture. Monasteries dotted along trade routes allowed monks, missionaries and merchants to criss-cross for ideas, technologies, languages, and commodities to flow in a seamless manner to be exchanged and renewed. This concept was amply illustrated using iconic, well-researched examples of Buddhist art, some of which are only seen in text books or museum catalogues and have never been seen outside of their museum stores such as the Sir Aurel Stein collection of Buddhist antiquities from famous sites such as Dunhuang.

50 Years of India-Singapore Diplomatic Relations Celebration

Singapore and India celebrated 50 years of bilateral relations with an exhibition on 'Treasures from Asia's Oldest Museum of Buddhist Art — the Indian Museum, Kolkata' (18 June to 16 August 2015) at the ACM jointly curated with the Indian side. The exhibition was a visual biography of sacred and sublime examples of Buddhist art of the Indian subcontinent from important Buddhist sites of Barhut, Mathura, Gandhara, Sarnath, Bodhgaya, Bihar and Bangladesh. This exhibition brought together some rare and well-known examples of Sunga, Kushana, Gandhara, Gupta, and Pala schools of sculptures and valuable Buddhist manuscripts from Nepal, nine of which were excavated from a Stupa in Lauriyan Tangai in the Peshawar region while some of the Barhut reliefs, and Gupta and Pala period sculptures were previously shown in the 'Way of the Buddha' exhibition organised by the ACM in 1993 and the Nalanda Trail exhibition in 2007–08.

In summary, Singapore-India bilateral relations, with an emphasis on cultural diplomacy, have developed decisively from the 1990s. These relations were spurred on partly by India's 'Look East' policy and partly by Singapore's wish to engage India more strategically. Buddhism and Buddhist art were highlighted as two avenues that established the existence of cultural exchange between the regions. I have personally been involved and witnessed how this has unfolded. I hope that this area of mutual interest and other academic research can further the interests of both countries as well as establish greater efforts in archaeological research and sharing of knowledge for future generations to savour. A concerted effort towards joint research programmes in tangible and intangible heritage is long overdue.

10

India's Economic Liberalisation: The Elephant and the Lion

M. Rajaram

It was Time!

"No power on earth can stop an idea whose time has come." When India's Finance Minister Manmohan Singh uttered these words, taken from the French novelist Victor Hugo, in his 1991–92 budget speech, it marked the start of the Indian economic reformation.

India was then in the midst of an unprecedented economic crisis. Soaring oil prices, resultant from the Gulf War, had caused the cost of India's imports to spike, which in turn drove its trade balances downwards. Weakened national reserves caused investor panic and the value of the Indian currency plummeted. Foreign exchange transactions were tightly regulated. Confidence eroded, the world shunned Indian investments and non-resident Indians wanted their deposits back in quick time. The country faced a double-digit inflation rate with essential commodities most hard hit. This caused extreme hardship, especially to the poorer segments of society.

In the meantime, a close trading partner and inspiration behind India's centrally-planned economy, the Soviet Union, had collapsed. With that, India lost not just a long-time trading relationship but perhaps, more importantly, also its equally long-held commitment to a centrally planned, socialist economic ideology.

India's inward-looking state-controlled five-year plans promulgating domestic industry protectionism and import substitution industrialisation had resulted in an insufficient foreign exchange buffer to withstand the effects of the 1991 events. India was on the brink of national bankruptcy and its reserves were sufficient only for payment for a few weeks of imports. India had to borrow from the International Monetary Fund (IMF) in exchange for Indian gold as collateral and, most significantly, upon the promise of economic reforms.

Previous attempts at opening up the economy had either been reversed, for example, under Indira Gandhi, with the nationalisation of banks being cited as the apogee of economic reforms, or stalled after initial enthusiasm, as during Rajiv Gandhi's government. The newly-elected Prime Minister P V Narasimha Rao knew that it was time to cross the Rubicon. While the balance of payments crisis and the strict conditions imposed by the IMF and the World Bank acted as triggers, there was no doubt that the time had come for the much-needed and long overdue overhaul of India's economy. Although Prime Minister Rao helmed a minority government, he and Dr Singh saw through a full five-year term to firmly set the economic reformation on track. While reforms did waver at various points in time, the days of a closed, insular Indian economy were over for good.

The Strategy and Challenges

The Indian government decided to act in phases. It first adjusted fiscal policies to stabilise India's macro-economics, with more drastic fiscal consolidation thereafter. During his budget speech in July 1991, Dr Singh also stressed that India "...must make a conscious effort to reduce the internal debt of the government and the external debt of the nation, so that we rely more and more on our own resources to finance the process of development." The laggard bureaucratic systems in the state dominated segments of the economy had to make profits rather than continue to incur excessive costs. The 'Licence Raj', whose *raison d'être* was to implement centralised planning and which became barriers to entry to protected sectors, had to be drastically overhauled to facilitate investment and growth. The overhaul of the financial sector was an integral part of the reforms. Financial institutions and financial systems had to be modernised to meet the needs of businesses operating in a market economy. Merchandise trade and the services sector, once the domain of the nationalised industries, now had to contend with foreign competition.

An even more gargantuan task was to change mindsets and attitudes. A high level of protectionism had allowed Indian industries in their formative years to grow without external competition. However, this was no longer feasible for a country that needed to plug into a global economy.

The guiding force of the economic reforms was to establish trade links and promote exports. Foreign direct investments (FDI) were no longer viewed as foreign exploitation of India but as providing access to capital investment, technology advancement, new markets and job creation. Competition in a market economy had to be viewed as market dynamism. Interestingly, Dr Singh, in his budget speech, reconciled liberal economic policies with India's socialist ideology. He described wealth as ultimately a social product which the rich should hold on trust for the benefit of society, especially the poor.

The 'Look East' Policy, 1991

The East Asian miracle had intrigued the world. With phenomenal sustained growth and reduction in income inequality, Japan, South Korea, Taiwan, Hong Kong, Singapore and Thailand had grounded their economies on the model of an export-driven market economy with domestic measures focused on building infrastructure and labour skills. India was part of Asia but neither benefitted from nor enjoyed the economic boom. With the 'Look East' policy, India sought to re-engage these countries.

Other than economic reasons, India's looking east was also motivated by China's rise. China's 'Open Door' policy in 1978 saw its economy accelerate whilst that of India remained stultified by its state regulated economy. Ironically, China's success resulted in suspicions of its commitment to a peaceful rise. India was perceived as the best candidate to balance China's rise. However, many smaller Asian countries still remembered India's Soviet-leanings which had been at odds with many of the Southeast and East Asian countries' pro-United States alignment. India had taken the Soviet side in its support of the Vietnam-backed Heng Samrin regime in Kampuchea. This was at odds with the Association of Southeast Asian Nations (ASEAN)-member states' non-recognition of the regime and of Vietnam's intervention in Kampuchean affairs, as illustrated by India's non-attendance of the 1980 ASEAN Dialogue which was unsurprising to critics.

Singapore's 'India Fever'

The close historical and cultural links between India and Singapore have been extensively described in other essays in this book. Although often described as an Asian Tiger, Singapore's multiracialism and multiculturalism set it apart. The common colonial heritage also meant that Singapore's legal and political system was similar to that in India. Most importantly, English was the common working language of business and government in both countries.

While Singapore's late Minister Mentor Lee Kuan Yew felt India's years of central planning, its caste system and constant conflicts with Pakistan weighed down its progress, he never wavered from his belief in India's potential. Well, prior to India's 'Look East' shift, the sagacious leader was already making multiple trips to India to observe developments. Then Singapore Prime Minister Goh Chok Tong was a champion of India-Singapore economic relations and spoke of sparking a 'mild India fever'. His enthusiasm did not go unreciprocated.

In 1993, then Foreign Minister George Yeo led a Singapore delegation to India. He returned with a positive report. That same year, the Confederation of Indian Industry (CII) organised a visit to Singapore. Representatives of the Singapore Indian Chamber of Commerce and Industry provided the working link between industry representatives and businesses of both nations. One of the first initiatives between both countries was the establishment of the International Tech Park (ITP) in Whitefield, Bangalore. Prime Minister Goh mooted the idea in 1992 and the joint venture was inked in 1994. The Bangalore ITP started operations in 1997 and companies from both countries committed to leases in a show of support. From Singapore, companies such as Siemens Components, Singapore Medical Centre, Singapore Technologies and Singapore Software Centre took up space. The fact that the huge project was completed in just three years would have been remarkable in any country; but for India, it signalled very clearly the death knell of the 'Licence Raj' under which approvals and permits would have taken more than three years. Today, there are ITPs in Pune, Chennai, Hyderabad and Gurgoan, modelled and run along the same lines.

Trade figures between the two countries in the immediate period post-reform were encouraging. Prime Minister Goh, in his speech at the banquet hosted by the CII, shared that trade had up to November 1994 increased by 19 percent compared to the same period in 1993 and Singapore's investments in India increased by 25 percent in 1993 over the previous year. In 2005, India and Singapore ties took a quantum leap with the signing of the India-Singapore Comprehensive Economic Cooperation Agreement (CECA). In June 2019, *The Straits Times* reported that Singapore was the largest source of FDI into India, with some S$22.1 billion flowing into India as of the last Indian financial year ending on 31 March 2019.

The Path of Economic Reformation — Faltering?

India took approximately two years to overcome its balance of payment crisis. Through macro-economic measures, including the devalution of the rupee, its foreign exchange reserves increased to an adequate level and it registered an average annual growth rate of nearly six percent from 1991 to 2000.

The liberalisation of the Indian economy ended certain public-sector monopolies and expanded the private sector. The deregulation contributed to a reduction in corruption: the lesser number of licences meant a lesser need for bribery to obtain them. However, as old licences became detritus from liberalisation, new licenses sprang up for other areas, for example, the environment, forests and land. The old cycle of impediments and corruption from pre-reform days was not completely eradicated. The manufacturing sector found itself benefitting less from the reform policies (compared with the services sector) because strict labour laws restricted, to an extent, the full leeway of operations in a free market economy.

The reforms reduced the *general* poverty ratio from 36 percent in 1993–1994 to 26.1 percent in 1999–2000 and grew India's middle class to more than 350 million people. However, growth was not uniform. Not all states enjoyed the benefits of FDI and job creation. The poorer states, which lacked basic infrastructure, a business friendly political environment and pool of educated and skilled labour, did not receive much investment, even though these states were the ones which most needed the fruits of the reforms. In the post-reform years, large pockets of inefficient public services remained. National schemes such as the Mahatma Gandhi National Rural Employment Guarantee Scheme were introduced in 2005 to remedy the imbalance of growth but these were riddled with "implementation complications, weak financial management and inadequate monitoring", according to a World Bank report.

Sceptics of the reforms have highlighted that India in the 1980s had seen a growth rate of more than five percent. They argue that the 1991 reforms should, therefore, not be credited for India's economic success. However, the counter-perspective is that the 1991 reforms brought about *sustainable* growth and fundamental structural changes, unlike the more fragile and tentative nature of the growth of the 1980s, as seen from the spikes and falls.

The Way Forward

From the outset of India's 'Look East' policy, Singapore was an unwavering proponent of India's re-engagement with ASEAN. Although largely characterised in terms of India's economic liberalisation, 'Look East' also encompassed political and diplomatic aspects. Prime Minister Goh, during the informal 1994 ASEAN Summit, mooted the idea of including India as an ASEAN Dialogue Partner. India was accorded this status the following year. Singapore was also instrumental in promoting India's participation in the ASEAN-organised inaugural 2005 East Asia Summit.

Indian Prime Minister Narendra Modi extended 'Look East' to 'Act East' in a policy announced during the 12th ASEAN-India Summit in 2014. However, in 2019, India declined to be part of the Regional Comprehensive Economic Co-operation (RCEP). Its concerns centre largely on the existing trade deficit with ASEAN and certain RCEP members and the impact of cheap goods from RCEP members on its domestic producers. However, as the Indian economy continues to evolve, it is plausible that India could be part of the RCEP.

The basic underpinnings of the India-Singapore relationship that made the two countries natural partners are unchanged. The economic relationship is not one way. Thousands of Indian companies have established financial and trading operations in Singapore. Many large Indian multinational companies and banks have made Singapore a hub for their regional and even worldwide operations.

11

My *Indianisation*

Ma Swan Hoo

Five years of courtship with an Indian did not quite prepare me for the complexities of all things Indian! My boyfriend, later husband, was born in Singapore and, for all intents and purposes, was Singaporean in every way. The only Indian characteristics he had were his moustache and his fondness for two shirts — one in shocking pink and the other in lime green, both colours of Holi! He was also a self-professed atheist.

My first immersion into Indian customs and traditions was on my wedding day. After our obligatory trip to the Registry of Marriages, we returned home to find several Indian women, close family friends of my in-laws, gathered there. My now husband and I were greeted with an Indian fire ceremony. A metal tray holding a coconut, a bunch of bananas and a little dish of fire was held by the women and moved three times in a circular motion in front of us. Thereafter, we were given a banana each to consume. My mother-in-law who had become a widow just several months earlier was hiding behind the kitchen door, not partaking in this very important part of the wedding rites. I learnt later that as a widow, it was inauspicious for her to be present as she might bring bad luck to the newly weds. Notwithstanding this, my husband led me to the kitchen where his mother was hiding and immediately prostrated at her feet to honour and show his respect for her. I was in great admiration of my husband's conduct. I followed suit. My mother-in-law was extremely moved and her eyes brimmed with happy tears.

Agni, the Sacred Fire, is integral in all Hindu weddings. It is the essence of life, of energy, of purity; it is wisdom, it destroys ignorance and delusions — all necessary elements for a successful marriage.

On the practical side, a marriage should result in plentiful children, though as abiding citizens during Singapore's then Family Planning campaign, we would have to stop at two! Bananas, which grow in bunches in large clusters, symbolise the perennial fertility and endless generations so much desired. Coconut is the quintessential fruit associated with selflessness as every part of the coconut — its trunk, leaves, coir and fruit — are all useful to man. During a wedding, the coconut is also a symbol of the womb — a symbol of life. At other times, the coconut is cracked to symbolise the destruction of self-ego.

Despite being born in India and migrating to Singapore only in adulthood, my mother-in-law had become quite a *kiasu* Singaporean in her approach to religion. She visited temples just once a year on New Year's Day when she would go to several different religious institutions to pray for blessings for her family. She was a very practical woman. On this special occasion of her son's wedding, although a secular one, she felt the need to bless the couple with what she was familiar with: the ultimate blessings of the Hindu deity and the associated symbolic fruits.

That evening, at our wedding reception, I was dressed in my first sari. It was a beautiful heavy red and gold sari, auspicious colours suitable for an Indian bride. My medical classmate, Dr Vijaya Karuppiah, had taught me how to drape the sari. The sari, with its six yards of flowing floor length fabric, has to be neatly pleated and tucked into the petticoat at the waist, with its long sensual pallu swaying gently from the shoulder. The sari is an elegant outfit and looks charming and particularly curious on a non-Indian woman. I learnt that sari-like drapery dates to the Indus Valley civilisation around 2800–1800 BCE. Women in exquisite saris have been described in Silappadikaram, the first Tamil epic, written in the form of a poem of 5,730 lines in the 5th/6th century CE.

Several years after our wedding, I had the honour of being selected by my mother-in-law to perform the simple abbreviated fire ceremony for my sister-in-law's wedding in the United States. When the couple reviewed their wedding video, they noticed that I had moved the fire in an anti-clockwise direction! To my great distress, I learnt then that the right way was to go clockwise! I am very relieved that my sister-in-law has a loving happy marriage blessed with two beautiful children and we remain the best of friends!

My first trip to India was in 1997 to Agra and to the world's most iconic monument of love — the Taj Mahal. And what better day to visit it than on Valentine's Day! My husband had to be in Agra for a neurosurgery conference and he thought this would be the perfect place to bring me to for my first trip to India. Upon arrival at the hotel, he told me, "There's no time to unpack the suitcases. Let's go!" I had read about and seen images of the Taj Mahal, one of the New Seven Wonders of the World but to see with my own eyes, the long reflecting pool with elegant slender trees lining either side, and directly beyond, this splendid monument built of ivory white marble, covered with beautiful Islamic calligraphy, inlaid with precious and semi precious stones — it was all too immensely enchanting.

The Taj Mahal was erected in the 1600s by Mughal Emperor Shah Jahan in memory of his favourite wife Mumtaz Mahal who died during the birth of their 14th child. It was built with the labour of 20,000 men and 1,000 elephants over 22 years. It was touching to see the cenotaphs of Mumtaz Mahal placed centrally and that of Shah Jahan beside it, albeit off centre. It was said that he had planned to have a mausoleum for himself built of black marble across the Yamuna River with a bridge to link the two mausoleums but, as fate would have it, he was deposed by his son Aurangzeb and imprisoned in Agra Fort where, through a little window, he was able to look at the Taj Mahal. I was moved by this man's great love for his wife and happy for him to be placed next to her, though only in death. Despite the numerous visitors there, a certain sense of tranquility and peace filled my heart as I looked across the Yamuna River and tried to imagine the Black Taj on the other side.

After this, we went to visit the Agra Fort nearby, particularly to check out the room with the window where Shah Jahan had spent endless hours gazing at the Taj Mahal and his beloved wife buried there.

The trip to Agra was indeed a charming way for a man of Indian descent to introduce India's beautiful heritage to his non-Indian wife.

The Taj Mahal left such an indelible impression on me that further trips to India were soon compelling. There was so much to discover about incredible India: the several millennia of complex and beguiling history, the spectacular monuments spanning different empires, the colourful festivals, diverse crafts, delightful cuisines and much more. Certainly, the exquisitely beautiful textiles of India were sights to behold in themselves. We made multiple trips to various parts of India: Tamil Nadu from where many Indians (including my parents-in-law) had migrated to Singapore: Thanjavur, Madurai and Kanchipuram/Mahabalipuram — strongholds of the Chola, Pandiya and Pallava empires respectively with their magnificent temples; the capital Chennai, formerly Madras under the British who rebuilt, in 1893, the Saint Thomas Cathedral Basilica which, in the 16th century, was erected by the Portuguese over the tomb of Saint Thomas, one of only three apostles to have churches built over their remains; Chettinad where massive mansions house the Nattukotai Chettiars who came to Southeast Asia as moneylenders. Other states explored and which offered much enlightenment to me into the mysteries of India included Kerala, Maharashtra, Gujarat, Rajasthan, West Bengal, Andhra Pradesh and India's capital, Delhi. A recent trip to Kolkata to search for the missing two fragments of the Singapore Stone, whose only extant fragment is exhibited at our National Museum, remains another highlight of my visits to India. There was a lot for me to learn and understand about all things Indian and I was enjoying it!

Further education in Indian culture and heritage arose during my now almost two decades as a docent at the various museums in Singapore, particularly the Asian Civilisations Museum (ACM) and the Indian Heritage Centre (IHC). When the ACM first opened at the Empress Place in 2003, I organised a study group to prepare our docents for guiding at this museum. The South Asia Gallery was the most difficult because of India's considerably long and complicated history from ancient and medieval to pre-modern and modern with its fascinating archaeological discoveries, numerous empires, periods of foreign rule and multiple religions, some with complex gods and goddesses or bodhisattvas which to the untrained eye, can look rather similar. This was when I learnt a lot about Hinduism, Buddhism, Sikhism, Jainism and Zoroastrianism, in addition to the heritage of Indians in Singapore, as showcased at the IHC.

During those years too, my husband had written the manuscript for a book on India. Sadly, he passed away too early at the age of 55. Together with the Institute of Southeast Asian Studies, I worked on getting the book ready for publication. The months of intensive effort on the book allowed me to discover more about India's rich history from the Indus Valley civilisation to the 18th century — the period covered in the now published book, *The Dancing Girl, A History of Early India* by Balaji Sadasivan.

Interestingly, following my husband's demise, I have become even more connected to and involved with the Indian community. I was invited to sit on the Content and Concept Subcommittee of the IHC during its planning stage and on its Advisory Board after it opened in May 2015. I am also on the Board of Apsaras Arts, an Indian Fine Arts dance company. These expose me to a large number of Indians in Singapore and India, allowing me to interact with them and to discuss various subjects and projects. There is a lot one can learn from the many great minds of the Indian men and women. Their genuine warmth, friendliness and kind hospitality are all very heartwarming. I am invited to the weddings of their children; I see the fire ceremony at temple weddings and realise how complex they are relative to my own wedding. The Singapore Gujarati Society always extends a very warm invitation to my family for their annual Navratri Dandiya night. I am beginning to appreciate the intricacies of Bharatanatyam, Odissi and Karthak dances and seem to be able to, very occasionally and with intense concentration, follow the beat of Carnatic music!

I enjoy the occasions to dress in Indian ethnic wear like saris and salwar kameez, and feast on Indian cuisines of the different states. My mother-in-law had taught me how to cook some Indian dishes, including chicken briyani, Indian curry and spicy prawn, with the recipes written in her stylish cursive handwriting. My education in this continues on YouTube and in workshops on Indian cooking and on banana leaf dining etiquette!

My most recent trip was with Apsaras Arts to Chennai to attend the Music and Dance Festival, where Apsaras Arts dancers performed to much acclaim. I gave the dancers a presentation on Mahabalipuram (one of my favourite destinations) before their trip to this UNESCO World Heritage Site, a place that captured international attention when Indian Prime Minister Narendra Modi hosted Chinese President Xi Jinping there during their India-China Summit in October 2019.

My *Indianisation* is very much work in progress and I am loving every moment of it!

12

Singapore's Pre-colonial Ties with India

Sureshkumar Muthukumaran

The Indic character of pre-colonial Singapore begins most conspicuously with its 14th century Sanskrit name. Singapura or 'City of the Lion' is hardly a unique toponym though; older namesakes exist in Vietnam, the Thai-Malay peninsula and eastern India. Toponyms apart, the meta-language of classical Southeast Asian cultures was overwhelmingly Indic. To date, the region's languages, scripts, literatures, belief-systems, monuments and material cultures bear witness to the millennia of impactful exchanges of peoples, ideas and commodities with South Asia. The 'Indianness' of Southeast Asia is, however, less a case of acculturating into a hegemonic colonising culture but more one of shared processes and simultaneous developments in which indigenous agency figures prominently in the selection and (re)interpretation of Indic models of polity and culture. The maritime confidence and technological proficiency of communities on either side of the Bay of Bengal ensured that regularised monsoonal contact with India was a recurring structural feature of Southeast Asia's history from distant antiquity.

Even a cursory reading of Singapore's pre-colonial past indicates she was no different from the rest of Southeast Asia in harbouring intimate links with India. It should be remarked at this juncture that it is wholly improper to consider Singapore's past with an isolationist paradigm. As the northernmost island of the Riau-Lingga Archipelago, which straddles the Straits of Malacca and South China Sea, Singapore's pre-colonial historical trajectory was intimately linked with the Riau Archipelago, Sumatra and the Thai-Malay peninsula. The documentary and archaeological evidence for Indic contacts is admittedly earlier on the mainland and Sumatra and manifests more forcefully in the form of durable buildings and art-historically valuable artefacts such as those found at the Bujang valley in Kedah. In considering the Indic links of pre-colonial Singapore, two strands of evidence, though by no means the only ones, come into prominent view: 1) the Singapore Stone, the singular surviving epigraphic record of pre-colonial Singapore; and 2) the Malay Annals (*Sejarah Melayu*), a 17th century historiographic text concerned with the genealogy of the Johorean ruling family which traces its lineage to 14th century Singapore via Melaka (now Malacca).

Since the Malay Annals, more accurately known as the *Sulalat al-salāṭīn* (The Genealogy of Kings), will inform our reading of the Singapore Stone as well, a few remarks on its composition will prove pertinent. Manuscript colophons securely establish a 1612 date for the earliest version of the Malay Annals which was redacted by the scholar, Tun Bambang, under the patronage of the Johor prince, Raja Bongsu, later Sultan Abdullah Ma'ayat Shah. An earlier prototype may have existed but the precise character of the urtext remains a matter of speculation. The *Sejarah Melayu* is hardly a sober and veracious account of the past by post-Rankean standards but more a storehouse of political myth preserving as the text itself claims information profitable to rulers, ceremonial protocol for courtly life and a genealogical record to support claims to legitimacy. A comparison with other written and archaeological records suggests some details recorded in the Malay Annals contain a kernel of truth in spite of the regular conflation, embellishment and distortion of past events. While operating in an Islamic milieu, the cosmological and political conceptions of the Malay Annals stem from an earlier Sanskritic Hindu-Buddhist stratum.

The Singapore Stone

The Singapore Stone was a large inscribed boulder about three metres in height which stood at the mouth of the Singapore River. It was obliterated by the British in 1843 in their efforts to expand Fort Fullerton. Of the fragments salvaged, those that were dispatched to Calcutta (now Kolkata) remain untraceable, leaving the single fragment at the National Museum of Singapore the only witness to this imposing epigraph. The published fragments indicate that the 50-odd lined inscription is a Sanskrit record in Kawi characters, a script widely used in the Archipelago, although it is too fragmentary to permit any meaningful reading. One clearly identified word which confirms the Sanskritic affiliation of the text is *kesara* which in the polysemic world of Sanskrit could denote hair, fibre, gold or saffron. Recently, Iain Sinclair has proposed the ending be restored as *kesarī* and hence denote a lion (lit. the maned animal). This appears plausible and it perhaps formed part of a royal title.

In palaeographic terms, the inscription dates between the 10th and 13th centuries and its scale suggests a royal commission. But by whom? The first narrative in the Malay Annals concerning the Singapore Stone recalls that it was erected to commemorate the adventures of Raja Chulan, a swashbuckling conqueror from India. Raja Chulan and a range of characters in the second chapter of the Malay Annals with dynastic names like Suran, Shulan, Chulin and Chulan are refracted versions of a Tamil dynasty called Chola. These characters are almost certainly a blurred memory of the historical Rajaraja and Rajendra Chola whose early 11th century naval expeditions led to the conquest of the Maldives, Sri Lanka, the Nicobar islands and the polity of Srivijaya whose territory extended from Sumatra to southern Thailand. The Malay Annals also accurately recalls that the stone was inscribed in an Indian language and refers to a Hindu-Buddhist *garbhanyāsa* (placing of the embryo) ritual involving the deposition of precious consecration deposits beneath the stela.

It remains to be seen, however, if the inscribed stone was really a record left behind by the Cholas. It could have equally been the handiwork of an aspiring potentate from neighbouring Sumatra. While Chola-style artefacts have been recovered from 11th and 12th century contexts in Sumatra and the Thai-Malay peninsula, none of these sites have produced a Sanskrit inscription in Kawi characters associated with a Chola ruler. The presence of a Sanskrit inscription in early historic Singapore is not, however, completely anomalous. A better-preserved, albeit short 13th century Sanskrit inscription in Nāgarī characters, is found southwest of Singapore on the island of Karimun Besar. This inscription refers to the presence of one Gautamaśrī, a Mahāyāna Buddhist scholar from Gaur in Bengal, suggesting the wider Riau region was well connected to pan-Asian Buddhist, and by extension, commercial-diplomatic networks.

The Malay Annals

While the Singapore Stone indicates some civilisational activity on the island between the 10th and 13th centuries, its pre-colonial heyday was the 14th century when it was host to a major emporium ruled by a dynasty of Indo-Sumatran extraction. For this period, there is now ample archaeological evidence, and the Malay Annals, despite its late dating and problematic narrative, serves as one of the key textual sources. The Malay Annals has no qualms articulating the Indic ancestry of the rulers of Singapore and, by extension, Melaka and Johor. From the vantage point of the 17th century, the Malay kings were simultaneously *bangsa Hindustan* and *raja melayu*. Incidentally, both *bangsa* (Sanskrit *vaṃśa*), meaning lineage, and *rājā* (king) are part of a vast corpus of lexical borrowings from Sanskrit into Malay.

Not only is Raja Chulan identified as the ancestor of the Singapore line of rulers, his progeny in India also produce another lineage which merges with the Singapore one in the figures of Talai Puchudi who marries her second-removed cousin, Sri Rana Wikerma, the third king of 14th century Singapura. Talai Puchudi is implausibly called a daughter of a king of Bija Nagara (Vijayanagara) named Jambuga Raja Mudaliar, a name not encountered in any Indic record. The Malay Annals at this juncture presents a dubious jumble of time-periods over and above mythic elements like murderous garfish, boulder-throwing strongmen and an underwater kingdom. Even the names of Utama, the putative founder of the Singapore dynasty, and those of his brothers (Maniaka and Sapurba) are utterly spurious, deriving from celestial damsels in Indic lore (Tilottama or Nilottama, Menaka and Suprabha). When they miraculously manifest in Palembang, the three brothers are described as youthful, adorned with gem-studded crowns and riding white elephants, resembling no doubt the white-elephant-riding storm god Indra in whose court resided the aforementioned damsels.

So what is one to make of the Malay Annals and its description of the fabulous Indianised kingdom of Singapura? All that can be said is that the historical memory of the Malay world unquestioningly accepted the Indic genealogy of its early rulers, which was furthered by matrimonial ties with contemporary Indian lineages. It is not at all unlikely that a 14th century ruler of Singapore contracted matrimonial ties with an Indian dynasty or a wealthy mercantile family. Such was certainly the case with the Melakan sultan Muzaffar Syah (1446–1459) who was of Tamil descent through his mother, a member of an influential Tamil Muslim mercantile family from Pasai in Sumatra. Returning to Talai Puchudi, the bizarreness of her name perhaps preserves some authentic nickname for a foreign-born royal woman in 14th century Singapura. The sobriquet, meaning 'one whose head is adorned with flowers' in Tamil, is highly unusual as it was routine for women to adorn their head with flowers in both South and Southeast Asia. Perhaps the queen was fond of elaborate coiffures with a proliferation of flowers — a

Singaporean Marie Antoinette? Her personal name, Nila Panchadi, is provided in some recensions of the Malay Annals. In any case, the story of Talai Puchudi bears testimony to the long-standing presence of Tamil speakers who continue to constitute the majority of the Indian population in Southeast Asia.

To conclude, I recall a well-known artefact from 14th century Singapore uncovered at Fort Canning in 1928: the gold armlet imprinted with a *kīrtimukha* (face of glory), a common apotropaic symbol in Indic ornamentation. The origins of the armlet remain indeterminate and scholars have posited both an Indian and Southeast Asian provenance. The ambiguity, I think, speaks strikingly to the seamless confluence of South and Southeast Asia in pre-colonial times.

13

An Extraordinary Affair

Uma Rajan

A question often posed to my father, Dr Shankar, was "Why did you join the Indian National Army (INA)?" His answer was "No single reason but I just had to." Looking at his life, I can identify several factors that influenced him to be part of the INA. Family friends who had been with him during the INA period shared their INA experiences with me.

World War II — a period when world politics, freedom struggle and wars raged — was unknown to me. I was too young to hear my father's INA story. We never had time to sit and have long conversations about his experiences though we did have some serious conversations when I was much older. It was quite painful for him to recollect the memories of atrocities he had seen or the despair, anger, depression, pain and suffering that surrounded him.

Reasons for Joining the INA

Circumstances — Family Situation

My father was a brilliant student and active in uniformed groups, arts (music and theatre) and sports. He first arrived in Singapore as a ship's doctor in 1938 when he was only 29 years old and stayed on to start his own clinic in Geylang. My mother joined him in 1939. I was born in March 1940. My mother and I left for Madras in June 1941. My brother, Kumar, was born in October 1941. We were due to return to Singapore when news came of the bombing of Singapore on 8 December 1941 and the fall of Singapore on 15 February 1942. My father was stranded in Singapore and very much alone. My grandfather sent a Man Friday, Maniam, to assist him in his clinic and home.

Passion for Social Service

My father had a passion for social service and nursed strong values of care and compassion, having watched his parents serve the less privileged and sick. He started devoting much of his time and energy towards this cause. This passion for social service and his being a doctor were strong motivations that led him to enlist as a medical officer in the INA.

Nationalism

It was a time when India's freedom struggle was gaining popularity and two different movements — the Gandhian and Nethaji movements — resonated with every household. My father was exposed to anti-colonial thoughts through radio broadcasts and newspaper reports, and he was inspired by the 'call for freedom'. Visits by nationalist leaders strengthened the nationalistic spirit in him as he heard, saw and felt the love of the people for their country. He listened to patriotic songs by the poet, Subramania Bharathi, and the poet and Nobel laureate, Rabindranath Tagore, and sang with emotion, yearning for a free India. He was an avid listener of stories on patriotic heroes and the need for a new India became deeply rooted in his mind.

Patriotism

Prior to World War II, the diaspora Indian community retained strong political, emotional and economic ties with India. The INA and Nethaji

Subhas Chandra Bose brought the spirit of nationalism to diaspora Indians. Patriotism was already a part of the daily life of many families and was one of the key reasons for my father joining the INA. He started taking part in INA events and activities from the formation of the first INA in February 1942 and its collapse and disbanding in December 1942. This was followed by the formation of the second INA headed by Nethaji, whose charismatic appeals at the Cathay building on 4 July 1943 and Farrer Park on 9 July 1943 for mobilisation of Indian civilians with no military experience to form a truly INA, touched many a chord, including my father.

Nethaji's magnetic oratory skills at the Padang mass rally drove the crowd to a feverish pitch and they responded rapturously. His fiery speech kindled a dignified patriotism in my father, along with a strong belief and conviction in the INA's aim of freeing India from British rule. He and his diaspora family in Rangoon donated funds to support the INA.

Friendship

While age, passion for social service, nationalism and patriotism could have been important reasons for my father joining the INA, it was his long-standing friendship as a doctor with Captain (Dr) Lakshmi Swaminathan, the Commander of the Rani of Jhansi regiment of the INA that was the final push. Both of them were from the Madras Medical College. My parents developed a friendship with Lakshmi upon her arrival to Singapore in 1940 to pursue academics and initiate her medical practice to take care of the Indian diaspora, along with several Chinese and Malay patients. Lakshmi also lived in the vicinity of my parent's residence. They met often, visited each other's homes and interacted professionally and as a family.

Lakshmi would come to our home to interact with my mother. She also played with me. My mother proudly announced often that Lakshmi carried me and attended my first birthday party. My father and Lakshmi spent time together even before the INA days and later on when he was alone in Singapore. Lakshmi's inspiring personality triggered the fire of patriotism in my father and many Indians to fight for a concept called 'Say India'. Her inspiration rallied many men, including my father, into action. He finally joined the INA as a doctor.

The INA in Singapore

Having enlisted with the INA on 5 September 1943, my father worked alongside Lakshmi to provide medical support. He knew life would never be the same again. In line with his experience in social service for the community, he knew that this would be the best way he could contribute to the cause.

His friends in Singapore remembered seeing him at the INA headquarters accompanying Nethaji and his Japanese counterparts in their regular walks along Waterloo Street and Bras Basah Road. He made his official medical rounds to tend to the wounded and sick in St Joseph's Institution, one of the makeshift hospitals of the INA. He would meet Lakshmi at the Waterloo Centre for the Rani of Jhansi regiment to discuss medical matters. Interestingly, some family friends shared that they also visited my father to provide volunteer support for his medical service.

The family in India was not aware of my father's plans and movements as communications, which were far and few, came to a standstill by the end of 1943. He had received my photograph as a three-year old, which he said he held onto tightly during his trek through Burma and while in internment in Red Fort in India. The family lived in the hope that my father was somewhere in Singapore or Burma.

Experiences in Burma

Once he enlisted, my father totally dedicated himself to the INA cause as a devoted medical officer. He highlighted that the training schedule for the INA's march from Singapore to Delhi through Burma was tough and involved tactical combat and weapon skills, including mastering the rifle, bayonet and grenade, among others, and living in very basic conditions — very unlike the world he was used to be a part of. After several months of intensive training in 1943, the INA was ready to free India and Nethaji planned to enter north-east India from Burma.

In January 1944, the INA headquarters shifted from Singapore to Rangoon to mount the final offensive. My father was an integral part of the medical support for the 2nd INA as it fought with the Imperial Japanese army against the British and Commonwealth forces in the Burma campaigns — at Imphal and Kohima — and later against the Allied retaking of Burma.

In March 1944, my father was with the INA when it successfully staged two offensive military campaigns and captured Imphal and Arakan. They crossed the border on 18 March 1944 and stood on Indian soil and hoisted the Indian flag in Manipur in April 1944. The plan to capture Kohima took longer than expected due to the arrival of the monsoon. He saw fierce fighting and, by 1 June 1944, the heavy monsoon made entry into Imphal difficult. Rivers overflowed with mud and transportation by river was difficult. The INA had run out of supplies and succumbed to starvation, injuries, illness and the war. Allies counter offensive forced the INA to be on the defensive and in retreat. The Japanese progressively withdrew from Burma while the remnants of the INA began their long march on foot towards safety in Bangkok in Thailand — the 'epic retreat'. My father continued on this march with the INA and provided medical support.

By March 1945, with the tide of war was turning against it, the INA leadership decided to beat a retreat before it could enter Imphal. On 20 March 1945, on the way to Maymyo, there was heavy bombing by the British. Broken shells were shattered all over the place and the INA went on a retreat. My father trekked through the swamps and forests of Burma to get fellow fighters back safely to their homes. He kept his spirits up singing patriotic songs and sharing family stories. He could hear the groans of the wounded through the occasional silent laughter of some soldiers. There was despondency and despair in the air.

The INA had more or less ceased to exist although some activities continued until Singapore was recaptured by the British. My father was very much aware of the likelihood of never returning to his family in India. He persevered, along with his colleagues, to tend and care for the wounded facing the hardships of camp life. He developed a hatred for fish as he had to spear the rivers in Burma for fish with his bayonet as it was the only source of food. In the months that followed, my father was heavily involved in rescuing wounded soldiers when the British bombed the Red Cross hospital in Rangoon. Rangoon fell in May 1945. The Japanese surrendered on 15 August 1945. The INA was dissolved in August 1945. Its effects continued to be felt in the Indian independence movement. Captured troops were transported via transit camps in Rangoon to detention camps all over India. By November 1945, many were released and returned to civilian life. My father was captured as a spy in Rangoon and sent to India to be interned at the detention camp in Red Fort for about six months. While at Red Fort, the interrogation process brought my father and his youngest brother in an emotional face-to-face encounter after six years. My father was not easily recognisable due to his moustache and beard. Following the intense interrogation process, he was released.

A Daughter's Feelings about the INA's Role in India's Struggle for Independence

My tears well up, a lump develops in my throat and my heart becomes heavy as memories of my father's life experiences in Burma flood back to me. I am reminded of my precious years of not being with my father. However, pride and respect for the INA engulf me when I recall the immense contributions and sacrifices made by the Indian community to the freedom struggle and that my father too had played a role in the struggle.

It is extremely gratifying that INA members like Lakshmi, John Thivy and John Jacob were widely commemorated and given important roles in public life in India and Southeast Asia. They continued to remain in touch with my father after the dissolution of the INA and we were closely associated with Nethaji Hindi School and Nethaji Library. My father was on the panel of doctors for the Indian High Commission.

Posterity will recall the INA and talk about the courageous role of its members. The INA is viewed with great pride and reverence in India and the Indian diaspora and it remains a popular and passionate topic in Indian culture and politics. The INA kindled in me the spirit of patriotism for India which has transcended over to Singapore, my beloved home, where I was born and where I have a stable secure life — one that I cherish.

14

Nalanda University in India: Reviving Ancient Glory

Hernaikh Singh

Established in 427 CE by King Kumaragupta of the Gupta Dynasty, Nalanda University was the world's first international university. The word 'Nalanda' translates to 'there is no stopping the gift of knowledge' in Sanskrit.

For more than 700 years, the university was a centre of learning for a wide range of subjects, including Buddhism, philosophy, mathematics, science and public health. It had thousands of students from all over Asia, including Southeast Asia. Sadly, it was destroyed by an invading army led by Muhammad bin Bakhtiyar Khalji in the 12th century.

The knowledge housed in Nalanda, including the thousands of books, was one of the most advanced in the world at that time. The destruction of the university was, therefore, not only a loss for India, but also for the rest of world.

The Revival

In 2006, then Indian President Dr A P J Abdul Kalam, a Muslim, proposed the idea of reviving Nalanda University. Excited at the prospect of a renaissance of ancient Asian knowledge and bringing South, Southeast and East Asia together again, then Singapore's Foreign Affairs Minister, George Yeo, a Catholic, took forward the idea and succeeded in securing its endorsement at the East Asia Summit (EAS) a year later.

A Nalanda Mentor Group was established in June 2007 to conceptualise the establishment of the university. Led by Indian Nobel laureate Professor Amartya Sen, it included Meghnad Desai, Baron Desai, a British economist; Sugata Bose, a professor at Harvard University; Professor Wang Gungwu, an eminent historian from Singapore; and Mr Yeo, among others. Singapore hosted the inaugural meeting of the group in July 2007 and, in November 2007, the Asian Civilisations Museum of Singapore organised a brilliant exhibition on the ancient Nalanda University and the spread of Buddhism from India to China and Southeast Asia.

Built next to the original site in Bihar, the university is a non-profit, public-private partnership. The Bihar government provided the land and funding as capital and recurring expenditure for the university. Financial contributions were also made by a number of countries, including China, Australia, Thailand and Laos. Deemed an international university, Nalanda University comes directly under India's Ministry of External Affairs, unlike other top academic institutions which report to the Ministry of Human Resource Development.

Challenges

Soon after its opening in September 2014, Nalanda University ran into several difficulties, which seriously affected its standing and reputation.

Ownership

First, the university fell victim to India's partisan politics and the deep animosity between the Bharatiya Janata Party (BJP) and the Congress Party.

In May 2014, the BJP-led coalition came to power on the back of a resounding general election victory. As the university was a brainchild of the Manmohan Singh government and the Congress Party, the ruling party showed little interest in it.

Bihar's Chief Minister Nitish Kumar, who was a prime mover behind the idea of reviving the university, was initially interested in it and even criticised the government for its interference in the university's administration. However, since partnership with the BJP is crucial for his political advancement, Mr Kumar has treaded carefully on the issue of the university with New Delhi.

Resignation of the Mentor Group

The first sign that all was not well at the university was when Professor Sen resigned as the university's first chancellor in early 2015. His replacement, Mr Yeo, also resigned as its chancellor in November 2016. His resignation came soon after then Indian President Pranab Mukherjee decided to remove the Mentor Group without consulting the chancellor. The government also decided to deny an extension to Dr Gopa Sasharwal's tenure as the university's vice-chancellor.

The Mentor Group's removal also saw the departure of Baron Desai and Professor Bose, who, like Professor Sen, were well-known critics of the Narendra Modi government. The Indian government proceeded to establish a Governing Board to replace the Mentor Group. While expressing his surprise at the decision, Mr Yeo pointed to political interference stating: "The sudden dissolution of the old Nalanda Board is bound up with Indian domestic politics, which I do not wish to be embroiled in."

However, the Indian government denied that the Mentor Group's removal was politically motivated. Then Minister of State for External Affairs, Dr V K Singh, clarified that the Mentor Group continued to function as the Governing Board for nine years though "...the Nalanda University Act, 2010, stipulates a tenure of only three years." Furthermore, the Governing Board should only comprise members whose countries have made financial contributions. Japan and Singapore did not. Additionally, it did not include members from the Bihar government, as stipulated under the Act.

Decision-making and Financial Management

The Indian government also raised questions about the decision-making process and financial management by the Mentor Group. It alleged that apart from the failure to submit its recommendations within nine months of its constitution as required, the group went ahead to make decisions on matters such as the adoption of statutes and rules and regulations despite not having any representation from Bihar. The Indian government also accused the group of other irregularities.

Progress Made

In spite of the trials and turbulences, the university has made some progress over the last few years.

Following its first cohort of 15 students and 11 faculty members in two schools, the university's intake increased to 130 students from 13 countries in 2016. Today, its five schools have 100 students in postgraduate courses and 650 in diploma and certificate programmes, with 26 faculty members, which include four foreigners. More than half of the students are foreigners.

The university is expected to start its PhD programmes in 2020 to complement its current offerings. It also has plans to launch three research centres — BIMSTEC-Centre for Bay of Bengal Studies; Common Archival Resource Centre; and Centre for Conflict Resolution and Peace Building. Additionally, it has inked memoranda of understanding with 19 countries supporting its revival, up from six during the EAS in 2007.

Spanning more than 400 acres, the new Nalanda campus will expand from its current five buildings to 110 buildings which will include 17 non-residential and 80 residential facilities. The new campus will be able to accommodate some 7,000 people at any given time.

In 2016, UNESCO added Nalanda University to its World Heritage list, signifying its importance as an archaeological site.

Moving Forward

Nalanda University cannot bring back the past. In its new incarnation, it must take account of the revolutionary changes which have taken place in the world. This does not, however, mean that the university cannot become a great, internationally-renowned academic institution. India has the ability, capacity and capability to make it happen. The country is home to some of the world's best institutes of management and technology, and their graduates rank among the brightest in the world.

However, India must address several key issues if it hopes the university will relive at least some of its past glory. These include an attractive pedagogy and curriculum, funding and infrastructure development. I shall not touch on all of these issues, save three — support, autonomy and international reputation — which, in my view, underpin the university's ultimate success.

Support and Autonomy

On 2 October 2015, Mr Ravi Velloor of *The Straits Times* wrote:

> ... [Professer] Sen [was] probably correct in asserting that Mr Modi should not interfere in Nalanda's academia. But the Indian leader certainly ought to involve himself more in executing the project, even if it was an initiative of the previous government. He should bring his doer's instincts to play and not only robustly back the project, but also monitor its implementation.

The university needs significant financial, logistics and administrative resources. The Indian government has these resources. The government should also outline the university's broad academic framework and national priorities. However, it must refrain from being involved in the university's operational management.

Both Professor Sen and Mr Yeo were critical of the government's involvement in the university's affairs. In his letter to the Nalanda University Board just before stepping down, Professor Sen expressed his regret at the government's interference: "...the academic governance in India remains so deeply vulnerable to the opinions of the ruling government." Similarly, Mr Yeo mentioned that when he succeeded Professer Sen as the chancellor, he was given repeated assurances that the university would retain autonomy. However, it was not the case.

The comments by and the resignations of key members of the board seriously impacted the university's standing. Mr Yeo explained:

> The circumstances under which the leadership change at Nalanda University has been suddenly and summarily effected [are] disturbing and possibly harmful to the University's development.

As a result of the delays and disputes, the Nalanda dream suffered a setback and interest in the initiative waned.

Building International Reputation

In March 2010, in a Singapore Ministry of Foreign Affairs press release, Mr Yeo said:

> Nalanda is an icon of the Asian renaissance in the 21st century and should draw students and scholars from everywhere as it once did. It should be a centre of civilizational dialogue and inter-faith understanding as it once was. It should again make available for the common betterment of all human beings, knowledge already existing in the world.

At its historical peak, Nalanda University boasted of more than 10,000 students and faculty members from all over the world. Even the famous Chinese monk, Xuanzang, spent time at the university studying Sanskrit and Brahmana philosophy.

The university needs to build its image beyond the Indian subcontinent. It currently has four international faculty members. It needs to attract a well-qualified cosmopolitan faculty with international connections. Similarly, its Governing Board must include scholars of world repute. It must also improve the diversity in its student population and curriculum. It must, in short, be distinguished and unique.

Nalanda, Singapore and Regional Partnerships

Singapore had contributed to Nalanda University's research through the establishment of the Nalanda-Sriwijaya Centre at the then Institute of Southeast Asian Studies (ISEAS) [now ISEAS-Yusof Ishak Institute] in August 2009. Mr Yeo was instrumental in its conceptualisation, proposing that the centre should be larger than just a Buddhist Study Centre, as originally planned. With Sriwijaya encompassing Indonesia, Malaysia, Singapore and Southern Thailand, Mr Yeo wanted the centre "...to go beyond national definitions". He even took the idea to Thailand and proposed the establishment of a Nalanda-Suvarnabhumi Centre in Chulalongkorn University.

For the next 10 years, led by Dr Tansen Sen, the centre in Singapore sought "...to promote the Nalanda idea of Asian achievements and mutual learning, and the Sriwijaya idea of Southeast Asia as a place of mediation and links across civilisations."

Through the centre, Singapore was intimately connected with the Nalanda initiative. Effort should be made to revive this collaboration which will reaffirm and strengthen Singapore's stake in Nalanda University and ensure that it does well in future. The Indian Heritage Centre could be the lead organisation from Singapore for this purpose.

Nalanda University's international linkages are largely with institutions in EAS-member countries. The most recent partnership was signed with Japan's Kanazawa University in 2017. Thus, in spite of the adversities it has encountered over the years, the university has been able to build some important links, in line with its original mandate of being an EAS project. This reflects some hope and the possibility that countries with which India has strong and established relations — Japan, Australia and Singapore — could be the partners that the university could bank on for its global brand-building.

Conclusion

India's decision to revive Nalanda University is a noble one. It made some headway in the initial years, winning the support of several EAS-member countries and putting in place a strong Mentor Group. However, the change of government in India in 2014 has altered the fortunes of the university.

Mr Yeo had previously stated: "Nalanda is an idea whose time has come. It is bigger than and will outlast any of us." He, like the other members of the Mentor Group and the initiators of the revival process, had a vision for the university. India has the potential to make that vision a reality.

15

Singapore-India Links through Hinduism

Vineeta Sinha

Scholars speak of waves of Indian mobilities outwards from the Indian subcontinent over time. There is overwhelming historical, archaeological and numismatic evidence of the early presence of Hindu and Buddhist elements — art, sculpture and architecture, music, dance, drama and literature, political and social institutions and religious traditions — outside the Indian subcontinent in regions and cultures, known post-World War II, as Southeast Asia. In the latter region, posts which served as halting stations for ships plying trade and maritime routes were located at the neck of the Malay Peninsula which facilitated mercantile and trading activities in the region. Singapore was placed firmly in regional maritime and commercial histories of these times.

The 1830s saw the forced global movement of Indians as labour to serve the needs of European colonial economies. It is estimated that, between 1830 and 1917, 2.5 million Indians were placed around the world as indentured labour to serve the burgeoning needs of industrial capitalism. Large numbers of Indians were brought in from South India, specifically Tamil Nadu, as cheap labour for estates and public works in British Malaya. Much of this labour was drawn from the lowest rungs of the Indian class and caste hierarchy, from the non-Brahmin, Adi-Dravida communities from rural parts of South India. Notably, between the 15th and 19th centuries, smaller numbers of Indians who travelled voluntarily as paying passengers and commercial and professional migrants also arrived on Malayan shores and to Singapore. The majority of the Indians who migrated to British Malaya were of a Hindu background, who formed about 80 percent of this group, others being Sikhs, Muslims and Christians. Other segments of the Indian population that migrated to Malaya belonged to the commercial, professional and clerical sectors. Sindhi, Punjabi, Gujarati and Tamil merchants had been present in Malaya from as early as the foundation of Penang in 1798. Of the huge numbers who arrived to these new shores, a majority eventually settled here, making a new home for themselves.

Historical data attest to the strong and early Hindu presence in colonial Malaya and the island of Singapore from the early decades of the 19th century. This is evident from the figures of Hindu arrivals to these shores, the widespread early establishment of places of worship dedicated to deities from South Indian *bhakti* tradition and village-based Hinduism, the records of the early observance of festivals such as *tai pucam* and *timiti,* both in the 'rubber estate temples' as well as those in the urban centres in Singapore, Kuala Lumpur, Penang and Malacca. The worship of village goddesses from Tamil Nadu was imported together with rituals and festivals widespread in mid-19th century rural South India. The village deities, male and female, accompanied Tamil, Hindu migrants to Malaya, as their *kula deivam* (household deity), *ista deivam* (personal, favoured deity) and as *ellai kaaval deivam* (guardian deities of boundaries), widely popular with low caste and Adi-Dravida communities in Tamil Nadu. These gods and goddesses (like Mariamman, Kaliamman and Periyacheeamman) were deemed to be central in managing pragmatic issues relating to fertility, health and well-being, and in affording protection from diseases and natural calamities. Male deities like Aiyyanar, Muneeswaran, Madurai Veeran, Muniandy and Karuppanasami, defined as guardian deities, security guards, bodyguards and attendants to female goddesses also arrived and were literally grounded in the local religious landscape.

In Singapore, the practice of building a *sami veedu* (Tamil for 'God's house') near residential spaces and work areas (such as ports, prisons and railway tracks) was widespread in the early decades of the 19th century, and the British colonial rulers were rather 'liberal' in allowing the natives to have their places of worship. The predominance of migrants from South India meant that a large number of temples were built for the gods of Tamil Nadu, especially those from folk, rural and popular forms of Hinduism. Interestingly, contemporary Tamil Hindus in Singapore have sustained, with vigour and enthusiasm, mother-goddess worship, veneration of *kaaval deivam,* celebrated festivals of *Tai Pucam and Timiti* and have adhered to the ritual complex of folk, village-based Hinduism, that is, the 'old ways' of their ancestors. At the same time, they have built and sustained agamic Hindu temples, where a text-based, theistic, *bhakti, devotional* tradition flourishes.

Hindu temple building in Singapore is dated to the 1820s, with the Sri Mariamman Temple being built in 1827. Over time, many of the early temples which had begun their lives as shrines grew into agamic temples. In addition to the numerous shrines dedicated to the folk deities of popular Hinduism on the island, agamised Hindu temples were built, including Srinivasa Perumal Temple (1855), Veeramma Kaliamman Temple (1834) and Sri Manmatha Karuneshwarar Temple (1888). Certainly, at the turn of the 20th century, the 'Indian connection' was seen to be important in the religious life of the migrant Hindu community in Singapore. The Mohamedan and Hindu Endowments Board was a statutory board set up by the British in 1905 to manage Hindu endowments in the Straits Settlements. Even for the British members of this board, the idea that the architecture of Singapore's Hindu temples needed to conform to Hindu and Indian precepts was crucial. The board members made efforts to establish what the 'Indian practice' vis-à-vis temple building was — as a guide for its own actions and turned to Indian experts. This relationship of dependence and connections with Tamil Nadu is instructive in revealing the continuing orientation to India as the locus and authority of Hindu affairs and in the early exporting of 'official Hinduism' in the model of agamic-style temples and the corresponding style of religiosity therein, to diasporic shores. Consequently, by the first decade of the 20th century, artists, sculptors, Hindu religious experts and Brahmin priests arrived in Singapore to conduct ritual in the newly-built Hindu temples.

The agamic temples were conceptualised, constructed and consecrated according to prescriptions outlined in the *Agamas* and were served by a retinue of trained ritual specialists (Brahmins and *Pandarams*) who hailed, then and now, mainly from Tamil Nadu. Especially salient is the fact that no community of Brahmins emigrated as ritual specialists to serve the local Hindu community in colonial Singapore. The building of agamic temples on the island (during this period) appears all the more ironic because up to the first half of the 20th century, for the largely non-Brahmin, Adi-Dravida members of the migrant Hindu population in Singapore, agamic temples were as inaccessible to them as they had been to their ancestors across the oceans. Agamic temples were only opened to Adi-Dravida communities in Malaya and Singapore after World War II and in response to the removal of bans on temple entries in India itself.

An account of Singaporean Hinduism would be incomplete without acknowledging a range of social reform groups and new Hindu movements which were imported from India and today enjoy a popular local following. Some prominent examples include the Sri Aurobindo Society, International Society for Krishna Consciousness, Radha Soami Satsang, Brahma Kumari Raja Yoga Centre, Sai Baba Movement, Amma's Society and the Art of Living Centre, among others. Having been introduced into Singapore in the 1960s, these movements have attracted a substantial following, not just from within the Indian-Hindu community.

Historically, access to ritual objects has especially been a challenge for diasporic Hindu communities. India is viewed not only as the sacred centre for Hinduism, but, more importantly, also as a key market for securing a range of ritual objects as commodities — seen to be crucial for expressing Hindu religiosity. Commercial ties and kinship alliances amongst the diasporic Indian community in Singapore and India are not new. Travel to parts of India has long been regular and frequent for Singaporean Indian Hindus. Over time, changes in the modes of transportation have dramatically reduced both travel time and cost, making it possible to undertake these trips. The 'Indian connection' has thus been maintained with enhanced possibilities for moving back and forth easily across these regions. For local Hindus, religious ties have been kept alive through allegiance to ancestral villages, household deities and family temples. Scores of Singaporean Hindus, even today, support and nourish their family temples (located in Tamil Nadu villages) financially and in other ways and make regular trips to be present at important ritual ceremonies there. Many others also regularly undertake pilgrimages to key Hindu sacred sites across India.

Demographically, Singapore's contemporary Hindu population is fairly young. By 1980, 93.09 percent of the local Hindu community belonged to the resident population of Singapore and 83.41 percent were Singapore citizens. In 2010, the Hindu population in Singapore stood at just about 5.1 percent, a significant upward shift from the 2000 Census figure of four percent. To-date, Hindu temples and the festivals of *Tai pucam* and *Timiti* are visible in this densely urban cosmopolitan city-state. For Singapore, the cultural connectivity and interactions with India continue to be renewed well into the present with new Indian Hindu arrivals (since the 1990s), many of whom have established community associations which represent their cultural and religious interests. Singapore's layered and textured Hindu communities have sustained vibrant manifestations of devotional Hinduism, both in public and in households. The small Singaporean Hindu community has energetically and doggedly sustained Hindu traditions and rituals imported from Indian shores but also introduced innovations to produce a specifically Singaporean version of Hinduism.

16

Madame High Commissioner

Karen Tan

When asked to contribute an essay for the book, Ambassador Tommy Koh gave me a free rein to pen my thoughts on a subject of my choice. Recalling an article, *'My Faith in India',* he had written for *The Straits Times* while I was still at post, where he cited, among India's challenges, "the discrimination of girls ..." and the fact that "Indian women are not treated with sufficient respect and equity", it occurred to me, as Singapore's only female High Commissioner to serve in India (so far), that I too could offer a unique perspective on the subject through my own experiences.

My own journey to India was fairly straightforward. The offer of the assignment was made while I was serving as Singapore's Permanent Representative to the World Trade Organization and the World Intellectual Property Organization in Geneva. Back home for a short break, the Permanent Secretary asked to meet me. I am not sure whether lunch was thrown in as a sweetener, but as a long-time fan of India and all things Indian, I did not need to be convinced to take up the post. Rather, I felt honoured to be considered for the position. We were experiencing an uptick in our relations, with a surge in economic ties and investments, greater military engagements and more flights between Singapore and destinations in India. In addition, we were benefitting from the cultural and people-to-people exchanges that were already taking place. I was excited at the prospect of being able to play a role in further intensifying our ties with the subcontinent. The accreditation from New Delhi to Bhutan and Nepal were added attractions.

I presented my credentials to the President of the Indian Republic, Mdm Pratibha Patil, on 25 February 2011 at the Rastrapathi Bhavan, the Indian equivalent of Singapore's Istana. Coincidentally, I was Singapore's first female High Commissioner to India and President Patil, the first female President of India. Prior to me, 11 men had served as Singapore's High Commissioners to India since we established diplomatic relations on 24 August 1965.

Being the first female Head of Mission in New Delhi had not struck me as being out of the ordinary. After all, I had the necessary subject expertise. I had served as the Director overseeing *inter alia*, South Asia and had travelled to India on several occasions, most memorably, when Prime Minister Goh Chok Tong was invited as the Chief Guest for the Republic Day celebrations on 26 January 1994. Moreover, throughout my career in the foreign ministry, I have found it to be generally gender neutral when it came to postings overseas. Several female Foreign Service Officers had served in the New Delhi mission prior to my arrival and continue to do so, as have those from other ministries and agencies.

For many of my Indian interlocutors, however, it was somewhat of a talking point, especially during my first few months at post. I found this observation and reaction (to the fact that I was a woman, single and relatively young) somewhat puzzling as the Indian establishment is no stranger to having women in high-level positions. In addition to the President, the Head of the Indian National Congress, the party in power at the time, was a woman, Sonia Gandhi. Indira Gandhi had served as Prime Minister twice. There were also several powerful Chief Ministers in office then such as Jayalalitha Jayaram in Tamil Nadu, Sheila Dikshit in Delhi, Mamata Banerjee in West Bengal and Mayawati in Uttar Pradesh. At the federal government level, there were woman Ministers,

Permanent Secretaries (the Foreign Secretary at the time was Nirupama Rao) as well as the Speaker of the Lok Sabha or the Lower House of Parliament, Meira Kumar (coincidentally the first woman to be elected to the position) and a good number of female Members of Parliament (MPs), some in their thirties.

The late Sushma Swaraj, who became Minister for External Affairs under Prime Minister Narendra Modi, was among those I had the good fortune to work with when planning a visit to Singapore. Others included the late Chief Minister Dikshit who oversaw the setting up of the first Singapore Skills Centre in New Delhi and Chief Minister Banerjee who graced the welcome of the inaugural SilkAir flight to Calcutta. When I called on the late Jayalalitha in Chennai as part of my introductory calls, I presented her with a huge bouquet of pink and white lilies on the advice of our Consul-General Ajit Singh. An imperious figure from behind her large desk, she broke into a wide smile to welcome me. During these interactions, what always struck me was that these rather diminutive women commanded an army of officials and oversaw regions and populations many times the size of Singapore.

These recollections of interactions with powerful women remind me of a recurring experience I encountered in casual settings outside the bubble we diplomats moved around in. To those unaware of my 'lofty' position, when dressed informally in *kurtas* (loose collarless shirts) or jeans on weekends or holidays, I was often mistaken for a salesgirl or the service staff in a supermarket or shop. I never thought to question why there was this case of mistaken identity until the penny dropped during a conversation with a friend in the hotel industry. The service industry in New Delhi and other metropolitan cities is largely populated by Indians from the Northeastern states, such as Assam. They are sought after, as someone has explained, because of their "distinct appearance and English language skills". Since I was female, spoke good English and "looked the same" as a Northeasterner, that is, more Chinese than Indian, it was not surprising for me to be mistaken as a local, and pigeonholed. I personally found this all rather amusing, but it made me think not only about the systemic prejudice that exists in Indian society, but also the bias that still prevails in all our societies. There is scope for greater elaboration on this subject but I will leave it to the experts to do so.

Another example of discrimination, this time because of my gender, came from within the High Commission itself. A long-serving local staff member wrote a letter of complaint against me, probably unhappy that a woman had taken a decision not to extend his service beyond the retirement age, and to offer his position to a woman. To give him the benefit of doubt, he was just trying to keep his job, but the nature and tone of the letter was clear, at least to me.

Barring these instances, I never felt that my gender was a factor in my ability to conduct my duties as High Commissioner. I have often wondered whether this was because I was THE High Commissioner. Although the caste system is from a bygone era, it still permeates Indian society, and rank and position are still strongly respected, especially one accompanied by the waving country flag affixed to an official car or following the two letters of the alphabet, HE (His/Her Excellency). As I was to find out on many an occasion, being a talking point could also be parleyed into an asset. However, beyond the title and, more importantly, Singapore's close and extensive ties with India, built up and nurtured over the years by my predecessors as well as Singapore political leaders, provided a good foundation on which to further broaden and deepen our bilateral relations.

So, while I could characterise my experiences during my two-and-a-half years in New Delhi as empowering (and satisfying), I also witnessed and lived amidst this tension between women who wielded a great deal of power and those that barely eked out a living — poor, discriminated against and vulnerable. I have spoken about the women who were in positions of power and influence. However, on the other extreme, I also saw those who toiled under the scorching sun as daily-rated labourers, using their bare hands to break stones to construct, inch by inch, mile-long stretches of highways. As there was a slum adjacent to the Singapore High Commission's premises, I noted that it was mainly the women who queued for and carried the water when the municipal tankers made their regular stops. They were the ones who had the indignity of having to stoop by the roadside to defecate because of the lack of toilets and basic sanitation. The most abhorrent was the violent gang rape of "Nirbhaya" (meaning "fearless") in December 2012 which triggered demonstrations and protests all across India. Among these acts of violence against women, this case still resonates with me as a critically-ill "Nirbhaya" was medevaced to Singapore for treatment but died from her injuries two days later. In March 2020, four of the perpetrators of this heinous act were executed, more than seven years after the crime. To this day, I have not been able to reconcile how these two extremes coexist in a modern India. Much more needs to be done, for starters, by the many female role models that exist today — whether in government, business or the cultural and education sectors and civil society — to change mindsets, attitudes and behaviours.

While not trivialising this continuing challenge, let me end on a happier note. I remain a fan and consider myself a friend of India. Like Ambassador Koh, I have great faith in the country. The achievements and world class Indians, both men and women, continue to propel the country forward. We have much to learn from India. Looking back, I was fortunate to have had a front row seat to witness India's economic success, to experience its cultural and religious diversity, engage in its intellectual vibrancy and enjoy, share and delight in its rich and varied history. When I left New Delhi for New York in June 2013, it felt as if it was a 'mission unaccomplished'. What was meant to be a five-year assignment had been halved due to an unfortunate run-in with cancer and, later, exigencies of service. Of its 29 states, I had only managed to visit 11 for work purposes, including Bihar where we were working to establish a university in Nalanda. Among the tourism sites, I had wanted to visit the tea plantations of Assam, the UNESCO World Heritage sites of Ajanta and Ellora, the temples of Tamil Nadu, the former French settlement of Pondicherry and the backwaters of Kerala. I did not have the opportunity to stay on a houseboat on Dal Lake in Kashmir or meet the Dalai Lama who has residence in Dharamsala. I felt that I had only skimmed the surface of what made India, India. I would miss the pre-dinner drinks (whiskey and Old Monk rum) with journalists, MPs, business tycoons, and civil servants on the political issues of the day, the machine-gun back and forth of the political commentators on television, cluttered and cramped bookshops, the cricket matches that saw the whole country unite behind the tricolours of saffron, white and green, Bollywood and serene misty walks in Lodhi Park. The list goes on.

Today, I have daily reminders of my India sojourn when I get up in the morning and step on the Kashmiri silk carpet I bought when I first visited Agra and the Taj Mahal more than 20 years ago or whenever I pass the photograph of me together with President Patil and where I recall her, on accepting my credentials with a knowing smile, addressing me as "Madame High Commissioner".

17

Historical Ties between India and Singapore

Tan Tai Yong

The histories of Singapore and India are intertwined in many aspects. A direct connection was formed during the period of British rule but there is evidence that linkages between Singapore and India go back even longer. Scholars have suggested that Tamil merchant guilds had started establishing their presence in Southeast Asia as far back as the 10th century. In the 11th century, the Chola Kingdom was thought to have launched a series of naval campaigns in the region in order to advance its trading interests as well as draw the Melaka Straits port-polities into its orbit. There is archaeological evidence to suggest that from the 13th to 15th century, Temasek (or Singapura) had economic relations with India.

The establishment of Singapore as a trading post in 1819 was in large part influenced by British interests in India. It is important to realise that commercial interests and European rivalry, which led to the acquisition of Singapore, were motivated by the broader British strategic concern of safeguarding their empire in the Indian subcontinent. The need for a secure base east of the Bay of Bengal had been evident to the East India Company (EIC) since the early 18th century. Prior to the British staking a claim on Singapore, India's eastern flank lay exposed to a Dutch controlled sea east of the Bay of Bengal. In the East Indies, the British had been all but squeezed out by the Dutch, apart from a little foothold in Bencoolen in Southwest Sumatra. It was primarily the concern over a gap in the defence of India against the Dutch, who the British considered a potential European foe in the east, that led to the British establishing bases in Penang in 1786, the Andaman Islands in 1788 and, subsequently, Singapore in 1819. The British acquisition of Singapore thus marked the culmination of the EIC's search for a strategic foothold along the Straits of Malacca. It would allow the British to counter Dutch influence in Southeast Asia as well as safeguard the India-China trade route.

In 1826, Singapore, together with Penang and Malacca, formed the Straits Settlements that were ruled directly from Calcutta (Kolkata) as part of the Bengal Presidency. In 1851, the Straits Settlements were transferred from the Bengal Presidency to the direct supervision of the Governor-General and the supreme government of India. Singapore was to remain administered from India, on behalf of the British crown, until 1876 when the Straits Settlements were brought under the control of the British Colonial Office. For nearly half a century, Singapore was effectively a part of India.

The legacy of this period on the development of modern Singapore was significant. Institutions and systems that were developed by the British in India were similarly implemented in Singapore. To a very large extent, Singapore's administrative and legal systems were based on the British-India model. Not only did the island come under the authority of the legislative council in India, the civil service in Singapore was also regularly staffed by former members of the Bengal service as well as officers from the Madras Army whose experience in India must have left an imprint. The Indian penal code, which was adopted in the subcontinent the 1860s, was brought into effect in Singapore in 1871 and it continues to leave its imprint on the latter's legal system.

Although Indian rule over Singapore was terminated in 1876, relations between the two colonies did not cease. By the latter half of the 19th century, India-Singapore linkages were sustained by immigrants from India who started arriving in Singapore in large numbers and who made significant contributions to the development of the island colony.

The earliest Indians to set foot in Singapore arrived in 1819 as part of Stamford Raffles' entourage. Among them were 120 sepoys and lascars, assistants and domestic servants as well as a Hindu trader from Penang, Naraina Pillai. Their settlement in Singapore marked the beginnings of an Indian community in modern Singapore. In the first few years of Singapore's establishment as a trading post, the number of Indian immigrants, however, remained small. The Indian population grew when Singapore was made a penal colony after the signing of the 1824 Anglo-Dutch Treaty. The Indian government found Singapore to be an ideal replacement for its former penal colony at Bencoolen. The newly established island colony faced a shortage of labour which could be met by Indian convicts and there was plenty of work such as the construction and maintenance of public roads and infrastructure. In April 1825, the first batch of prisoners was transferred from Bencoolen to Singapore. Despite the protestations of the local European community, the arrival of the Indian convicts to Singapore was fortuitous as they provided an invaluable source of manpower. They were assigned to often difficult and dangerous work: clearing of swamps and jungle cover, hunting down tigers menacing the interior of the island and the construction of roads and buildings. The contributions by Indian convicts were crucial to the growth and development of modern Singapore long after the island ceased to be a penal colony in 1873.

It was only in the second half of the 19th century that the large-scale voluntary immigration of Indians to Singapore occurred, coinciding with the consolidation of British rule in Malaya. As the British Empire expanded, so too did the need for unskilled and skilled labour to develop its colonies. This demand was met by immigrants from the Indian subcontinent. The British Indian administration allowed for the free circulation of goods, capital and services within and into India. Likewise, the British saw no reason to restrict an outward flow of labour to places where they were needed. In the 1830s, Indian labourers, mainly Tamils from South India, were brought to Singapore through the indenture system and, later on, the *kangani* system, to work on general municipal and other development works. By the 1850s, the bulk of the Indian community in Singapore was of the labouring classes, mainly from South India. Many of the south Indian Tamil workers were employed on plantations and government public works departments. They featured prominently in the harbour, transport and conservancy workforce as well as in the British naval and military bases.

Not all Indians who immigrated to Singapore were labourers. There were some who came in search of trading opportunities in the port city while others who had the benefit of an English education in India, for example, the Malayalis and Sri Lankan Tamils, found employment as civil servants, clerks, teachers and doctors. In the inter-war years, the growing British naval and military presence in Singapore proved to be a boon for educated Indians seeking white collar work. Some Indian communities came to be closely identified with particular occupations because of their dominance in those professions. The Sikhs were one such example. In India, 'martial races' like the Pathans, Punjabis and Rajputs from the Punjab and the Northwest Frontier were regularly enlisted for colonial security forces and deployed to British colonies. In 1879, Singapore received its first batch of 200 Sikh policemen which had been recruited to augment the local police force. As word spread of their policing skills, they were increasingly sought after as security personnel. More Sikhs started making their way to Singapore and Malaya in increasing numbers in search of job opportunities. Those who were unable to meet the strict enlistment requirements were employed as watchmen, security guards and bodyguards. Sikhs also found work as bullock-cart drivers, dairy farmers and shopkeepers.

Commercial migrants too came seeking their fortunes and the Indian business community grew to include shopkeepers, pedlars, petty traders as well as merchants and financiers with substantial capital. Traditional merchant groups like the Parsis, Marwaris, Bengalis and Gujaratis were joined by large numbers of Sindhi and Punjabi commercial migrants in the pre- and post-war years. Sindhi and Sikh textile merchants set up shop along High Street and, for several years after the war, they dominated the wholesale textile trade in Asia through networks that spanned Jakarta, Bombay, Hong Kong and Kobe. The Natukkotai Chettiars were another prominent group of commercial migrants whose financial activities oiled the wheels of commerce in colonial Singapore. They first arrived in Singapore in the 1820s and, by the mid-19th century, these south Indian moneylenders were a well-established presence in Singapore.

Many Indian immigrants in this period regarded Singapore as a temporary abode. Few opted to settle in Singapore permanently. Fresh immigration from India, periodic trips back to India for those who could afford the expense as well as visits to Malaya and Singapore by prominent Indians like Rabindranath Tagore, Pandit Jawaharlal Nehru and E V Ramasamy Naicker meant that ties with India remained strong. In the late 19th and 20th centuries, an increase in education and improvements in communications resulted in the spread of modern ideas such as Indian nationalism and Pan-Islamism into Singapore. The Singapore Indian Association, which was set up in 1923 and whose members were predominantly middle-class, was an attempt at creating a pan-Indian fraternity but it made little headway. For much of the 1920s, the association functioned primarily as a social club. There were also attempts to advocate for the interests of the local Indian population to the colonial government. Yet, such efforts were ultimately hampered by a community very much split along lines of class, occupation, ethnicity, religion and caste. Moreover, most Indians identified more with India or the Ottoman Empire (pan-Islamism) rather than to Singapore or even Malaya.

A galvanising force for the Indian community was its experience with the Indian National Army (INA) during the Japanese Occupation

(1942–1945). Led by the charismatic nationalist Subhas Chandra Bose, the INA was formed by the Japanese with the hope of deploying it to fight the British Raj and liberate India. Local Indians and prisoners of war were recruited to fill the ranks. Bose was a skillful orator who delivered electrifying speeches to the Indian community. The INA failed in its goals when it was defeated at the Battle of Imphal by the British but it proved to be an important influence in the shaping of Indian nationalism in Singapore. Independence for Singapore in 1965 also meant that the Indian community began gradually to shift its political allegiance away from the subcontinent and focused more on local concerns.

In the post-colonial period, India's relations with Singapore went through a period of ups and downs. As new members of the Commonwealth and the Non-Aligned Movement, India and Singapore enjoyed warm relations. This was followed by a period of 'benign neglect' (of Southeast Asia) when India shifted its focus away from the region and its foreign policy came to be influenced by Cold War dictates. India's re-engagement with Singapore and Southeast Asia began in earnest when India was propelled by a severe economic crisis in the early 1990s to take decisive steps toward economic liberalisation, which in turn led to a corresponding strategic shift in its foreign policy. This shift was articulated as the 'Look East' policy by then Indian Prime Minister P V Narasimha Rao during his Singapore Lecture in 1994. The 'Look East' policy, in which Singapore would play a major role, has led to the establishment of closer diplomatic ties between India and the member states of the Association of Southeast Asian Nations.

The Indian leader, Jawaharlal Nehru, had regarded Southeast Asia as a region whose history, fate and destiny were linked with that of India. For centuries, trade and migration had sustained, and will continue to do so in different forms, networks which connected maritime Southeast Asia and the Indian subcontinent.

18

Singapore-India Defence Relations: The Singapore Perspective

Jonathan Tow

As independence was thrust abruptly on Singapore in 1965, one crucial matter of state carried out on 9 August was Prime Minister Lee Kuan Yew's urgent request to India for military assistance to raise and train our army. This was an important consideration for a newly-independent nation, especially one as small and vulnerable as Singapore. Hence, we can only imagine Prime Minister Lee's thoughts when he did not get what he hoped for. Fortunately, Singapore defied expectations following independence to develop rapidly and, at the same time, build up a modern and capable military. As we progressed, defence relations with India evolved and have today become as important a pillar in our account as the political and economic agendas.

To understand how we reached this juncture, perhaps we can group the story of our defence ties into four broad phases. The first was from Singapore's independence to the beginning of India's 'Look East' policy in 1991. The second focused on trust building through joint naval exercises. The third was formalising relations through the Defence Cooperation Agreement (DCA) in 2003. The fourth was the signing of the India-Singapore Strategic Partnership in 2015 which elevated the DCA to the ministerial level.

The initial period from 1965 to Narasimha Rao's election as Indian Prime Minister in 1991 saw few bilateral military interactions of significance. Although culturally intertwined and with a common colonial past, Singapore and India chose different paths of development during the Cold War era. However, at the dawn of the 1990s, the energetic dismantling of India's socialist-era economy by Finance Minister Manmohan Singh and the introduction of India's 'Look East' policy shifted the country's gaze strategically towards Southeast and East Asia. Singapore was quick to recognise these changes and understood India's vast economic and strategic potential. We offered early and strong support to help integrate India into the region, starting with being an ASEAN Sectoral Dialogue Partner in 1992 and then to other ASEAN-centric memberships.

The second phase was a natural outcome from the impact of India's 'Look East' policy and Prime Minister Goh Chok Tong's igniting a "mild India fever" in Singapore. Prime Minister Goh and Prime Minister Rao felt the timing was right to initiate defence cooperation and launched naval interactions to build confidence and trust. The navy seemed to be a good starting choice as it was easier to arrange for exercises in the open seas rather than having larger-scale army or air force manoeuvres. In 1994, both sides began conducting annual bilateral naval exercises, first known as Exercise Lion King, before being renamed Singapore-India Maritime Bilateral Exercise (SIMBEX) in 1999. The exercises were conducted either in the Andaman Sea, Bay of Bengal or the South China Sea. By 2019, SIMBEX had completed 26 editions and exceeded expectations by its growing scale and complexity, and is the longest uninterrupted bilateral naval exercise that India has with any other country. Arising from the long-standing relations cultivated through SIMBEX, Singapore and India signed a Navy Bilateral Agreement in 2017 to expand and institutionalise the relationship.

The third phase was marked by the signing of the DCA in 2003. Relations were on an upswing and Singapore and India were then negotiating the Comprehensive Economic Cooperation Agreement (CECA). The DCA broadened military involvement to include the army and air force and established a Defence Policy Dialogue (DPD) at the Permanent Secretary-level. Significantly, it paved the way for the Singapore Armed Forces and the Republic of Singapore Air Force (RSAF) to train on Indian soil and airspace. In 2004, the first bilateral air force exercise, the Singapore-India Defence Exercise (SINDEX) took place at Gwalior in Madhya Pradesh. This was followed by the first bilateral artillery exercise in Devlali in Maharashtra in 2004, and the first bilateral armour exercise in Babina in Uttar Pradesh in 2005. Importantly, it was the first time India granted a foreign army the privilege of hosting personnel and equipment in India. Shortly after, in 2007, the RSAF concluded the Air Force Bilateral Agreement and bilateral air force training was shifted to Kalaikunda Air Force Station in West Bengal under the aegis of the Joint Military Training. This too was the first time India granted such a privilege to a foreign military. The Army Bilateral Agreement was subsequently concluded in 2008.

The bilateral agreements provided an important framework for the services to cooperate and foster professional trust. They were not symbolic agreements but offered professional value to each other. For example, the RSAF regularly exercised its F-16s with the Indian Air Force's fighter aircraft, which was mutually beneficial as pilots from both sides could train alongside different types of combat aircrafts. Furthermore, the gradual inclusion of advanced training scenarios showed the high professional regard for each other. The Air Force and Army Bilateral Agreements have both been renewed twice since. At the policy level, the DPD meets annually to set and oversee the agenda, often floating new ideas along the way. The DPD also provides the opportunity for senior defence officials to get to know each other personally.

The fourth phase coincided with the 50th anniversary of diplomatic relations in 2015. The India-Singapore Strategic Partnership, signed by

Prime Minister Lee Hsien Loong and Prime Minister Narendra Modi, is a forward-looking vision for bilateral ties. The DCA, which was separately revised, signalled a maturing of defence relations and a growing convergence of strategic interests and included the establishment of a Defence Ministers' Dialogue (DMD). Singapore also encouraged India to engage the region closer through the ASEAN Defence Ministers' Meeting (ADMM)-Plus process. During Prime Minister Modi's keynote address at the Shangri-La Dialogue in 2018, he announced that India and Singapore would conduct a trilateral maritime exercise in the Andaman Sea. The initiative demonstrated India's commitment towards the region and the exercise was successfully inaugurated in 2019 with Thailand as the third country. Singapore and India have since agreed that the exercise would be conducted on an annual basis and, from this initiative, kicked-started a modest but important beginning that could lead to more participation in the future.

Finally, the leadership of the defence ministers should not be understated. After four DMD meetings from 2016 to 2019, the Singaporean and Indian defence ministers have injected greater impetus and vision to the relationship. Cooperation has quickly moved beyond traditional exercises at the services-level to exploring the possibility of Singapore using India's Chandipur Integrated Test Range in Odisha, to conduct missile testing and live firing. Singapore officials will also study opportunities to collaborate with India's Defence Testing Infrastructure Scheme and step up cooperation in capacity building and joint operations in humanitarian assistance and disaster relief. The broadening of the agenda suggests that our defence cooperation is valued at the highest levels. This augurs well for the defence account as it could potentially herald more exciting possibilities over the horizon.

As we look back, Singapore-India defence relations have come a long way. Credit is due to the quiet confidence building measures undertaken by the army, air force and navy in building the early foundations. Together with the active leadership of the ministers, we can expect cooperation to continue in a strategic manner. In addition, the different defence-related strengths Singapore and India have acquired over the years can complement and build up each other's capabilities. Hence, as we look ahead, there are opportunities for defence cooperation to grow. This could include increased complexity of bilateral military exercises as well as research and development collaboration on defence technologies, cyber security and joint commercial defence production, wherein India had previously shown interest in Singapore's field artillery. We can also use our shared experiences to bring together like-minded defence partners to promote confidence building and greater familiarity in the region and contribute towards peace and stability.

As the next phase of the Singapore-India defence relations continues to be written, it would be well for us to reflect on the past journey as a reminder and inspiration of the possibilities that could lie ahead.

19

Remembering the India Connection

Walter Woon

I once had lunch under the glare of a mass murderer. It was in a restaurant in a luxury hotel in Singapore. The theme of the restaurant was the British Empire. The décor was meant to evoke a sense of nostalgia about colonial times. The food and service were very good, and I have no complaints there. It was only at the end of the meal that I noticed a framed photograph of a British officer staring down at the diners. It was a photograph of Brigadier-General Reginald Dyer, otherwise known as the 'Butcher of Amritsar'. To the credit of the hotel, the staff took down the photo immediately when I pointed this out to them.

For those who do not remember, while Singapore was celebrating the centenary of British rule in 1919, Dyer perpetrated the infamous Amritsar Massacre on 13 April 1919 in Jallianwala Bagh. Visitors to Amritsar will find a memorial to the over 300 civilians — men, women and children — who were killed when Dyer ordered his troops to fire on a peaceful gathering of Indians. According to *Encyclopedia Britannica*, a further 1,200 were wounded. Dyer was unapologetic. In his own words: "It was no longer a question of merely dispersing the crowds but one of producing a sufficient moral effect, from a military point of view, not only on those who were present but more specifically throughout the Punjab."

Lest anyone be under any illusions about the benign nature of British colonialism, Dyer's actions were applauded by the White community in India. A British newspaper organised a subscription which made Dyer a rich man when he returned to England. The British House of Lords presented him with a sword inscribed 'Saviour of the Punjab'. Lord Sinha, the sole ethnic Indian member of the House of Lords, dissented strongly.

In contrast, the massacre of unarmed civilians provoked a storm among non-Whites. Nobel laureate Rabindranath Tagore renounced his knighthood in protest. Mahatma Gandhi launched his first non-cooperation movement. The Amritsar Massacre pushed India towards Independence and the dismantling of the Raj as Indians realised that the continuance British rule was predicated not on any supposed moral superiority, but rather on the threat and actual use of deadly force, even against unarmed British subjects.

In Singapore, *The Straits Times* (then run by the Whites) published an editorial on 31 May 1920 supporting what Dyer had done. Their view was that his actions had saved the White community from slaughter. This is unsurprising, given that there had been a mutiny in Singapore by the 5th Light Infantry in 1915 (which is the subject of a recent book by Ambassador Umej Bhatia, *Our Name is Mutiny*, as well as an essay in this publication). The British were always deathly afraid that their subject peoples would rise up against them.

All this has been forgotten in Singapore a century on. During our Bicentennial celebrations (as with the Centennial celebrations in 1919) much of the focus has been on the British. Yet, Singapore's connection to India goes right back to the foundation of the modern city.

Every school child knows that modern Singapore was founded by Sir Stamford Raffles in 1819 when he installed Tengku Hussein Shah as Sultan of Johore and later induced him to cede the island to the British. What many do not recall is that in 1826, Singapore became part of India, together with Malacca and Penang, when the Straits Settlements were established as a Presidency (shortly thereafter reduced to a Residency under the Presidency of Bengal). The Straits Settlements were transferred to the direct control of the Governor-General of India in 1851. It was only in 1867 that the direct link with India was broken when the Straits Settlements became a Crown Colony.

It was during the time when Singapore was part of India that the Indian Mutiny (also known as the First War of Independence) broke out in 1857. This was put down with great ferocity. Thereafter, the spectre of such a rising haunted the British not only in India, but also in Singapore. British heroes of the mutiny are commemorated by street names like Outram Road and Havelock Road.

The Singapore connection with India did not end in 1867. Resistance to British rule continued not only in India, but also among the Indian diaspora. Indian revolutionaries were inspired by the example of the Irish, who rebelled in 1916 and finally shed the British yoke in 1922. Some like Gandhi advocated non-violent resistance. Others like Subhas Chandra Bose preferred more direct methods.

Bose was detained by the British at the outbreak of the Second World War. He escaped, made his way to Germany and was instrumental in forming the Free India Legion (*Azad Hind Fauj*) from Indian prisoners of war in February 1942. Meanwhile, on 15 February 1942, the Japanese administered the biggest drubbing ever to have been meted out to a British army when they took Singapore. Later that February, over 25,000 Indian prisoners of war volunteered for the Indian National Army (INA) [also known as the *Azad Hind Fauj* and which in fact had been established in Taiping in December 1941] at a meeting in Farrer Park. This was commanded by Captain Mohan Singh, late of the 1/14th Punjab Regiment, who was raised to the rank of General.

Bose was taken by German U-Boot to rendezvous with a Japanese submarine in the Indian Ocean. He eventually found his way to Singapore via Tokyo. There, in the Cathay Building, he declared the independence of India in October 1943. Eamon de Valera, the President of the Irish Free State, sent felicitations.

Bose was, of course, anathema to the British and, after the return of the King, anyone in Singapore who admitted to admiration for him risked prosecution. However, Kolkata's airport is named the Netaji Subhas Chandra Bose International Airport.

Interestingly, at the beginning of 2020, Amazon Prime Video launched a mini-series titled 'The Forgotten Army' (*Azaadi Ke Liye*). In the first episode, a young Singaporean Indian, who knows nothing of Singapore's connection to India, grumbles at having to give up his room to the 'weirdo' brother of his dying grandmother. After talking to the old man and doing some research, he discovers the part that Singapore played in Indian history during the Second World War. He then shows his visitor the INA Memorial on the Esplanade. This triggers off the old soldier's recollections of his days fighting the British for India's independence as a member of the INA.

How many Singaporeans are today ignorant about all of this, like the young man in the Amazon mini-series? It is time to address this historical amnesia. People of Indian descent form nine percent of our population. The link to India is part of our national heritage. It is ironic that running right next to the Indian Heritage Centre is Clive Street. Robert Clive was the victor of the Battle of Plassey in 1757 (exactly a century before the First War of Independence or the Indian Mutiny). The East India Company's army defeated the Nawab of Bengal, setting the stage for the subsequent British Raj in India. Clive Street may perhaps be renamed. My suggestion is call it the Rani of Jhansi Street. Rani Lakshmibhai was one of the leaders of the mutiny, having been dispossessed by the British who refused to recognise her as heir to the late Maharaja and annexed her state.

There is a Singapore connection to the Rani of Jhansi. The original INA was sidelined by the Japanese and its commander, Mohan Singh, exiled to Pulau Ubin after he refused to let his troops be used as labourers rather than fighting for Indian independence. Bose reinvigorated the INA when he got to Singapore in 1943. He instigated the formation of an all-women unit in Singapore — the Rani of Jhansi Regiment (documented by Joyce Lebra in her book, *Women Against the Raj*). It was commanded by another Lakshmi, Dr Lakshmi Swaminadhan, who worked in Singapore. The personnel of the Regiment (mainly Tamils) were recruited from British Malaya, including Singapore.

Some may say: "Nothing to do with me, I'm not Indian." That would be unfortunate and inimical to societal cohesion. Our shared history cannot be seen through a narrow ethnic lens. The Ranis are as much a part of Singapore's history as Major-General Lim Bo Seng (whose rank was posthumously awarded by the Republic of China, for whom he fought in her struggle against Japan) and Second-Lieutenant Adnan bin Saidi (an officer of the Malay Regiment which tried so valiantly to keep Malaya and Singapore in the British Empire). Knowledge of where we came from is vital in appreciating what we are today and understanding where we should be heading in future.

A final footnote — In 1983, I was in Cambridge and watched the United Kingdom (UK) general election in which Mrs Margaret Thatcher won a resounding victory. Last year, I was again in Cambridge and watched the UK general election in which Mr Boris Johnson won another resounding victory. What struck me was the difference in the media personalities who covered the elections. Back in 1983, the presenters and commentators were uniformly White. In 2019, a significant proportion were of South Asian ethnicity. Mrs Thatcher's cabinet was overwhelmingly Caucasian. Mr Johnson's cabinet has three members of Indian ethnic origin (one born in Agra). If, in 1919, British society was as accepting of other races, instead of honouring war criminals like Dyer, they might still have an empire.

Section II

THINKING ABOUT THE PRESENT

20

India is an Enigma

Zulkifli Baharudin

It is amongst the most promising emerging economies in the world. Although long touted as the world's biggest democracy, every aspect of life and society in India is hardly democratic. It has a sizeable and potentially lucrative domestic market with a huge appetite for consumption which continues to remain unmet. This economic giant has been in a deep and long slumber.

The difficulties of doing business in India have been well documented and remain relevant — excessive bureaucratic regulations, poor infrastructure and a legal system that lacks transparency and prone to persistent political interference at all levels of the government. Yet, this is still the same country that has some of the most cultured people in the world. It is also home to some of the most leading-edge companies and it is known worldwide for exporting some of the most skilful and talented people in all endeavours of economy and society, including to Singapore. More than any other country, the sons and daughters of India are visible as celebrated corporate honchos in some of the biggest companies in the world. These include Google, Microsoft, Nokia, Adobe, Cognizant, PepsiCo and MasterCard, among others.

The pertinent questions here are that, given its vast global talent, why hasn't India been able to produce such global champions at home and why has it not able to retain some of its best talents? Without addressing both these questions, India will remain a country incapable of achieving its true potential.

At the risk of oversimplification, this is where a comparison with China is useful. Perhaps, China's early national strategy of courting some the world's best to outsource its low-value manufacturing and production is a key difference between the two countries. China's attempt to attract capital, technology and skilled expertise from the very best in the industry is unmatched. China was well prepared to open up its domestic market to foreign competition as an added incentive to attract multinationals into the country. Its leaders realised this would be a small price to pay for its greater ambitions of building world class enterprises as its own state enterprises were then riddled with corruption, under-performance and failure. This was part of China's larger and comprehensive strategy to remake the country and claim its rightful place in the world.

Soon, it became obvious that Chinese entrepreneurs were capable of manufacturing products for global corporations. China created an entire new class of global workers and professionals. Farmers from the interior of the country were introduced to global standards of work. This has had a pervasive effect on work and life. Over time, a whole new generation of workers, professionals and leaders emerged, completely transformed and educated within the walls of factories and industries. This is the genesis of China's industrialisation. The rest is history!

My own experience bears a similar story. In 1992, I was tasked to set up a logistics facility in Shenzhen where insoles, leather and shoe boxes were brought in from Oregon in the United States (US) to feed into a shoe manufacturing plant. Thousands of workers were each tasked with a simple process on the assembly line. The work was laborious. They were allowed a 10-minute break after each hour. They followed the policy diligently. Discipline is an acknowledged prerequisite of work. Right from the start, top political leaders in the province took personal charge to support and ensure the success of the project. I remember teaching night classes to staff all eager to learn skills and processes completely alien to them even when they had only a limited understanding of what I was communicating. I was unable to converse with them in Mandarin.

Today, China is home to the biggest and most sophisticated shoe and apparel industry in the world. Insoles, leather and boxes are of course no longer brought in from the outside.

On the other hand, India has been incredibly surprising. I went to India around the same time as I did to China to set up a logistics facility for a US computer company in what was then Madras. I was immediately taken in by the attractive charm and beauty of culture, history and a sophisticated elite class living in luxury. Here, I was first introduced to the trappings of luxury hotels with butler service. Looking back, I was probably naïve to think that the common language of English would make my task easier as compared to that in China.

In India, one can only be bowled over by its promises and presentations which are all too familiar by now. The immediate reality of stretched timelines and cavalier attitudes to the promises and commitments and the myriad of regulatory hurdles soon become a daily pre-occupation of new entrants into the country. Not to be cowed and defeated, I stayed put for extended periods to learn about this country and its people. I struggled with its work ethics and discipline as workers are always not at their places. Each and everyone will somehow have an incredibly convincing excuse.

I tried hard and in fact developed an intoxicating fascination for the country. However, I was tormented by the fallacy that others can never understand India and that a foreigner can never have the country's collective interest at heart, that is, to put India first. I was subjected to these accusations on numerous occasions by Indians at just about every level of society, each using this argument to justify his or her position. Indeed, many have eloquently and elegantly perfected this defence to an art form.

The result of all these myriad of obstacles and confusion is a compromise of standards and expectations and, of course, a sense of doubt and cynicism on the part of practitioners like me, permanently bruised by the experience. As such, the logistics facility I sought to set up, has to this day, not generated the progress and transformation expected of it and as seen at facilities elsewhere.

Yet, this is the country that has produced the first wave of immigrants mainly from Tamil Nadu to work in the rubber estates of Malaya. Subsequent generations have successfully integrated into Singapore society and have done exceeding well. Even the more recent migrants to the island state have shown to possess global talent and expertise that many occupy positions of strategic importance. Singapore is indebted to the thousand of workers whose hardwork, sweat and toil have been so crucial to the growth and development of Singapore. Here, they have demonstrated the important traits of discipline and work ethics not synonymous with the perceptions back home.

On reflection and with the passage of time, I have come to realise that perhaps this is part of a larger cultural and ideological challenge confronting India. It has not been able to cut itself off from the self-limiting aspects of its culture and history. Social class, culture and tradition, which are steeped in Indian life, remain frustrating impediments for many Indians at home. Until India is liberated from these constraints, its best potential will continue to elude it and its people.

For now, India is a place where only the few brave ones are prepared to tread!

21

India's Business Environment as Seen by the Singapore Private Sector

Gautam Banerjee

In January 1994, Singapore's Prime Minister Goh Chok Tong started a 'mild India fever' with his visit to India with a group of Singapore business leaders from both government-linked companies and the private sector. During that visit, he laid the foundation for the Bangalore IT Park, a joint venture between a consortium of private sector and government-linked Singapore companies, and India's Tata Group, one of India's largest and most respected private sector groups.

For Singapore businesses, the joint venture encapsulated both the 'highs' and 'lows' of doing business in a newly-emerging market like India. It demonstrated that for foreign investors to succeed in India, not only do they need tenacity and perseverance, but also a strong local partner to navigate domestic laws and regulations and the many road bumps they are likely to encounter. In addition, if it is a large project in the public eye, one has to clearly demonstrate that it is a 'win-win' for all stakeholders, not just for the foreign investor. This is particularly true of infrastructure projects which require land and a host of planning-related and other permits and clearances by a variety of government departments. These projects usually have multiple stakeholders and are likely to be in the public domain, which means they can potentially be subject to scrutiny. The invaluable practical experience gained by early Singapore investors in India such as the consortium involved with the Bangalore IT Park project has over the years been socialised with a wider group of Singapore companies with an interest in investing and doing business in India. These include government agencies such as the Economic Development Board and International Enterprise Singapore (now part of Enterprise Singapore), and business federations such as the Singapore Indian Chamber of Commerce and Industry and the Singapore Business Federation as well as professional services firms and advisers. All of these entities are part of an important ecosystem available to guide and advise Singapore businesses looking at India as an investment destination.

Since the start of the 'mild India fever', there has been a steady stream of Singapore companies investing in India. This is not surprising, given that India, for the last several years, has been one of the world's fastest growing large economies, growing at an average rate of 7.3 percent between 2016 and 2020. This has increased the ranks of the middle class in India and this, coupled with a youthful population, means that economic growth in India should be sustainable for the foreseeable future as India cashes in on its demographic dividend. The emergence of India as a global centre for outsourced business and technology services anchored by globally competitive Indian technology service companies such as Wipro, Tata Consultancy Services and Infosys, among others, has also had a beneficial and multiplier impact on foreign investment in India. For example, this has spawned world class business and information technology (IT) parks with tenants such as global banks and financial services companies, telecommunications and technology companies, pharmaceutical companies and the like. Many Singapore companies are involved in this sector across the value chain from owning, building and managing these business parks to housing part of their operations in these facilities to get access to qualified staff at competitive prices.

Moreover, the Indian government under Prime Minister Narendra Modi has set an ambitious growth and development agenda with an aspiration of doubling India's gross domestic product to US$5 trillion (S$7.1 trillion) by 2024. If India is to achieve this ambitious target, it will need to radically overhaul its infrastructure (new smart cities, roads and airports), grow its manufacturing sector and make it globally competitive by becoming an integral part of global supply chains, diversifying its service sector and reducing its reliance for economic growth on IT and software services. India has to work with overseas financial and strategic investors to provide both capital and expertise to do justice to these opportunities. Singapore companies are well represented across all the sectors and include companies such as Singtel, Sembawang, Ascendas, Singapore Airlines, Meinhardt and Lee Kim Tah, just to name a few.

India's youthful population also means that there will potentially be a million new entrants into the country's workforce annually for the next several years. For India to reap full advantage of this demographic good fortune, it needs to equip these individuals with the appropriate skills to make a positive contribution to the country's growing economy. New technical colleges and vocational institutions will have to be set up to augment existing institutions of higher learning. Here again, the opportunity is so large that India has had to work with overseas partners. Singapore educational institutions, particularly in the areas of vocational and technical training, have been active in India. They have been welcomed by the Indian government as they are helping to train young Indians in the hospitality, tourism and other relevant service sectors, thereby helping to promote youth employment in India which is a top priority for both the central and state governments in India.

In my various past and present roles, I have had the privilege of not only having a ringside view of Singapore companies operating in India, but also being closely involved as an insider with Singapore businesses and their investments and operations in India. How do Singapore companies see the business environment in India? While the vast majority of Singapore businesses see India as a land of opportunity, the ones which have been successfully operating in India for a while are realistic enough to know that as in many places, doing business successfully in India requires a deep level of experience and understanding. These companies have made the effort to understand what it takes to be successful in India:

1. Have a clear and detailed business plan for your India business or investment, prepared after a robust feasibility study by a multi-disciplinary group, including managers with a strong 'hands-on' track record of operating in India;
2. Develop a sound understanding of business dynamics in India and how it differs from other markets. India is not a homogenous country. Every state is different and there are important variations and nuances in the relationship between the central government and different state governments. This means that no one authority can give a foreign investor a blanket clearance or even a high degree of assurance on important investment-related matters in the way certain countries like China are able to do quickly and reliably. India is justifiably proud of its democratic traditions and vibrant free press, but in a large developing country with a significant rural population, this slows the pace and increases risk and uncertainty of outcomes that foreign investors seek to avoid when they invest overseas.
3. Appreciate that India is not an easy place to do business because it has a proliferation of laws and regulations. This requires investing time to understand the laws, regulations and judicial processes of its central and state governments, which vary greatly by state. India inherited its legal system from Britain. However, the speed at which and how the laws are enforced is vastly different from the British system. Although India has moved up in global tables which measure the ease of doing business, it still has some way to go. The good news is that from Prime Minister Modi downwards, Indian government officials, both at the centre and in the various states, are committed to simplifying and providing regulatory and policy certainty on key matters important to foreign investors. There are also positive signs that the Indian government is listening to the business community and making meaningful changes for the better. For example, in the recent central budget, Finance Minister Nirmala

Sitharaman did away with the dividend distribution tax, lowered corporate tax and announced incentives to promote start-ups and financial inclusion. As this is still work in progress, investors will need to have patience, resilience, nimbleness and agility to succeed in India. It is also clear from looking at the successes and failures of Singapore businesses in India that, as an investment destination, India is not for everyone. To succeed in India, foreign companies must have a sound business case with demonstrable competitive advantage be adequately capitalised, and have experienced leadership with a long term outlook and either a strong local partner or experienced and trustworthy local managers in India.

There has been much progress in the three decades since former Prime Minister Goh started the 'mild India fever' by promoting bilateral trade and investment between Singapore and India. In my opinion, the single most positive development has been in the mindset of Singapore business leaders, the majority of whom today see the business environment in India and the accompanying opportunities as a glass half full rather than a glass half empty.

Before concluding, I would like to share a few quotations from Singapore business leaders with first-hand experience of doing business in India which capture very succinctly their views on the business environment in India:

> Singapore has a deep social connect to India through the local presence of the Indian diaspora for many generations. This gives Singapore and India a very close personal connection and understanding of each other that is quite unique. So I find Singaporeans appreciate the challenges that India faces as a large, diverse and developing country with strong democratic traditions. Furthermore, while India may still be a developing country, it has a rich history and culture which has a positive impact on all aspects of society, including commerce and business. — *Mr Kishore Moorjani, Senior Managing Director, Blackstone Singapore*

With its young and digitally savvy population and an emerging and aspirational middle-class, India presents huge demographic dividend opportunities. The scale and size of the Indian market provides a significant multiplier effect for businesses. The digital India initiative (that is, digital and financial inclusion for all) is a potential boon for the Indian economy and for businesses as it will allow companies to tap India's massive population at a lower incremental cost. However, regulatory, tax and legal uncertainty and unpredictability can dilute the attractiveness of the market. Rules and regulations must be clear, transparent and consistent for businesses to do their investment planning and execution successfully and within an acceptable time frame. — *Mr Arthur Lang, Chief Executive Officer International, Singapore Telecommunications*

India's local capital markets are still small and relatively unsophisticated which means that it presently does not have a domestic market for assets of scale. Over time, the development of markets for insurance companies, REITs and the like will help the Indian capital market to broaden and mature. Investing prior to a rerating is a huge potential opportunity for foreign investors. — *Mr Alan Miyasaki, Senior Managing Director, Blackstone Singapore*

It is important to understand and appreciate the business environment of any country you wish to do business in. You can always internationalise your presence and technology but each country's business culture is unique and India is no exception. The way to conduct business in India is to build trust and long-term relationships at all levels in the system. Long-term commitment to the country is essential for success. You simply cannot have a short-term investment horizon in India. We only wish the tax, remittance and dispute resolution systems were simpler and faster, which sometimes worry foreign investors. — *Dr Shahzad Nasim, Group Executive Chairman, Meinhardt (Singapore)*

The views expressed in this essay are the personal views of Gautam Banerjee and do not necessarily reflect the views of The Blackstone Group Inc.

22

India's Challenges

Manu Bhaskaran

As we head into a new decade, it is fair to say that the recent deterioration in the economy has deflated the high hopes that many observers had for a resurgent India, one that would reclaim its long-lost position as one of the world's pre-eminent powers. Economic growth has slowed noticeably, financial stresses have emerged at many levels and the spectre of sectarian strife has re-appeared. The COVID-19 crisis will place an additional burden on an economy that is ill-prepared for such shocks. It would appear that deep structural factors underlie this underperformance, some of which are discussed below.

The risk is that rather than the 'determined marathoner', which the report by the Asian Development Bank and Centennial Group (2009) on India had hoped for, it appears to some that India might only be capable of occasional spurts of growth, followed by periods of weak performance. If that is indeed the case, then India will not succeed in gaining entry into the top tier of global powers.

Indeed, it would appear that the challenges India faces as it seeks to transform itself are proving formidable. This essay seeks to understand these challenges in order to better assess India's prospects. By challenges, we mean the factors that hinder India from pulling off a rapid transition to an affluent society, one that delivers a high quality of life to its people in a politically and environmentally sustainable manner and which underpins a secure geo-political position for the country in a turbulent world.

Progress has been Made; the Question is Whether that Progress is Enough

In the past decade, India has moved forward in several areas as it tries to establish the foundations for greater prosperity:

First, there has been a big push for better infrastructure. Some of India's new airports are as well designed and as efficient as the best in the world. Highways are being built, as also smaller roads in the rural areas where most people still live. The rail network is improving, electricity is being brought to virtually every village in India and more piped water is now available for the poor. The mobile telephony revolution adds to the greater connectivity that even rural India now enjoys. Cumulatively, the improvements will help overcome the infrastructure constraint on economic growth and competitiveness.

Second, game-changing moves have been introduced by successive governments. By replacing a plethora of confusing state taxes with a unified federal tax, the Goods and Services Tax (GST) has created a single national market for the first time in Indian history. The *Aadhaar* scheme of a 12-digit unique identity numbers for citizens opens the way for many innovations while also enabling greater financial inclusion. The Insolvency and Bankruptcy Code helps to tackle a perennial problem — the difficulty in managing corporate distress and non-performing loans — that precipitated multiple financial crises in the past. The introduction of digitalisation and other efficiency-raising initiatives in government is also helping to raise public sector efficiency. Anecdotal evidence suggests that high-level corruption has been reduced.

Third, the government has swept away red tape, producing a dramatic improvement in India's ranking in the World Bank's Ease of Doing Business 2020 survey to 63rd in the world, up from 133rd in 2010. Problems with its business eco-system have been seen as a major hindrance by both domestic as well as foreign investors. If this progress can be sustained, then we could see a rise in the investment share of gross domestic product, which could then translate into a higher rate of economic growth.

Fourth, indeed we are already seeing India gaining more favour with global businesses: foreign direct investment has risen impressive. It was up 16 percent in 2019 to reach S$67.8 billion.

This is real progress. Yet, India's socio-economic performance remains unimpressive.

Economic growth has decelerated markedly from a peak of 13 percent in early 2010 to just 4.7 percent in the last quarter of 2019. The banking and non-bank financial sectors are saddled with mountains of bad debts, severely reducing the flow of credit in the economy. The balance sheets of large companies are so weighed down with debt and excess capacity that they are not undertaking the investment needed to generate high growth.

India is also not creating enough jobs for its people, especially the young — the male youth unemployment rate is 20 percent. Where jobs are created, too many are in the informal sector where workers have few rights and little expectation of the skills development that would lead to higher productivity and eventually progressively higher wages. Comparing indicators such as life expectancy and the share of the population in poverty, Bangladesh, with a lower per capita income, has performed better than India. Of the 10 most polluted cities in the world, nine are in India.

The list can go on but the point is clear — the Indian economy is not making enough progress to deliver the improvement in living standards that the people deserve. The promising surge in growth in the 2000s has petered out, raising questions about India's long term prospects.

What Lies at the Root of this Under-performance?

At the root of India's challenges is the state's failure to provide public goods — essentials that only the state can provide efficaciously.

A society cannot progress well and an economy cannot advance rapidly without critical public goods such as a national consensus on vital issues that is needed for a cohesive society; a well-functioning legal-regulatory system; good infrastructure; an effective education system; investment in research and development; astutely negotiated economic partnerships (including free trade agreements [FTA]) with other countries); macro-economic stability; and an effective administration that can implement policies smoothly.

Many of the problems that bedevil India today can be traced to this failure. Here are some recent examples where the state has been unable to deliver what the country needs:

i. A substantial relocation of production facilities out of China is now underway as a result of China's rising costs and its trade dispute with the United States. This relocation is a unique historical opportunity for developing economies to rapidly expand their manufacturing sectors, move up the value chain, generate a huge number of jobs for their people and create immense business opportunities for their companies. Yet, hardly any of this relocation is reaching India. Vietnam, Bangladesh, Malaysia and Thailand are winners in this relocation. Even with the improvements in the ease of doing business, India's business eco-system is seen as too difficult — regulations on land and labour, in particular, are perceived as onerous and its infrastructure is still woefully inadequate. The tax authorities are also seen as unreasonable and difficult to deal with. Indonesia too has not benefitted much from this relocation. However, Indonesian leaders have confronted this failure head-on: they have now introduced a courageous reform bill in parliament, including labour market reforms that will improve Indonesia's ability to do better. It will be easier to hire and fire workers subject to some limitations while what was seen as excessively high redundancy payments for retrenched workers will be reduced. There is no similar move in India. While it is encouraging that a few states have now said they would deregulate labour restrictions as part of the response to the pandemic, it is not clear if these changes will indeed be implemented permanently and be sufficiently bold to address the fears of investors.

ii. The GST reform should have been a boon for the economy but poor implementation has diminished its benefits. The large number of rates for various categories of products and services has caused confusion and added a large administrative burden, particularly for small- and medium-sized enterprises.

iii. India also suffers from the lack of integration with its neighbours which deprives it of important synergies which, for example, the Southeast Asian economies have gained from the various integration initiatives there, such as the Association of Southeast Asian Nations (ASEAN) Economic Community. India's difficult relationship with Pakistan makes such productive regional engagement difficult. The way out of this dilemma was for India to seek integration beyond its immediate hinterland. In fact, both geo-political and economic factors argued for India to be part of the Regional Comprehensive Economic Partnership (RCEP), an FTA that brings the 10 ASEAN-member states, China, Japan, South Korea, Australia and New Zealand to create the world's largest free trade area. India had valid reservations about certain aspects of the RCEP such as the lack of services sector liberalisation. Yet, when it came to the crunch, Indian trade diplomacy could not persuade its trade partners to compromise on its reasonable requests.

iv. Over and over again, India's economy has been tripped by crises in its financial sector. Yet, the regulatory and supervisory institutions that oversee the sector have not been overhauled to prevent their recurrence. Failure resolution frameworks remain inadequate to the task. The Insolvency and Bankruptcy Code, mentioned above, for instance, was a good idea but its implementation has been slow. However, the biggest issue is the dominance of state-owned banks where question marks over corporate governance and risk management have been raised for a long time but have yet to be answered.

v. Finally, India faces the risk that its vaunted demographic dividend may not yield the economic advantages that were hoped for

> because of inadequate skills development. According to data put together by the Global Business Coalition for Education, the Education Commission, and United Nations Children's Fund, more than 50 percent of Indian youth will lack the skills necessary for employment by 2030. While India has some excellent institutions of higher education such as its much-admired Indian Institutes of Technology and the Indian Institutes of Management, there are concerns over curricula and infrastructure. A particular area of weakness is vocational training.

Thus, the overarching challenge for India is to create a governance structure which will enable the state to deliver the public goods that it is currently unable to.

For this to happen, there has to be the same single-minded focus in the government on achieving socio-economic goals that countries such as Japan and China demonstrated. The state cannot be distracted by other agendas. To the outside observer, it seems that India is doing the opposite, engaged in a battle for its soul between inclusiveness and majoritarianism — and shifting away from the successful management of diversity that kept its polity intact for the past 70 years.

Conclusion

India is in a position to generate about 4.5 to 5 percent growth over the next few years, given the demographic dividend it is enjoying, urbanisation and the improvements in infrastructure and business eco-systems mentioned above. However, this will not be enough to create the number of formal sector jobs to absorb the entrants to the workforce. Nor will it be enough to generate the resources India will need to sustain its geo-strategic position at a time when a giant rival is rising and the world is turning more turbulent.

What India needs to do to perform better is generally well known. What needs to be answered is whether there is the political will to do so.

23

Arbitration and Dispute Resolution: Thinking of India

Lawrence Boo

Historical Link — The East India Company

The legal history of Singapore and India started with a company that carries 'India' in its name — the East India Company (EIC). A company, set up in 1600 with 125 shareholders and £72,000, still exists today, and now prides itself as having been "founded to explore the mysteries of the East... mapped trade routes through unchartered territory and changed social customs, tastes and ways of thought to influence the very fabric of our lives today." As romantic as it may sound, the adventurers of this company fought the locals in India and replaced the Mughal legal system to set up the first British-style courts in India in 1726. In Singapore, the EIC, after setting up a trading post in 1819, went on to obtain a Royal Charter from the British Crown in 1826 to set up law courts in Singapore, replacing the role of local chiefs and their traditional Asian laws.

Curial Attitude to Arbitration

While the arbitration and mediation in civil law jurisdictions grew with specialised institutions and the support of their courts, the English common law courts guarded their jurisdiction jealously, declaring any attempt to oust its reach and jurisdiction as being against public policy. Although non-institutional (ad hoc) arbitration and mediation were allowed to co-exist, the same monopolistic attitude towards dispute resolution outside the curial system permeated into India and Singapore for much of their judicial history, with courts treating them as inferior subordinate tribunals, for which the courts retain the right to scrupulously supervise and often intervene. At the same time, English arbitration laws were enacted with little change as local legislation in both countries, all of which rang with implicit undertones that the courts reserved the right to intervene in all references outside the curial system.

Backlog of Court Cases

While the scale of the problem might be vastly different, the courts in India and Singapore suffered from the usual problem of a growing population and a developing economy. Court cases rose exponentially and no sooner got inundated with matters far beyond their capacity to dispose. India had long held the pole position for the number of pending case in its courts' dockets. Attempts to stem its growing numbers and reduce its backlog have not thus far seen success. According to the National Judicial Data Grid, as at 2 June 2020, there are 2,040,267 civil cases pending in the Indian High Courts of which 15.6 percent have been pending for 10 to 20 years and 19.5 percent pending for 5 to 10 years. In Singapore, this prompted the appointment of a new Chief Justice in 1990 with the immediate mandate to reform the backlog of some 2,000 cases which would need to wait five to six years before they could be heard. New court procedures were introduced, electronic technology was deployed, specialist courts set up and new judges appointed. Within five years, the backlog was cleared. Unfortunately, in India, the backlog problem is far too huge and complex and remains an issue that has to be addressed.

Institutional Arbitration

Although the Singapore International Arbitration Centre (SIAC) was established as part of Singapore's long-term economic strategy, its setting up in July 1991 acted as a secondary prong in reducing the flow of cases to the courts. The SIAC brought Singapore very quickly into the forefront of developments in international arbitration and mediation in Asia. The SIAC supported the adoption of the UNCITRAL Model Law on International Commercial Arbitration (MAL) by Singapore which resulted in the enactment of the International Arbitration Act in 1994 (IAA) to regulate the arbitration of international cases, introducing with it the concepts of party autonomy and prohibiting judicial intervention in arbitration unless expressly permitted under the IAA.

Throughout its formative journey, the SIAC received tremendous support from the International Chamber of Commerce International Court of Arbitration (ICC), the American Arbitration Association (AAA) and China International Economic and Trade Arbitration Commission (CIETAC) and the Secretariat of UNCITRAL. By 2004, regular joint colloquiums and conferences were staged by the SIAC, ICC, CIETAC, AAA and UNCITRAL with the objective of educating the legal and user community on the use of institutional arbitration and mediation.

SIAC in India

During a visit led by Mr Mah Bow Tan, Singapore's Minister of National Development, to India in September 2003, the Construction Industry Development Council (CIDC) of India, a quasi-government body under the Planning Commission (chaired by the Indian Prime Minister), enquired about the possibility of working with Singapore institutions to chart ways for the Indian construction sector to expedite the resolution of large infrastructure construction disputes. Mr Mohan Pillay, a partner at Wong Partnership, very quickly connected the CIDC with the SIAC, the Singapore Mediation Centre and the Law Faculty at the National

University of Singapore (NUS). The SIAC saw this as an opportunity as well as a duty to call attention to the Indian business and legal community on the use of a disciplined and structured institutional process of arbitration. It interacted with the CIDC and the Confederation of Indian Industry as well as several large Indian construction corporations through meetings and seminars. This quickly bore fruit in the form of the setting up of the Construction Industry Arbitration Council (CIAC) by the CIDC and the SIAC. The first industry-based arbitration institution in New Delhi, the CIAC was inaugurated by the President of India, Dr A P J Abdul Kalam, on 15 November 2006. The CIDC and the SIAC agreed to provide seed funding and administrative back-up to the CIAC in its initial five years. With support from the SIAC, the CIAC obtained an observer seat at the UNCITRAL Working Group in 2008. The CIAC continues today as an important player in the resolution of construction disputes in India.

The SIAC's venture with the CIDC in India attracted much attention within India and its presence felt in many arbitration conferences in the major cities in India, prompting other international institutions to follow suit. The London Court of International Arbitration (an arbitral institution based in London) started an Indian branch in New Delhi in 2009 but closed it five years later. The SIAC set up its first office in Mumbai in 2013 and a second in the Gujarat International Financial Tec-City, Gujarat, in 2017. Seminars for the legal profession, law students, corporations and conferences (often over-subscribed), graced by ministers and Supreme Court judges, both from Singapore and India, were organised frequently with local Indian bodies as well as in collaboration with other international institutions. They propagated the resounding messages of the efficacy of institutional arbitration and on the need for the institutionalisation of arbitration in India.

It is no secret that the number of Indian parties in the SIAC cases has risen considerably over the last 10 years. In 2019 alone, 429 Indian parties were involved in 479 of SIAC's cases. The success of the SIAC thus far owes much to the support of Indian users. As such, when we think of the SIAC, we think of India!

Birth of Indian Arbitral Institutions

In the wake of the efforts by the SIAC, a number of institutions were established in India. They included the Delhi International Arbitration Centre in 2009, the Bangalore International Mediation Arbitration and Conciliation Centre in 2013 and the Mumbai Centre for International Arbitration in 2016. More recently, the New Delhi International Arbitration Centre Ordinance 2019 was promulgated by the President of India to set up the New Delhi International Arbitration Centre which seeks to serve as the leading body, taking over the role of the International Centre of Alternate Dispute Resolution. It is interesting that a common observation by the initiators of such moves was the SIAC's significant share of Indian cases. It appears that, in India, when one speaks of institutional arbitration, he or she would invariably think of the SIAC.

A Place for Indian Arbitrators, Parties and Counsel

To Indian parties, Singapore is an easy choice as the place of arbitration. It is near, secure, accessible and less costly than London or elsewhere in Europe. As a dedicated dispute resolution facility, Singapore's Maxwell Chambers hosts many users from India. Some of the largest Indian cases not involving the SIAC have been heard or decided in Singapore. Arbitrators based in Singapore are sufficiently exposed to Indian parties, their lawyers and other professionals appearing before them. Doubtless, Singapore arbitrators do have India much on their minds.

Similarly, Indian arbitrators often sit with others in Singapore, and lawyers representing Indian parties frequently appear in such arbitrations with or without local assisting counsel. More significantly, the Singapore High Court recently granted admissions to Indian senior advocates to appear before it in a case arising from an arbitration involving Indian parties, a privilege usually extended to English Queen's Counsel and, even so, only in exceptional cases. It appears that the Singapore courts also think of India.

Education in Alternative Dispute Resolution

In education and training in alternative dispute resolution (ADR), Singapore academics and practitioners make frequent appearances at teaching seminars and workshops in Indian cities and universities. Each class, seminar and conference would often be oversubscribed. The hunger for knowledge and learning with Indian professionals and students encourage us to often go the extra mile. This same quest could be seen from programmes held in Singapore as well when, in August 2016, the NUS Law Faculty started a Master of Laws in International Arbitration & Dispute Resolution. Since its launch, each cohort has had a significant proportion of students from India. In the latest cohort for the academic year 2019/2020, about 90 percent of the students are Indian nationals. In ADR education and training, we think of India!

Indian Law Reform — A Great Move

In 1996, the Indian legislature made its first change to the law of arbitration, replacing its Arbitration Act of 1940 with the Arbitration and Conciliation Act, adopting many of the features of the MAL, yet maintaining certain features reminiscent of the old English mindset to arbitration. Bolder legislative steps were taken in 2015 and, more recently, in 2019 to remove vestiges of the old arbitration regime. These encourage judges to support rather than intervene in ongoing arbitration and the outcomes of arbitration.

A refreshing change in the Supreme Court rulings on arbitration augurs a new era of judicial support for international arbitration. These appear not to be more than mere exhortatory but are firm strident moves indicative of a serious change of course. Indian courts could, henceforth, play a leading instrument in the international arbitration orchestra.

24

A Country of Contrasts: A Young Singaporean's Perspective of India

Chan Jia Hao

"Have you been to India?" was the first question the recruitment manager asked me when I applied for an internship at the Institute of South Asian Studies (ISAS) in the National University of Singapore (NUS) in 2017.

I instantaneously replied no but, in the same breadth, added that besides China, Singapore has been looking at India as a potential market for years. "I would like to get a sense of how Singapore can build forward and backward linkages with India for the benefit of Singapore businesses and our citizens", I sincerely asserted. I was eventually given the internship at ISAS. Following my graduation from NUS, I joined the institute and until my departure in September 2020, I belonged to a very small group of Singaporean researchers looking at India's and South Asia's linkages with Singapore and the Southeast Asian region.

In July 2019, I made my maiden trip to New Delhi as part of an ISAS administrative team for the India-Singapore Strategic Dialogue (ISSD), a 1.5 Track dialogue between the two countries. I was in New Delhi again in December 2019 for another work trip. I was also part of an ISAS team involved in a project on trade connectivity and institutions in South Asia with the Confederation of Indian Industry and the Department for International Development (United Kingdom).

Before my visit, my preconceived notion of the Indian society was very much influenced by popular movies like 'Slumdog Millionaire' and '3 Idiots'. While these movies may not reflect the total reality of a country as vast as India, they, nonetheless, suggested how the typical Indian society could look like — cosmopolitan yet traditional; progressive yet poor; competitive yet supportive; and cities bustling all-day with motorists sounding their car horns non-stop on congested roads.

Let me, as a young Singaporean, share some personal perspectives on the Indian society, economy, cuisine and culture and heritage.

During the free time on my trips, I took the opportunity to venture around the city. At the end of each journey, I always found myself at the famous Khan market, either checking out the bookstores or trying out new dishes at the cafés. I was told that you can find any book under the sun at the bookstores there and that was certainly the case. The same applied to the amazing variety of food available at the place. At the whip of my Uber application, my curiosity also brought me to an equally charming boutique shopping area called Hauz Khaz Village where affluent Indians from South Delhi drop by for tea and a stroll in the reservoir park. This was my first impression of a city of contrast and with that, a country rich in diversity.

Perhaps my most unforgettable moment in New Delhi was the trip to Majnu-Ka-Tila (Manju's hillock) which has been home to many Tibetan refugees and their Indian citizen children since the 1960s. On the way there and in the hillock, I witnessed people living under overhead bridges and in tents by the side of Delhi's Yamuna River and beggars approaching cars stopped at traffic light junctions. From the looks on their faces, they seem to accept that their fate was sealed and this was their place in life. These sights and the existence of slums right in the heart of New Delhi reflected another stark disparity in the Indian society.

During my first visit, another occasion also intrigued me about the nature of Indian society. I was invited to a farmhouse for dinner as part of the ISSD delegation. We were taken by bus to a village-like district with locals cycling on congested roads lined with small shops and stalls, and families rearing cattle in the area. Suddenly, a big gate beckoned and we were driven into the compound. From the gate, we travelled about 300 metres to a huge mansion with tennis courts and a swimming pool. When I turned back to look at the street outside, I must admit that I had to pinch myself to see that I was not dreaming. Such contrasts were, in fact, evident in many parts of New Delhi.

When in the capital, more than once, I exclaimed, "What a dynamic city!" The city was not just like what I saw in the movies or read in books, but it was also the case in reality. Never in my life, as a Singaporean, have I seen such drastic differences in lifestyle in a single location. Yet, my travels made me understand that, seen through the lens of New Delhi, India is, in fact, developing very rapidly. This progress in turn has benefitted many Indians while many others have been left untouched by the transformation. The images of disparity in the Indian society and economy that presented themselves to me will remain etched in my mind for a long time.

When in New Delhi, I also found myself enjoying the various cuisines while keeping in mind the danger of falling prey to the infamous 'Delhi belly'. I tried the *momo* (steamed filled dumpling), a dish similar the Japanese *gyoza*, and 'chow mien' and 'hot and sour soup', which had a canny resemblance to the Sichuan dishes found in South-western China. These were on top of the usual *kebabs* (meat or vegetable dish grilled on a skewer) and *briyani* (mixed rice dish). I also thought that New Delhi's Indian food, while comparable to that in Singapore, was different in terms of portion, spiciness and combination. The Indian dishes had an abundance of all these items. It was also not uncommon to have both North and South Indian dishes in the same eating house. Even in its cuisines, India is a country of culinary variances.

I observed that, while New Delhi is fast modernising and developing, there are proactive efforts to keep the heritage and culture alive. There are many town quarters that invoke one's reimagination of Delhi during the days of Mughal Empire — places like Humayun's Tomb Red Fort, Qutub Minar and Jama Masjid so easily transform one back into India's glorious past. So do the colonial-style buildings at Connaught Place, constructs of more than 150 years of British imperialism. Modern sites like the Akshardham complex and Lotus Temple also attempt to promote traditional religious beliefs. The former has included boat rides and a musical fountain as a means to attract visitors to the place. It reminded me of Singapore's Haw Par Villa, a theme park rich in Chinese tradition and religious beliefs.

My Singaporean friends did not believe me when I returned to depict the modernity, richness and glamour of India I experienced just by being in New Delhi. Neither could they imagine the skyscrapers in the city, similar to those found in Singapore — a city-state they associate with development and prosperity. They were also amazed by the many contradistinctions that New Delhi offered.

The reality is that, despite Singapore being highly globalised and cosmopolitan, many Singaporeans, particularly young Singaporeans, have not been to India. According to India's tourism ministry, Singapore tourist arrivals in 2019 accounted for only an average of one to two percent of total tourist arrivals to the country every month. Their disinterest in India, as in my case previously, was the outcome of their understanding of India acquired through the media and hearsay, and one that is based on an imagined notion of what India is.

The Singapore heartland, no doubt, has helped to portray the image of India in the form of *roti prata* (*paratha* [flatbread]), Bollywood, sarees, alongside a spice-friendly Little India neighbourhood. When one craves for *masala chai* (tea mixed with Indian spices) and *biryani*, one instinctively travels to Mustafa Centre or its vicinity, the de-facto 'epicentre of India' in our small city-state. Further away from the heartland, Singaporeans may also have unapologetically, in their internet-driven imagination, conceive of India being made up of rural villages surrounded by people living in poverty with no or poor access to basic amenities. At the workplaces in Singapore, however, many Singaporeans, like me, have the fortune of learning about the country from Indian colleagues. After all, Singapore is home of a group of highly relevant, innovative and enterprising Indians, particularly in the financial and services sectors.

I wonder at times if the impression of India for the majority of Singaporeans is based largely on the country's social and cultural landscapes rather than its political and economic transformation. Some young Singaporeans I know do actually recognise Amit Shah (India's Home Minister and former President of the Bharatiya Janata Party) and even Chandrababu Naidu (former Chief Minister of Andhra Pradesh). At present, to many, India means Prime Minister Narendra Modi. Some of these young Singaporeans are aware of big Indian companies like Reliance and Tata. However, very few can identify the sectors that India is willing to liberalise with Singapore in an exchangeable manner under the India-Singapore Comprehensive Economic Cooperation Agreement.

I have been constantly asked for the rationale for my focus on India and South Asia, for that matter. "Why, of all regional research, did you choose South Asia and India?" "Why research on a country that only sends thousands of migrant workers to our small country to steal our lunch?" I also have friends who lament that India and Singapore's development standards differ significantly and, as such, what Singapore could offer to India will never equate to what Singapore would receive in return. These comments and queries intrigue me as they reveal biases, doubts and definitely a lack of awareness of the relevance of India as an economic partner to Singapore. However, such remarks also exhibit a sense of anxiety and fear and an 'us versus them' attitude where a zero-sum game shall prevail at the end of the day.

Personally, I do not think the above (mis)perception of India is healthy and good for Singapore and Singaporeans. In a highly globalised and competitive 21st century, the lack of appreciation by young Singaporeans of the trade and investment opportunities emanating from emerging economies like India is worrisome. We need to adopt a more positive approach to India. After all, it is expected to become the world's third largest economy by 2025.

I must quickly state here that, sadly, India is not the only victim of young Singaporeans' indifference or one for which they have limited knowledge and understanding. Some still conceive of the West as the almighty, the omniscient and omnipotent. Apart from India, they also imagine emerging countries like China as dirty and backward despite China's rapid development in the last two decades being well documented. Many also tend to overlook the fact that China is the second largest economy in the world today and the fastest-growing trillion-dollar economy.

It is opportune for young Singaporeans to visit and spend some time in India to better understand this highly diverse country. They have nothing to lose by taking the first step out of Singapore to India. Young Singaporeans should start re-imagining India based on their own personal experiences rather than one based on social media, news and second-hand impressions. They will be amazed by what this country of contrasts has to offer.

25

Heavenly Tryst Postponed: Amaravati and Beyond

Francis Chong

On 9 September 2019, at the 'India-Singapore: The Next Phase' conference, Singapore diplomat, Professor Tommy Koh, asked Andhra Pradesh's Finance Minister, Buggana Rajendranath Reddy, and Singapore's Foreign Minister, Vivian Balakrishnan:

> One of the bilateral projects between India and Singapore, which has caught the imagination of many Singaporeans, is a project to build a new capital city in Andhra Pradesh called Amaravati. So my question to the two Ministers is: Is Amaravati sick, very sick or dead?

As the audience buzzed and the ministers answered diplomatically, I recalled a more optimistic period five years earlier in June 2014. India's Prime Minister Narendra Modi had just announced India's 'Smart Cities' vision. From recently bifurcated Andhra Pradesh, Chief Minister Chandrababu Naidu sought Singapore's help to masterplan a new state capital city eventually named Amaravati. After discussions at the highest levels, the Andhra Pradesh and Singapore governments, with the Indian government's blessing, cooperated to create three masterplans for

i) the Amaravati Capital Region; ii) Amaravati City; and iii) a detailed Seed Development area within Amaravati. These were completed by Surbana-Jurong Pte Ltd and delivered by July 2015.

The next phase of cooperation was hampered by political rivalries and legal manoeuvrings in Andhra Pradesh but in May 2017, the Andhra Pradesh government and a consortium of Singapore companies — Ascendas-Singbridge Pte Ltd (now CapitaLand Pte Ltd) and Sembcorp Development Ltd — agreed to form a joint venture company to master-develop the Amaravati Start-Up Area. Simultaneously, the Andhra Pradesh and Singapore governments agreed to cooperate in: i) master-developing a start-up area within Amaravati; ii) supporting Andhra Pradesh's broader economic development through encouraging Singapore companies to explore economic opportunities in the state; and iii) enhancing the capabilities of Andhra Pradesh institutions through capacity-building programmes, 'deep dive' workshops and expert advice on planning and governance.

Singapore's Ministry of Trade and Industry (MTI) established the Amaravati Partnership Office (APO) to explore, initiate and design partnership activities among the public, private and people sectors of Andhra Pradesh and Singapore. The APO's mission was to support Andhra Pradesh's developmental plans; encourage Singapore companies to pursue business opportunities in Andhra Pradesh; and strengthen people-to-people ties between Andhra Pradesh and Singapore. The small APO team's capacity to respond to Andhra Pradesh's needs was greatly augmented by its Singapore partners: other government agencies, companies and business associations, educational institutions and non-governmental organisations. The 'P' in APO stood for 'Partnership', which expressed the APO officers' conviction that the cooperation between Singapore and Andhra Pradesh was not a transactional arrangement in an urban development project, but also a broad-based partnership for mutual benefit.

Five years of furious activity in expanding areas of cooperation came to an abrupt standstill in May 2019 when elections brought to power another political party. Andhra Pradesh's new leaders set different priorities that diminished the importance of both Amaravati and Andhra Pradesh's partnership with Singapore. While Singapore is ready to resume activities under the partnership, it acknowledges the prerogative of the new Andhra Pradesh government to determine how it wants the partnership to progress.

Given the theme of this book is *India On Our Minds*, the next part of this essay shares some of what went through the minds of the APO officers as we watched developments in Andhra Pradesh unfold from the time each of us joined the team to the present. The personal accounts are told in our own voices. They provide a glimpse into the thoughts, feelings and motivations of Singapore civil servants who, though not of Andhra Pradesh, nonetheless committed deeply and personally to make the Andhra Pradesh-Singapore partnership a success:

> Amaravati was a dream … but not an impossible one. After all, shouldn't dreams be lofty? It could have brought benefits to many people, and be a gateway for ideas and solutions from all over the world to enter Andhra Pradesh and India. The question is how to be on India's mind? Our typical approach as a partner is to either offer capacity-building programmes pro bono and/or introduce Singapore companies with solutions to the concerns of Indian government agencies. However, we struggle to be a priority on the agenda of our Indian partners. Beyond the alternatives of paid or pro bono engagements, perhaps it is investment — impactful and profitable — that will succeed in attracting India's attention. — *APO Officer 1*

> In our collaboration, there were times our Indian partners surprised us by delivering on their commitments just when we thought they would not pull through. While the effort was, at times, trying, we sought to understand the perspectives and actions of our partners, and made it a point to be a committed partner ourselves. I believe we learnt a valuable lesson in working with India: changes in vision can happen, and we need to learn how to hedge risks to ensure continuity. It is

also important to define what it means to continue if goals have been shifted. — *APO Officer 2*

No matter the setbacks or challenges, one cannot deny the importance of engaging India. I quickly noticed the rigour and commitment from my team mates: there was a tremendous amount of work and coordination to provide leadership and direction to multiple agencies. It is an advantage to know the right people at the right time. Such is the dynamic nature of Indian politics. — *APO Officer 3*

I was drawn to the APO because of Amaravati. I came from the construction industry, completing project after project, but never had I brimmed with much purpose for an incredible opportunity to build a brand new capital city. Even more amazing was it being in India, which was filled with mystery for me. We worked very hard for Amaravati, though it does not belong to us. I felt like a foster parent: nurturing a city from birth, celebrating little milestones towards the Big Plan. Now our work on Amaravati has halted: the buzz is gone. My purpose for Amaravati, once fired up within, is extinguished. I never imagined a political change in a state of India would have such an effect on me, a Singaporean. — *APO Officer 4*

In my mind, India was and still is an adventure. Being in the APO enabled me to get closely acquainted with an Indian city and its people and play a part in fulfilling their vision. It is tempting to think that Singapore has a lot to offer the Indians, but experience has taught me that we have to pursue her and make ourselves relevant to earn the chance to partner her on her growth journey. What is an adventure without a few bumps? Let's keep going! — *APO Officer 5*

Some vivid memories will stay with me. Watching the masterplan take physical shape on the ground every month I am there — I think those are the foundations of the Chief Secretary's house! — the strong sense of mission of its officials and the faith of villagers who contributed their lands inspired me. When India and its leaders apply themselves to a united vision, they are formidable! However, while

> Amaravati is a greenfield city, it is firmly situated within the cultural, social and political spaces of Andhra Pradesh and India. To be an effective partner, we need to understand how this unseen, rich and complex context should guide our efforts. I don't want to shy away or be daunted, but instead I want to develop the right skills, insights and perspectives to work with it, and within it. India presents an opportunity for us to learn to operate amid diversity and complexity. If successful, our capacity to adapt to the changing global headwinds will be enhanced. — *APO Officer 6*

Some would regard Amaravati as an object lesson in the need to be 'realistic' about the difficulties and the risks of investing huge efforts to engage with India. To others, the visible failure of the project was outweighed by the subtle gains. It changed Singaporean mindsets to be more flexible and agile; it provided deeper knowledge and skills to operate more effectively; and it resulted in wider networks of contacts to help identify and participate in India's vast and varied opportunities.

Ultimately, India's strategic importance to Singapore and the determination not to waste the lessons of failure led to the decision for the APO to be reincarnated as the Singapore-India Partnership Office (SIPO). On 1 February 2020, the SIPO was inaugurated with the mission to engage India, beyond Andhra Pradesh, through partnerships for mutual benefit, while applying the lessons of Amaravati to increase its effectiveness and mitigate risk. To signal its resolve, one of the first decisions of the SIPO team was to choose as its motto the following quote by American singer, actor and businessman, Jimmy Ray Dean: "I can't change the direction of the wind, but I can adjust my sails to always reach my destination."

26

Singapore-India Cultural Collaborations

Rosa Daniel

If culture is defined as the arts and heritage of any grouping of people, it is no exaggeration to say that for Singapore and Singaporeans, culture has contributed to our sense of national identity and helped build our confidence as a modern country with deep historical roots.

It would also be a fair observation that our cultural expressions over more than five decades of nationhood have become a source of strength for our international relations. Singapore can take some pride in the way culture now serves as an anchor for our bilateral relations, giving authenticity through institutional and people-to-people linkages. In the case of India, our cultural ties stem from our shared heritage and the new collaborations that have been forged over the past decades.

Singapore — A Diverse City-State

While Singapore is a small city-state in Southeast Asia, it is home to diverse cultures, including a sizeable Indian community. When the British East India Company established Singapore as a free port in the early 19th century, economic opportunities quickly attracted migrants from India, China, the Malay Peninsula, the Indonesian Archipelago and even Europe.

Singapore's resident population is highly multi-racial and multi-cultural. The Department of Statistics Singapore stated that in 2019, 74.4 percent of the population was Chinese, 13.4 percent Malay, 9 percent Indian and 3.2 percent other residents. Another unique feature is that Singaporeans have preserved their distinct ethnic cultures within a shared heritage and national identity. Singapore has been acknowledged as the world's most religiously diverse nation. The Department of Statistics Singapore, in its General Household Survey 2015, stated that 43.2 percent of the population was then Buddhist or Taoist, 18.8 percent Christian, 14.7 percent Muslim, 5 percent Hindu, 0.7 percent other religions, and 18.5 percent professing to no religion. It is this multi-ethnic and multi-religious social fabric that has sustained our rich connections to India.

The Indian Community in Singapore

The Indian community in Singapore is a diverse group. It includes those who migrated from the subcontinent as British colonial subjects and those born in the Straits Settlements (mainly Penang, Malacca and Singapore). Added to this are migrants who arrived in Singapore's post-independence era. Ethnic Tamils form slightly more than half (54.2 percent) of Singapore's Indian community. According the General Household Survey in 2015, the other community groups include the Malayalis, Sikhs, Punjabis, Hindustanis, Gujaratis and Sindhis, among others. Hinduism, followed by Islam, is the dominant religion.

Right from the first wave of migration to Singapore, many Indians settled here and made important contributions to the development of modern Singapore. They also enriched our broader social tapestry through food, customs, festivals, skills and trades that are part of our precious intangible cultural heritage. Today, Indians continue to come to Singapore, drawn by jobs and opportunities. They refresh our historical linkages and help to anchor our bilateral relations.

India — An Important Cultural Partner for Singapore

The formal cultural linkages between the two countries go back many years. In 1993, Singapore and India signed a standing memorandum of understanding for cooperation in the arts, heritage and archives. This agreement launched several fruitful exchanges at the institutional and community levels. In the same year, both countries concluded the first of six Executive Programmes (EP) which set out specific areas of collaboration and projects in the fields of arts, heritage and archives. These EPs have signalled high-level support by both governments to boost our exchanges of artists, arts groups and heritage professionals. In 2015, both countries extended the loan agreement for artefacts between the Archaeological Survey of India (ASI) and our Asian Civilisations Museum (ACM).

Institutional Exchanges

While state-level agreements have been forged, the key progress has been among arts and cultural institutions. Singapore's cultural institutions have built on a long history of collaboration with their Indian counterparts and pursued numerous initiatives. One of the most significant was the National Museum in New Delhi hosting the Peranakan exhibition from the ACM titled 'The Peranakan World: Cross-cultural Art from Singapore and the Malacca Straits' in 2015. Then-Singapore President Tony Tan launched the exhibition during his state visit to India. It was the key commemorative event celebrating the 50th anniversary of bilateral relations between our two countries.

In 2015, the ACM reciprocated by hosting an exhibition titled 'Treasures from Asia's Oldest Museum: Buddhist Art from the India Museum, Kolkata'. Several existing artefacts on loan from India are currently on display at the ACM. Our institutions are also keen to engage Indian experts in the preservation and restoration of monuments, and in intangible cultural heritage. For example, the Hindu Endowments Board and the National Heritage Board are in discussions with ASI to tap on its expertise to restore Hindu temples in Singapore.

Indian Heritage Centre — A Proud New Institution

One new institution in Singapore is the Indian Heritage Centre (IHC), the first museum in Southeast Asia to focus on the diverse heritage of the Indian communities in Singapore and Southeast Asia. This heritage institution, located in Singapore's Little India precinct, was launched in May 2015 in conjunction with Singapore's 50th anniversary celebrations. For its opening, the Indian government donated four busts of eminent Indian leaders, Netaji Subhas Chandra Bose, Mahatma Gandhi, Jawaharlal Nehru and Rabindranath Tagore. During the Shangri-La Dialogue in 2018, the IHC proudly hosted a visit by Indian Prime Minister Narendra Modi.

It is no mean feat to distil 4,500 years of rich history, connect the dots from India to Singapore and Southeast Asia and tell stories of the Singaporean Indian community. This would not have been possible without the strong support from the entire Singapore Indian community. The curatorial storyline was the result of consultations with more than 50 Indian organisations, associations and groups, and many individuals deeply interested in Singapore's Indian heritage. In fact, almost half the artefacts on display at the IHC are either loans from or donated by members of the community.

Since its launch, the IHC has actively engaged in programming and outreach to promote intra- and inter-community awareness and appreciation. Inspired by the popularity of artisan craftsmanship, the IHC and the High Commission of India in Singapore launched 'Kala Sangam' in 2018, which features 12 traditional craftsmen travelling annually from India to the IHC over a five-year period to demonstrate their crafts and interact with the local community. The IHC also partners the community to celebrate Deepavali, Pongal and other Indian festivals to promote intangible heritage and culture, and add vibrancy to the Little India precinct.

Artistic Exchanges

On the artistic front, the National Arts Council (NAC) supports many diverse activities to profile Indian culture. In 2018, one of Singapore's foremost groups, Shantha Ratii Initiatives, received support from the NAC to present a multi-dance presentation at such venues in India as the National Centre for the Performing Arts in Mumbai and the Ganesham Black Box in Thiruvananthapuram, Kerala.

Another group, Apsaras Arts, has been provided with support to organise the annual Dance India Asia Pacific, which brings dance practitioners from the region together to learn from leading international dance artists. The Esplanade, Singapore's national performing arts centre, presents many Indian artists, and Indian art and culture shows almost throughout the year. However, the highlight has been 'Kalaa Utsavam — Indian Festival of Arts', a 10-day performing arts festival presented every year by the Esplanade since 2002. The festival, featuring artists and arts groups from Singapore, India and the Indian diaspora, attracts an audience of 40,000 yearly.

Over the years, every Indian High Commissioner to Singapore has played an active role in supporting and facilitating cultural exchanges. To commemorate the 50th year of diplomatic relations between India and Singapore, the Indian High Commission in Singapore, together with the country's Indian Council for Cultural Relations, organised a year-long 'Festival of India' in Singapore from August 2014 to September 2015.

In 2019, Shubigi Rao, a Singaporean multidisciplinary artist, a naturalised citizen originally from Mumbai, did Singapore proud when she was selected by the Indian organising committee to curate the fifth edition of the Kochi-Muziris Biennale, which is South Asia's biggest visual arts event. Shubigi was Singapore's sole representative at the fourth edition of the Biennale.

In the area of literary arts, writers from India are regularly featured in platforms such as the Singapore Writers Festival. The NAC also supported the Association of Singapore Tamil Writers in setting up a Singapore Literature Booth at the Chennai Book Fair in 2016 and

2017. Another initiative has been the National Library Board hosting the significant Tamil Digital Heritage Collection, a repository for more than 350 literary works, some of which are out of print. In addition to physical resources, this digital collection facilitates access by a younger generation of tech-savvy Tamil Singaporeans.

Culture — Navigating Uncertainties

In a time of increasing geopolitical uncertainties and technological developments where societies are becoming increasingly complex and polarised, culture has the power to bring people together. It is a universal language that transcends boundaries and fosters people-to-people affinity across regions and cities. Being able to get the Indian community in Singapore to appreciate its cultural links with India will help build an important stakeholder community for Singapore-India relations, one that will further strengthen the relationship between the two countries.

Fortunately, many Indian Singaporeans, both local-born and new citizens, still retain strong ties to their ancestral homeland which contribute to growing economic, political and cultural linkages between Singapore and India. It is important that Singapore's cultural institutions and artistic community continue to engage the diverse local Indian community to serve as a cultural link between both countries.

Cooperation aside, there have been occasional allegations that Singapore's cultural institutions, among other international museums of high standing, possess artefacts alleged to have been looted from India. Singapore has viewed these allegations seriously, taken steps to verify the claims and acted in accordance with the frameworks and guidelines expected as a member of the International Council of Museums. We have also established open communications with Indian authorities and centres of expertise such as the ASI. These actions have ensured that we sustain our long-standing friendly cultural ties with our Indian counterparts.

Looking Ahead

Our museums have responded positively to India's recent request to support its current efforts in setting up new museums with a view to using technology to enhance visitor experiences. The National Heritage Board has identified Singapore companies specialising in exhibition designs and interactives which can contribute to India's efforts. In research, Singapore has also agreed to work with India on its Project Mausam research initiative which focuses on spice routes in the region.

India continues to be an important cultural partner for Singapore, with our agencies and institutions keen to work further with their counterparts across a wide range of areas. We are looking to renew our EP on Cultural Cooperation (a 7th edition) and build on the deep and sustained engagement between the cultural institutions of both countries. We continue to view our cultural relations as a source of strength in anchoring our overall bilateral relations with India.

Beyond bilateral collaborations, Singapore is privileged to have many extensive partnerships with other international counterparts at the state and institutional levels. Moving forward, Singapore and India can build on our respective partnerships with other countries to jointly explore training and technical exchanges, for instance, in heritage conservation, to share best practices and develop capabilities. This will require greater coordination on research, innovation, documentation and sharing between our institutions and third parties.

The tumultuous events of 2020 during the time of COVID-19 have presented not only challenges, but also opportunities as we seek to sustain our cultural relations with key partners. With India's digital and technological capabilities, our cultural institutions, artists and arts groups can tap on new possibilities for collaboration with their Indian counterparts. As we have experienced thus far, our cultural ties have been robust through the changing times and generations. We should continue to draw inspiration and strength from these ties to achieve further mutual growth and development.

27

Financial System's Linkages between Singapore and India

Piyush Gupta

A question I am asked often by journalists is the defining moment when I knew that DBS Bank had to transform itself digitally or die. That moment was in 2014 when Alibaba was preparing to list in New York. DBS' Chairman, Peter Seah, and I had arranged a meeting with Jack Ma and Joe Tsai, and I walked away frightened out of my wits that they would change our industry forever.

That epiphany led to DBS' Board and senior management placing a S$200 million bet on digitalisation. One of the more radical questions we also asked ourselves was, "Can we launch an entire bank in a mobile phone?" In 2016, we unveiled digibank, a groundbreaking branchless, signatureless, paperless bank in India. We picked India as the first market for our bold foray into digital because it had the largest biometric identification system and a multi-layered technology stack on which we could tap. After India, we took the digibank concept to Indonesia and, today, we have 3.25 million digibank customers in both markets.

Another milestone in India was DBS being granted wholly-owned subsidiary status in 2017. This put us on par with local players in terms of activities we could do, including removing pre-existing branch limitations. The only other lender granted wholly-owned subsidiary status was the State Bank of Mauritius.

DBS' investments in India are just a microcosm of the extensive financial linkages that have long existed between Singapore and India.

DBS' presence in India spans just over 25 years, making us a youngster considering the history of finance between the two nations. The Chettiars of Tamil Nadu arrived in Singapore in the 1820s and were specialised lenders to local merchants, miners, planters, contractors and petty traders. Until their decline following World War II, they were a key source of finance for small business. The Oversea-Chinese Banking Corporation (OCBC Bank) transferred its headquarters to Bombay to preserve the bank during the Japanese Occupation. And the first Indian banks — Indian Bank, Indian Overseas Bank, United Commercial Bank and Bank of India — set up operations in Singapore in the 1940s to 1950s when Singapore was still under British rule. The State Bank of India (SBI), India's largest bank, has been in Singapore since the 1970s and was granted the Qualifying Full Bank status in 2008. As a result, SBI is allowed to carry out the full range of banking businesses permitted under the Banking Act, including retail deposit-taking.

Singapore's foreign direct investment (FDI) in India is testament to the two countries' continuing close business connections. In FY2018-2019, Singapore's FDI of S$22.1 billion made us the largest investor in India. We are also a leading investor in India through foreign portfolio investment (FPI). Last year, Singapore's FPI flows to India were S$60 billion, the fourth-highest after the United States (US), Mauritius and Luxembourg.

The reasons for this are manifold:

1. India has set its sights on becoming a US$5 trillion (S$7.1 trillion) economy by 2024 — about double its current gross domestic product (GDP). While this is not without challenges, and India's

banking sector, in particular, is beset by elevated levels of bad debt, the long-term prognosis is positive with GDP growth expected to stabilise between six and seven percent.

2. Singapore boosts a sizeable local Indian community, along with a growing Indian expatriate community, both of which have traceable roots back to India. This has led to a rise in demand for retail banking and wealth management services for non-resident Indians (NRIs).
3. As a global-Asia gateway for asset managers and investors with S$3.44 trillion in assets under management in 2018, Singapore is home to a large amount of funds in search of a good return.

Whether it is in the capital markets, derivatives markets, wealth management, remittances or banking, there has been tremendous inbound and outbound activity. Flows from Singapore to India have been on the rise.

- Singapore has always a healthy provider of offshore financing through the fixed income market. Today, there are about 200 debt securities from 100 Indian issuers listed on the Singapore Exchange (SGX). Singapore has also been the preferred capital market for Indian corporates raising 'Masala Bonds' denominated in Indian rupees.
- For the last two decades, foreign investors have been able to get exposure to the Indian equities market via derivatives, in particular, the Nifty 50 index futures, listed on the SGX. This has been an attractive proposition, given India's historically complex compliance norms, tough tax rules and other roadblocks. In FY2019, SGX Nifty futures were the fourth most actively traded contracts on the SGX. Plans are however in the works to move this equity derivatives market to the Gujarat International Finance Tec-City, which the India government has ambitions to make an international financial services hub.

- Globally, India is the highest recipient of remittances, with its diaspora sending back US$79 billion (S$112.4 billion) in 2018. While flows from Singapore amounted to less than US$1 billion (S$1.4 billion), this is likely to grow further, and the opportunity is well recognised by both DBS and other Singapore-based financial technology (fintech) providers.
- Singapore-based NRIs continue to invest into foreign currency non-resident deposit programmes offered in India for security against fluctuating exchange rates and attractive returns. Likewise, this segment has also been used by the Indian government to mobilise foreign currency when required. As an example, in 1998, India launched the five-year Resurgent India Bond in US dollar, sterling and the deutschemark, raising US$4.2 billion (S$5.7 billion). Of this, 50 percent came from NRIs in the Middle East, 30 percent from Europe and the US, and 20 percent from Asia.
- In banking, both DBS and the United Overseas Bank have an on-ground presence in India. OCBC Bank's private banking subsidiary, Bank of Singapore, entered into a partnership with India's Edelweiss Group last year to allow clients of both entities to tap on their respective product platforms.

Even as funds are flowing from Singapore to India, the converse is also true. Among them, the outbound Liberalised Remittance Scheme has been a huge draw among resident Indians seeking to invest overseas. The last 10 years have witnessed a strong performance of S&P 500/Singapore REITS, in comparison to a tepid performance by Indian equities. This has triggered a sense of urgency among high-net-worth individuals to diversify out of India. The depreciating rupee has also encouraged many Indian investors to diversify overseas.

Recently, the Reserve Bank of India changed regulations to allow Indian family offices to be structured as 'Core Investment Companies'. This, along with Singapore's family office regime, will enable outbound remittances for capital market investments.

The year 2020 will be particularly tough for India. The economy was experiencing a slowdown heading into the year, with deleveraging of corporates, banks and non-banking institutions already ongoing. The COVID-19 pandemic will further hamper growth as India's lockdown impacts real income, employment, households and businesses.

Nonetheless, strong linkages between the two nations will continue. There will be strong growth in outbound investments from India to Singapore, as growing onshore wealth increasingly diversifies overseas. Indian family offices in Singapore focused on private equity and venture capital will also grow. Finally, we can expect more in the way of fintech collaborations and partnerships. Singapore has a fintech-friendly regulatory framework, a digitally savvy workforce, sound infrastructure and is home to about 500 fintech companies. India was the third most preferred global destination for fintech investments in 2019, behind only the US and the United Kingdom. The fintech industries in both countries have significant synergies that should continue to be harnessed.

28

Why India's Economy Has Fallen so Far behind China's

Vikram Khanna

Over the last 30 years, China and India have been among the world's fastest growing economies. In terms of poverty alleviation, their achievements have been spectacular. Between them, they have lifted around one billion people out of poverty, with China accounting for about three quarters of the total.

However, while 30 years ago, the two economies were comparable in many respects, this is no longer the case. China's performance has surpassed that of India on almost every social and economic metric.

At US$14.1 trillion (S$20 trillion) in 2019, China's gross domestic product (GDP) — the second largest in the world — is almost five times that of India. China is far more integrated into the global economy. It is the world's largest exporter, accounting for 12.8 percent of global exports, compared with 1.7 percent for India. China has superior physical infrastructure and a more business-friendly environment. It is also well ahead in terms of social indicators. On the United Nations Development Programme's 2019 Human Development Index, which combines measurements of life expectancy, years of schooling and per capita income on a purchasing power parity basis, China was ranked 85th out of 189 countries, while India ranked 129th.

What explains China's outperformance vis-à-vis India? The divergence between the two has occurred in less than a generation. As recently as 1980, the per capita incomes of both countries were roughly equal at about US$250 (S$355). However, China's superior growth compounded over the period has made the difference.

There are many interpretations of why China grew faster than India. A big part of the story is that China embarked on its market-oriented economic reforms in 1978, more than a decade ahead of India, which, faced with a financial crisis, was forced into liberalising its economy only in 1991.

The nature of China's reforms was also different. It started with agricultural reforms which gave its farmers more control over their holdings and better prices. This raised the living standards of the majority of China's population. At the same time, China encouraged labour intensive industries, such as clothing, toys and light engineering goods, areas in which its cheap labour enabled it to quickly become competitive, aided by substantial foreign direct investment, initially from Hong Kong and Taiwan, which poured into newly-created special economic zones. As more workers moved to cities, China's urbanisation accelerated, creating 'agglomeration effects' — synergies resulting from multiple economic activities in close proximity. China's urbanisation rate increased dramatically from 18 percent in 1978 to 59 percent in 2018 (compared to 34 percent in India at present). China's manufacturing sector expanded in both size and sophistication after it joined the World Trade Organisation in 2001, and established itself as the biggest player in global supply chains for many manufactured goods, which led to further job creation as well as technology transfers as global companies established production operations in China.

India's 1991 reforms dismantled some elements of the 'License Raj' — a panoply of bureaucratic obstacles to business — and partially liberalised imports and foreign investment. While these were significant reforms that also spurred higher rates of investment, including foreign investment, they largely bypassed the farm sector, where the majority of the population lives, and thus did not lead to mass job creation as in China. The services sector expanded and is now the largest in the economy. Many manufacturing activities were reserved for the small-scale sector and they were thus unable to scale up. India failed to address the biggest constraints to the expansion of manufacturing, notably rigid labour laws and problems with land acquisition, which persist to this day and have deterred both Indian and foreign companies from investing in mass manufacturing, despite a major 'Make in India' initiative launched by the government in 2014. India's participation in global manufacturing supply chains, which have expanded since the 1990s, was, therefore, limited.

In short, after an impressive initial burst in the early 1990s, India did not persist with its reforms. Only much later, in the last five years, did it push through important reforms such as the introduction of a biometric national identification system, a national Goods and Services Tax and a bankruptcy code.

China, by contrast, maintained a continuous process of reform, which included institutional reforms such as allowing private, foreign and collective-ownership companies to operate, privatising state-owned enterprises, strengthening property rights and, more recently, expanding the digital economy.

Beginning in the 1990s, China started to ramp up its infrastructure spending and now has the world's largest network of high-speed rail and expressways, which India is in the relatively early stages of building. Here, it is important to correct the popular myth that India's infrastructure deficit vis-à-vis China is a major cause of its relative underperformance. As Professor Yasheng Huang of the MIT Sloan School of Management has pointed out, up to the 1990s, China had poor infrastructure, but still grew rapidly. China built its infrastructure ***after*** — not before — more than a decade of high growth. "The 'China miracle' happened not because it had glittering skyscrapers and modern highways but because bold economic liberalisation and institutional reforms...created competition and nurtured private entrepreneurship", he points out. Infrastructure may have helped to sustain China's rapid growth but did not cause it.

Nor, to correct another myth, is China's superior infrastructure the result of its one-party system — other countries have managed to build good infrastructure without such a system. It is the result of many years of rapid growth and sustained reforms which generated financial resources.

However, China's system of government has led to a state that is, in many ways, more effective than that of India. This has long been true: China has had a stronger state than India throughout much of its history and has been better able to mobilise society for state aims. Its state has also been more innovative, engaging in experimentation and piloting, for example, in the creation of special economic zones. The differences in state capacity between the two countries are a major determinant of the differences in economic performance.

India is widely viewed as having an overbearing state. While indeed India's bureaucracy has been intrusive and obstructive, especially in the economic realm, political scientists point out that far from being excessively large, India's state is among the smallest in the world relative to its population. According to India's 7th Pay Commission, India had just 16 government employees per 1,000 population in 2015 (the latest year for which data is available), compared to 51 in China. India's public sector employment has been declining since 1991 even as the population has increased and there are significant vacancies in even essential public services such as the police and the judiciary. While India's state has been extremely effective in major undertakings such as organising elections for 850 million voters, responding to natural calamities and managing a large space programme, it has not been able to deliver on core functions such as providing basic public goods, which impact peoples' daily lives.

Two areas in which the gaps between China and India are especially glaring are healthcare and education.

China has long had an extensive national network of healthcare services, starting with barefoot doctors and commune clinics in the 1950s. It has also emphasised public health measures. India has done nothing comparable. Even before China's reforms in 1978, its life expectancy was 68 years, while India's was 54 years. While the gap in this particular metric has narrowed (China's life expectancy is now 76 years while India's is 68 years), there remain significant differences in nutritional and other health-related indicators which means that China has long had the benefit of a healthier and more productive workforce. The differences in the emphasis on healthcare persist to this day. Currently, China spends more than six percent of its GDP on healthcare, while India spends 1.5 percent.

China has also consistently invested more in education, resulting in a higher literacy rate, particularly of women, and higher school and college enrolments as well as more spending on research and development. While India is catching up — and there are big differences in educational attainments among its states — decades of lagging behind China in education has left India's workforce and technological development at a significant disadvantage.

Many economists, including India's Nobel laureate Amartya Sen, point out that the gaps between the two countries in the critical areas of healthcare and education are the most important determinants of the differences in their economic performance.

While that is the story so far, it could change in the future. At least as far as economic growth is concerned, India, with its younger population, has a demographic advantage. Its less mature economy could also mean potentially higher growth than China over the medium term, provided it manages its economy astutely and improves its state capacity.

China will also face new challenges. Besides dealing with an ageing population, as a middle-income country, it will have to contend with difficult reforms, especially in the context of a one-party state, including instituting the rule of law as well as better regulating its capital markets and improving its corporate governance, areas in which India is ahead.

Politically, while India's democracy is well entrenched, some observers believe that China may face an uncertain political transition. Geopolitical issues, including relations with the United States, could also impact the future of both countries.

Therefore, much remains to be played out. However, for now, as their economies go, China and India are at different stages of development.

29

Culture Hopping from One Democracy to Another

Asad Latif

I came from India to Singapore as a journalist in 1984 and became a citizen in 1999. Looking back, I could, like thousands of other immigrants, speak of the push and pull factors that brought and kept me here. Looking ahead, I could offer some thoughts on how India's diasporic relationship with Singapore might evolve. These are ways of celebrating India's presence in Singapore and Singapore's attractiveness to Indians.

However, let me proffer a simple political connection between the two countries: Both are democracies. Then I shall describe some facets of the cultural transition that I faced in hopping from one democracy to the other.

It is not difficult to travel between democracies, live in them for a while and even to settle in one of them eventually. For all their demographic, cultural and economic differences, democracies everywhere share a quintessential principle: The people form the nation and own the state. It is not the other way around: The state does not form the nation and own the people. In totalitarian systems, people are not citizens but merely subjects. In theocratic states, religion sanctions the only common denominator of belonging. In democracies, the citizens are the masters. They remain masters wherever they go in the democratic world.

I came from India to Singapore. It was not a political journey. I came here to make money, multiplied automatically by the exchange rate differential between the Singapore dollar and the Indian rupee. I wished to strike up friendships and return to India with my money and my networks. I could then live on my Singapore earnings, supplemented by other work.

It was not to be. I stayed on and on, falling in step with a new people because they were not that different from old compatriots. I was born and grew up in the city of Kolkata, capital of the Indian state of West Bengal. There is a joke about Bengalis, whether they live in West Bengal or Bangladesh, erstwhile East Bengal. The joke is that one Bengali gives you one Bengali, two Bengalis give you two poets and three Bengalis give you three political parties! The imaginative, argumentative and fractious nature of Bengali culture serves to uphold the diversity of the South Asian mindscape which is nothing if it is not a speculative and combative celebration of difference.

In a democracy, all existence is infectious. Lives are shared far more freely and intimately than they can be in a theocracy where faith contours social possibility, or in an autocracy which segregates people into graded orders of political legitimacy, acceptance and belonging. A democracy is different. It is an invitation to freedom from birth. Democracies give people the freedom to become the nation by accepting the supremacy of the Constitution, the rule of law and universal suffrage. Democracies are defined by the degree of civic nationalism which they possess, that is, by the extent to which citizens owe allegiance to them because of their equal political rights and responsibilities, not because of their privileged faith community or elevated economic status or superior social standing.

The democratic India of my birth was an open house for the everyday festivity of an infectious nationalism that cut across inherited and inbred boundaries of creed, caste and region.

So it is in democratic Singapore. Hindus in India and Chinese in Singapore constitute overwhelming demographic majorities. However, just as India is a secular democratic state, so is Singapore. The India in which I grew up possessed no sense of subjugating its religious minorities in order to assimilate them into a nation ruled by the ethnic majority. Singapore exhibits the truth of this principle in equal, if not in greater, degree. Singapore is a Chinese-majority state: It is not a Chinese state.

Interestingly, both India and Singapore survived the majoritarian threat to their democracies inherent in the circumstances of their birth as independent nations. The Partition of British India in 1947 into India and Pakistan, the latter envisaged as the homeland of South Asian Muslims, did not lead India to proclaim itself as the homeland of South Asian Hindus. Singapore's separation from Malaysia in 1965 did not make the republic stray from multi-racialism towards Chinese majoritarianism.

Recent controversies over the religious dimension of Indian nationalism will be subsumed ultimately, I believe, by India's timeless ability to survive dissension. Meanwhile, Singapore's astute management of racial and religious differences should give hope to secularists in India.

When I decided to apply for Singapore citizenship, some well-wishers warned me that I was giving up a passport that was thousands of years old for one of extremely youthful provenance. I thanked them for their concern but reminded them that both passports are tied to republics of fairly recent vintage: India from 1950 and Singapore from 1965. They smiled in shy agreement.

Looking ahead, I hope that India and Singapore will draw closer as two democratic pillars of an unsteady world that needs support. Identity politics in the form of exclusive ethnic affiliations is now an international menace. Such politics militates against the civic inclusiveness which defines the nation-state as a protective entity for all its citizens, an entity that rises above divisive self-identification made on the basis of racial or religious majoritarianism.

As a Muslim, I was part of a minority in India. As an Indian (and a Muslim), I am part of a minority in Singapore. I owe it to myself to be a democrat. That is because democracies preserve the itinerant identities of people like me who remain ourselves wherever we go.

Cultural Transition

How do people like me remain ourselves? We do so when the laws of the state and the customs of society allow us to become citizens, not by forsaking who we are but by relocating our old selves to new surroundings without cultural injury. Singapore consists of the descendants of its original inhabitants and the descendants of immigrants who are joined continuously by fresh arrivals. Most Singaporeans lay claim to this land by virtue not of native ancestry but of ancestral or personal settlement. This psychological recognition underlines an important element of Singapore nationhood. Even after generations, the descendants of original inhabitants and those of immigrants do not reserve for themselves the right to belong to Singapore and deny that right to those still coming. Singapore nationalism is not exclusive but inclusive, not foreclosed but open-ended. Today's Malays, descendants of the original inhabitants, have created the cultural basis of this national inclusiveness through an instinctive hospitality to newcomers that has made successive waves of Chinese, Indians and Eurasians as Singaporean as Malays are.

True, Singapore lately has witnessed a degree of resistance to foreigners but this resistance has to do with economic insecurities over access to jobs, education and public transport. That those sentiments have abated in the wake of remedial public policies reinforces the fact that the resistance was not territorial. Singaporeans were not saying: "I do not want you in my country because you do not belong here." They were saying: "I do not want you to upset my access to opportunities." Singaporeans use economics as the gauge of destiny. They do not treat the good life as a function of ethnicity.

That is why I found the cultural transition from India to Singapore seamless. I did not have to stop being the Indian that I had been born, to be reborn as a Singaporean. I did not have to abjure the Bengali roots of my verdant Indianness. Bengali, my mother tongue, remained mine. When my son and I eat mangoes, their sweetness shapes itself into Bengali words. I would not be able to discuss mangoes with him in Singlish. I am not good at learning new languages.

Of course, there are cultural differences between India and Singapore.

Indians are an extremely public people. West Bengal, for example, is defined by its face-to-face societies, localities called *paras*. In *paras*, every saint or sinner has a name, a history and an address which obliges each of them to exist in fated proximity. Saints take the form of the shy girl who made it to Calcutta Medical College, the boisterous geek who entered the Indian Institute of Technology at Kharagpur or the radical debater who joined the bourgeois elite at Presidency College. The sinners are more numerous. School dropouts, unemployed graduates and members of street-corner groups curse the passing successful under their breath. Yet, it is the malodorous sinners who become indispensable when an aged husband suffers a stroke and his distraught wife runs down the stairs to beg the vagabond sitting nearby to do something. Half-drunk, he and his cohort of sinners nevertheless accompany the patriarch to hospital on a taxi. The saints are busy meanwhile studying Medicine, Engineering, Law, History or English. If the old man dies, his illustrious daughters and sons will appear dutifully at the crematorium or the graveyard. The vagabond too will be there. Later, he will return to the street, smoking and drowning away his sorrows in the certainty that, like him, his social betters will pass. It is all a matter of impartial time. Street corner gatherings lie at the heart of the Bengali public sphere, providing concrete evidence every day of the capacity for companionship that makes humans a gregarious species of saints and sinners.

Singaporeans, by contrast, are a rather private people. That is because the state has all but taken over the functions which chance performs elsewhere. Housing and Development Board precincts are not *paras*. No distraught spouse has to run down the stairs to summon help. Ambulances come with attendant personnel bearing stretchers. No one has to fight with the hospital authorities to get anyone admitted. Social anonymity is the prerogative of citizens of an affluent and well-ordered society.

Yet, people are people everywhere. So many years after having arrived here, I realise that I never left India. I simply brought it with me to Singapore. Even today, I look for overlaps between the life processes of people there and here. And there is no greater overlap than their shared heritage and promise as democracies.

30

The Indo-Pacific — Eye of the Beholder

Lim Thuan Kuan

Much has been written about the Indo-Pacific. As a geographic concept, alongside others such as Asia Pacific or East Asia, it is not new or novel, having been mentioned many times over many years by many people. What is new and why it is currently generating so much interest is that some countries are actively pushing to give it more structure or definition and some degree of collective organisation.

Whilst our region has had some successes in creating or embedding institutions within geographic concepts such as the Asia-Pacific Economic Cooperation and the East Asia Summit (EAS), getting to that stage is often highly challenging. Geo-strategic considerations play a big part in the process. The proponent of the initiative and the timing are also crucial, as are the dynamics and interactions between the major players during discussions and negotiations. The twists and turns in the establishment of the EAS is a case in point. The EAS originated from the earlier idea of an East Asia Economic Group (EAEG), a proposal advanced by then Malaysian Prime Minister Tun Dr Mahathir Mohamad. It evolved through several phases from the EAEG to the East Asia Economic Caucus and a proposal for an East Asia Community before eventually morphing into the EAS. Discussions at the various stages were bogged down by minute details which were considered as having major ramifications such as whether it should be 'East Asia' or 'East Asian' and whether 'community' should be spelt with a capital 'C' or small 'c'. Behind these seemingly small details lay a bigger strategic concern, that of the eventual shape of the geo-strategic landscape in the region. The elephant in the room was membership and this came down to the geographic concept of East Asia.

To cut a long story short, the EAS was eventually born, which included the 10-member states of the Association of Southeast Asian Nations (ASEAN), India, Australia and New Zealand as well as the United States (US) and Russia, in addition to the ASEAN+3 countries of China, Japan and Republic of Korea. However, the idea behind original EAEG and the subsequent East Asia community remains very much alive through existing mechanism such as the ASEAN+3 and in discussions on evolving regional developments and in regional initiatives. Even while the EAS was formed, there were clear boundaries that it was a forum for discussion, not decision-making. Hence, no formal institutionalisation was envisaged. The EAS is an example of a successful establishment of an entity which started life based on a geographical concept of East Asia. Even then, it took many years, with the final outcome perhaps not one envisaged by the earlier proponents of the EAEG.

The discussions around the concept of the Indo-Pacific could have gone on indefinitely had there not been a push to turn it into something that had some collective bite, much like what the EAEG sought to achieve. There are always reasons why initiatives emerge at any one time, and the push for the Indo-Pacific at this point in time is no exception. The genesis of the current move on the Indo-Pacific can be traced to Japanese Prime Minister Shinzo Abe. According to Gaimusho, what was to become the 'Free and Open Indo-Pacific Strategy' (FOIC), was first mooted by Prime Minister Abe at the 6th Tokyo International Conference on African Development in Nairobi, Kenya, in August 2016. Thereafter, the proposal was systematically introduced to regional players, including India and ASEAN, and the US. The seriousness with which the Indo-Pacific concept and the FOIC were pursued led to many questions being asked in the regional capitals as to what was envisaged. After all, there have been past attempts at creating additional or overarching regional structures or mechanisms which have, in the main, been diplomatically discouraged due to the potential disruptions they could create to the existing finely balanced geo-strategic landscape. Australia's failed attempt to establish the Asia Pacific Community (APC) around 2010 is a case in point. Countries balked when it was represented (or misrepresented) as a 'concert of powers', leading to obvious questions over what it was intended to achieve, membership, and, where ASEAN was concerned, where it fitted into the new proposed structure. The default position of countries to such initiatives is always one of caution. Hence, many questions were raised as to what exactly was envisaged with the FOIC. While many speculated the reasons behind the initiative, the key to whether support could be extended depended on what was being supported. Was it support for a common objective or the establishment of an entity in the pursuit of common objectives? Without such clarity or a clearly defined end goal, countries danced around the concept as each had to factor in its own set of strategic considerations.

For Japan, ASEAN and India were the key components to the success of the FOIC. However, the same issues and considerations which be-devilled the APC and dictated the way in which the EAEG evolved stood in the way. With the US joining in with its own version of the Indo-Pacific, similarly named the 'Free and Open Indo-Pacific', the initiative expectedly drew the ire of countries such as China and Russia, which saw it as being targetted at them and exclusionary. India, which did not want to disappoint Japan nor antagonise the Chinese and Russians, eventually took the middle path.

During the keynote speech at the June 2018 Shangri-La Dialogue in Singapore, Indian Prime Minister Narendra Modi said that India did not see the Indo-Pacific region as a strategy or a club of limited numbers.

Neither should it be a grouping that seeks to dominate or is directed against any one country. He then went on to spell out a set of principles which should guide the Indo-Pacific — free, open, inclusive with ASEAN at the centre, freedom of navigation, etc. A year later, the ASEAN Outlook on the Indo-Pacific was released, which also expounded the principles of openness, inclusivity, rules-based framework, governance, etc., together with a set of areas for cooperation. India was naturally happy with the ASEAN Outlook as it supported the approach it took.

The position that India adopted on the Indo-Pacific preserves its manoeuvring space as it pursues its policy of 'strategic autonomy' and non-alignment. India, under the Modi government, seeks for itself a greater role in global and regional affairs in pursuit of its national interests, and not just for pride of place. A greater India in the international and regional space translates to greater influence which it can wield multilaterally, regionally and bilaterally. In the emerging global competition between the western and eastern blocs, India is already well placed to play both sides. Its diverse and multi-layered memberships in bilateral, regional and multilateral mechanisms afford it the space to adjust and shift when the need arises. For example, while India is part of the Quadrilateral Security Dialogue (that also includes the US, Japan and Australia) and the US-Japan-India Trilateral, it is also a member of the Russia-India-China grouping as well as the Shanghai Cooperation Organisation.

Being the common denominator in such groupings also gives India a certain leverage which it can use when the need arises. As for the FOIC, given its likely orientation even amidst an inclusive narrative, India would have had to make a choice which it felt it did not need to make. As a former Indian Ministry of External Affairs (MEA) official told me, if one was looking for an inclusive Indo-Pacific mechanism, the EAS was already there.

So where does that leave the concept of the Indo-Pacific? Has anything changed? Where India is concerned, the Indo-Pacific concept is, in essence, a geographic framework, a reference point upon which countries can adopt in defining their national interests, as well as a means to analyse regional or country developments bringing the totality of the Indo-Pacific region into play. It is up to each country or regional grouping to decide how best it should go about defining its own interests, and the Indo-Pacific framework is one such way to do so. It means, for example, the FOIP strategy is Japan's way of operationalising its objectives in the Indo-Pacific, as conceived by Japan. Other countries or regional groupings could do likewise.

A very senior ex-Indian diplomat once told me that among countries in our overall region, only China could be said to have been practicing an Indo-Pacific approach and all the others are playing catch up. What this means for India is that instead of looking at developments in the Indian Ocean separate from developments in other regions, it should be aware of the dynamics of the wider canvas and how one development could relate to another, particularly in areas where India interests are impacted. Hence, the ASEAN Division within the MEA has now been subsumed under the newly-created Indo-Pacific Division, which also covers the EAS, Indian Ocean Rim Association, Asia-Europe Meeting and Mekong Ganga Cooperation. As India re-orients its perspectives, it may do well for ASEAN to also review its role and strategic value to others in an ever-evolving regional landscape.

31

Vocational and Technical Education

N. Varaprasad

In 2018, India's working-age population (people between 15 and 64 years of age) became larger than the dependant population (people outside the same age range) at 50.2 percent. Every year, 12.5 million young people enter the labour market. This bulge in the working-age population is projected to last till 2055, or for another 37 years. The potential of this 'demographic dividend', as defined by the United Nations Population Fund, if harnessed properly and creatively, could bring about a period of great growth for India, or huge social problems, if not.

Many Asian economies such as Japan, South Korea, Singapore and China were able to use this demographic dividend to generate a seven-fold increase in gross domestic product. Singapore enjoyed a demographic dividend from pre-independence until it ended in 1979, due to rapidly falling fertility rates and increasing life expectancy. In India, the latest jobs data (2018) show that only half of the working age population is engaged in any economic activity, with the labour force participation rate (LFPR) falling below 50 percent. India, with a current median age of 26.6 years, has a huge number of young people hungry for jobs. Given that there are also now greater educational opportunities for women who are entering the job market in larger numbers, the utilisation of the demographic dividend is a cause for concern. According to the 2017–18 data, male LFPR is about 75 percent and 25 percent for the women. The need of the hour is, therefore, for industry-based skilling of very large numbers of young people in vocational and technical skills.

Singapore, on the other hand, has experience in maximising the potential of its people to achieve high employment rates and high growth through proactive skills development policies which are closely tied to economic development strategies. Singapore's Institute of Technical Education (ITE) and the five polytechnics are internationally lauded for providing market-oriented and responsive education and training, leading to one of the highest youth employment rates in the world.

India's central government and the various state governments have, over time, become familiar with Singapore's education and skills development strategies and the implementing institutions. During his trip to Singapore in 2015, Prime Minister Narendra Modi visited various ITE facilities, including the maritime training centre, the aerospace hub and the precision engineering section, all of them representing high value-adding economic sectors. As an immediate outcome of that visit and discussions with Singapore's Prime Minister Lee Hsien Loong, Prime Minister Modi lay the foundation stone for the Indian Institute of Skills (IIS) in Kanpur in Uttar Pradesh in December 2016, a collaboration with Singapore's ITE. Following the first IIS in Kanpur, the foundation stone for the IIS in Mumbai in Maharashtra was laid in September 2019. The foundation stone for the IIS Ahmedabad campus was laid in January 2020, but it is planned to function from a temporary campus. When operational, these three institutes target the graduation of 5,000 trainees every year with 70 percent placement in employment.

Singapore's experience in vocational and technical education, which has evolved over three decades in tandem with the nation's economic progress from basic manufacturing and high-technology industries to sophisticated services and an entrepreneurial, innovation-based economy was a good fit for India's current need.

Singapore has been supportive of India's skill development journey through a number of notable initiatives.

First among these was the Indian government's World Class Skill Centre (WCSC) in Delhi, established with the assistance and training from Singapore's ITE under a Technical Assistance agreement with GovSG, offering courses in hospitality operations, retail services, software testing and finance. This was a first test case of the skills transfer model, including both the hard and soft training infrastructure (including a Train-the-Trainer component on Singapore). It was also a test of Singapore's disciplined and systematic approach working with India's more complex decision-making and execution practices. Prime Minister Modi's 'Skill India' initiative, launched in 2015 to train more than 400 million people in different skills by 2022, has been a great contributor to the success of this project. To quote the WCSC project director, Dr D P S Verma: "The results are amazing, and we've maintained a consistent benchmark (of full employment) in the last three years." All batches of graduates have found sustainable employment, including some who found work outside India. To cope with the increasing demand, a 37-acre satellite campus is under construction in Jonapur, South Delhi.

Several Indian states were not far behind in seeking assistance from Singapore. Rajasthan (2015), Madhya Pradesh (2016), Assam (2017) and Odisha (2018) received expertise and technology transfer from Singapore's ITE to establish various skills training centres. The programmes of study range from tourism and beauty and wellness to retail services and hotel management.

The transfer of knowledge between Singapore and India is not limited to vocational skills. An example was the establishment of an Aerospace and Aviation Centre of Excellence in Advanced Skilling in Bangalore in Karnataka. This was led by the National Skill Development Corporation (NSDC) of India, together with Singapore Polytechnic and Terra Orient Skills Academy. These centres of excellence will focus on high-end skill domains such as the automotive, logistics, aerospace, aviation and related technology sectors. According to Mr Jawed Ashraf, India's former High Commissioner in Singapore:

> These are all priority sectors under 'Skill India' and 'Make in India' programmes, which require a large workforce with advanced technical skills... Singapore is a leader in aviation services, including maintenance, repair, overhaul services as well as skill development across various sectors

Real transfer of knowledge happens less in the establishment of training institutes, but more when instructors and managers of such institutes are provided with the tools and techniques to be able to manage these centres independently and in the creation of more of such centres. Hence, the collaboration among the NSDC, Singapore Polytechnic and Temasek Foundation International to develop Centres of Excellence for the Training and Continuous Development of Trainers and Assessors is a step in the right direction. This is a programme to build the capabilities of 300 educational leaders and specialists in technical and vocational education and training who will manage these academies across India. Mr Manish Kumar, Managing Director of the NSDC, succinctly explains why this is important:

> This will help us develop best in class framework for vocational training and quality assurance in India and will further help in scaling-up various initiatives under Skill India mission.

Moving on to future skill needs, the Singapore e-Government Leadership Centre at the Institute of Systems Science (ISS) at the National University of Singapore (NUS) and the NSDC will work together to develop and implement skill development programmes across emerging technology areas like data analytics, artificial intelligence and robotics. They will also collaborate in vocational training and new-age technology, training of trainers and assessors and promoting life-long learning. Mr Khoong Chan Meng, Chief Executive Officer of NUS-ISS, explains why he supports this initiative: "This collaboration with [the] NSDC also aligns well with our vision of enabling a digital economy that is always learning and always leading."

Perhaps more than anything else, this encapsulates why tiny Singapore is doing its part to assist India to develop its human capital. It may not appear much in the larger scale of what needs to be done but it is very significant for a small country. By contributing to India's growth, we are also learning while sharing. Just as we have participated in China's early phase of industrialisation by collaborating with the development of the China-Singapore Suzhou Industrial Park 25 years ago (and subsequently with Sino-Singapore Guangzhou Knowledge City and Sino-Singapore Tianjin Eco-city) and Vietnam-Singapore Industrial Parks, Singapore continues to pay it forward in sharing its expertise and experience to build a better world, based on multilateralism and inter-state relationships founded on international rules of engagement.

The collaboration with India has also provided an opportunity for Singapore educators and trainers to understand and even appreciate the country's deep culture and the mindset of its people. It is only by facing outward that Singapore has survived, and it is only by engaging in more of such collaborations that Singapore will secure its place in the world.

32

Evolution of ASEAN-India Relations

Ong Keng Yong

Southeast Asia and India are no strangers. The links date back to more than 2,000 years, with trade and human migration connecting maritime Southeast Asia to the Indian subcontinent. These linkages manifest themselves in the many historical monuments, rich cultural heritage, religious affiliations, diverse culinary delights and linguistic influences in Southeast Asia.

The contemporary relationship between Southeast Asia and India was shaped by events of the time. Being the largest democracy in the world, India was an inspiration for the newly-independent nations in the region, and there was recognition on the need to develop strategic ties with one another. In fact, the Indian navy held its first-ever naval exercise outside the Commonwealth with the Indonesian navy in 1960 and the two countries also signed a bilateral cultural agreement in the same year.

Unfortunately, even as Indonesia and four of its neighbours established the Association of Southeast Asian Nations (ASEAN) in 1967, relations between them and India remained lukewarm. They diverged in ideological outlook and security relationships during the Cold War. Their economic development strategies also differed.

Relations took an upwards trajectory with radically altered geopolitical realities and circumstances following the end of the Cold War.

The acceleration of economic reforms in India in the early 1990s, coupled with efforts by Indian and ASEAN leaders, led to an incremental growth in India-ASEAN relations. India became a Sectoral Dialogue Partner of ASEAN in 1992, focusing on economic and development cooperation. This was the first defining moment in ASEAN-India partnership.

Subsequently, at an informal meeting of the 1994 ASEAN Summit, Singapore's Prime Minister Goh Chok Tong proposed granting India full Dialogue Partner status. Despite initial reservations in some ASEAN quarters, a consensus soon emerged among the leaders, and India became ASEAN's fifth Dialogue Partner in 1995. This was the second defining moment in ASEAN-India relations. India's Foreign Secretary Krishnan Srinivasan acknowledged Singapore's role saying, "Singapore was the first and, at the time, the only ASEAN country to take India seriously." Soon after, in 1996, India made its maiden appearance at the ASEAN Regional Forum (ARF) and the ASEAN Post-Ministerial Conference (PMC) meetings.

The third defining moment occurred when India became a Summit Level Partner of ASEAN in 2002. At the Second ASEAN-India Summit in Bali in October 2003, the leaders signed the Framework Agreement on Comprehensive Economic Cooperation, paving the way for a free trade area by 2010 and India's accession to the ASEAN Treaty of Amity and Cooperation.

ASEAN formally accepted India's admission as a founding member of the East Asia Summit (EAS) in 2005, together with Australia and New Zealand, thus effectively recognising India as a regional player that could help shape the political and strategic landscape of Asia and the Pacific. The EAS is a key component of an open and inclusive regional architecture, and the region's only leaders-led forum.

ASEAN and India have made progress on a wide range of issues facilitated by 30 platforms for cooperation, including the annual Leaders'

Summit and various ministerial dialogues across multiple sectors. New Delhi set up a separate diplomatic mission to ASEAN in Jakarta (where the ASEAN Secretariat is located) in April 2015 to supplement the efforts of bilateral Indian embassies in Southeast Asia.

These developments owed much to the efforts of the respective Indian Prime Ministers in strengthening relations with ASEAN since 1992. Leaders matter. A brief review of what happened during their time in office is germane.

P V Narasimha Rao: 1991–1996

ASEAN-India relations saw a quantum leap with the 'Look East' policy, which was an effort to forge political contacts, economic integration and security cooperation with the Asia Pacific countries, initiated during the prime ministership of P V Narasimha Rao. It emerged as an important foreign policy initiative of India in the post-Cold War period, marking the potential convergence of ASEAN and India's national interests. The initial engagement by both sides was primarily economic-oriented as the Rao government sought more trade and foreign direct investment flows from Japan, Korea and the ASEAN countries to bolster its economic reform programme.

H D Deve Gowda: 1996–1997

The elevated interactions kick-started under Prime Minister Rao's initiative continued under the short tenure of his successor, H D Deve Gowda. During the ASEAN PMC in Jakarta in July 1996, the ASEAN-India Joint Cooperation Committee (JCC) was established. A significant outcome of the JCC was the establishment of the ASEAN-India Working Groups on Science and Technology, and Trade and Investment. New Delhi also inaugurated the India-ASEAN Eminent Persons Lecture Series in December 1996 to promote increased awareness of ASEAN-India partnership. Since then, lectures have been delivered in India and the ASEAN countries by various distinguished speakers.

I K Gujral: 1997–1998

Although Prime Minister I K Gujral held the prime ministership for a brief period, he left a lasting imprint in India's foreign policy. He is best known for formalising what became known as the 'Gujral Doctrine'. This advocated a conscious policy of conciliation with neighbours with no use of force and settling all pending issues by negotiations, unilateral gestures of goodwill without waiting for reciprocity from smaller states and moving away from fixed positions to examine alternatives when an issue seemed intractable. The 'Gujral Doctrine' bears similarities to ASEAN's way of conducting regional affairs through consensus and consultations, and facilitated India's involvement in ASEAN-led mechanisms like the ARF and ASEAN PMC meetings.

Atal Behari Vajpayee: 1998–2004

When the Atal Behari Vajpayee government came to power in 1998, the 'Look East' policy entered its second phase with four defining features: (i) expansion of its geographical scope; (ii) a strong focus on free trade agreements (FTAs) and the establishment of institutional economic linkages between the ASEAN countries and India; (iii) physical connectivity (including air and road links) to Southeast Asia; and (iv) a shift from trade to wider economic and security issues. Subsequently, India signed the Framework Agreement on Comprehensive Economic Cooperation for the establishment of an ASEAN-India Regional Trade and Investment Area, and the ASEAN-India Joint Declaration for Cooperation to Combat International Terrorism. Prime Minister Vajpayee also offered a unilateral 'open skies' arrangement which would allow ASEAN airlines to operate more flights to Indian cities.

Manmohan Singh: 2004–2014

The change of government in May 2004 under the prime ministership of Manmohan Singh did not see a major departure from the Vajpayee government's approach towards ASEAN. A major milestone of Prime Minister Singh's tenure was India's membership in the EAS in 2005. Singapore and Indonesia actively supported Indian participation. ASEAN's decision to invite India was the result of the latter's continued economic reforms and the larger perception in ASEAN of a more purposeful Indian diplomacy. By the time Prime Minister Singh left office, ASEAN and India had signed an FTA in goods which took effect in 2010. He also elevated relations with ASEAN to the level of 'Strategic Partnership' in 2012. India established the ASEAN-India Centre in New Delhi in 2013.

Narendra Modi: 2014 to date

Prime Minister Narendra Modi rebranded the 'Look East' policy as 'Act East' to emphasise greater activism and commitment on India's part, with commerce, connectivity and culture as the guiding themes to boost engagement with ASEAN. In January 2018, he hosted the 25th anniversary summit of the ASEAN-India Dialogue Partnership in New Delhi. He also invited all the ASEAN leaders to attend India's Republic Day celebrations at that time.

Prime Minister Modi's key proposals under the 'Act East' policy has been India's offer of S$1.4 billion Line of Credit to promote projects that support physical and digital connectivity between India and ASEAN. However, nearly 40 months after Prime Minister Modi made this offer, Laos is the only ASEAN country to have sent formal requests for digital connectivity projects under this initiative. The request has not made much progress due to bureaucratic issues. Surprised by this lack of interest from ASEAN, New Delhi decided to provide a grant of S$56.5 million for pilot projects in Cambodia, Laos, Myanmar and Vietnam to activate the credit line.

To enhance people-to-people exchange, India announced its offer of 1,000 scholarships to doctoral students in the Indian Institutes of Technology — the country's top technology institutes — and bestowed the Padma Shri, one of India's top civilian awards, on one eminent citizen from each ASEAN nation. Prime Minister Modi also unveiled another initiative to enhance ties between the ASEAN countries and India's northeast — an ASEAN Studies Centre to be created at the North-Eastern Hill University in Shillong in the state of Meghalaya.

Conclusion

The strategic rationale for India's deepening of its engagement with ASEAN is perhaps stronger today as the international community faces considerable flux in geopolitics. It is in the interest of ASEAN and India to stay engaged substantively and to enhance ASEAN centrality in keeping the regional architecture open and inclusive.

In economic terms, the numbers are compelling. Trade between ASEAN and India is progressing towards S$141 billion per annum. There are about 3,000 Indian companies operating in the ASEAN countries. In 2018, more than 4.6 million Indian tourists visited the ASEAN countries while almost one million Southeast Asians toured India. ASEAN looks forward to the eventual membership of India in the Regional Comprehensive Economic Partnership.

While ASEAN and India are busy engaging themselves to build a long lasting and durable partnership, both sides need to be vigilant or mindful of drawbacks that could momentarily cause irritation in the relations. Continued dialogue is crucial to ensure the two sides are on the same page. The momentum to enhance cooperation should not be held back by bureaucratic considerations and vested interests in the domestic arena.

ASEAN-India partnership is work in progress. It is continuous and evolving. Both sides need to provide new impetus to the partnership from time to time via innovation and strategic foresight. ASEAN and India have maintained and grown their centuries-old ties. Collectively, this connectivity will play a vital role in securing the peace and prosperity and delivering the mutual benefit all of us desire.

33

How Singaporeans Perceive Indians

Gopinath Pillai

It is not right to judge a man
— By hasty glance or passing whim,
Or think that first impressions can
— Tell all there is to know of him.
"First Impressions" by Alfred Grant Walton

I start my essay with a short verse from a poem which questions whether it is proper to fully judge a person on the basis of just one look (or a country through just one visit). I include this verse as a preamble to my essay. As a matter of fact, in my essay, I will move beyond just the perceptions of Indians by Singaporeans and look at the realities in the dealings between India (Indians) and Singapore.

The essay examines perceptions of India and Indians from the time of Stamford Raffles' arrival to Singapore in 1819 to the current period. However, I must hasten to add a caveat that Indians and all those who lived in the region interacted among themselves long before the arrival of the Western powers to Asia. I once asked Professor Wang Gungwu, an eminent historian based in Singapore, how India was viewed by the other countries of the region? He replied that everyone, including China, looked up to India as the source of knowledge in ancient times. Over the years, this changed due to internal strife, foreign invasions and poverty.

The officials of the East India Company perceived Indians as a pathetic group which performed menial labour to feed itself. While many Indians came to Singapore as indentured labour, there were others who came here as traders. However, the latter were small in number. For a long time, even up to World War II, poverty and menial jobs were associated with those who came from South Asia to work for the Europeans in the region.

In reality, Indians were not merely migrant workers who came here just to eke a living. They also contributed to society. In her working paper on *Grassroots Giving, Philanthropy, and the Identity, Singapore 1919–1959 — Philanthropy in Asia for the Asia Centre for Social Entrepreneurship & Philanthropy* at the National University of Singapore, Ms Ooi Yu-lin highlighted some of these contributions. As early as 1921, public subscriptions were called to create a fund to help Indian coolies. By 1929, the Agent of the Government of India and the Singapore Indian Association were mandated to ensure the well-being of Indians in the region. By 1932, following the Great Depression, an unemployment fund was initiated for Indians in Singapore. In 1935, the Lotus Club, established by a few rich Indian women, raised funds to help the victims of the Quetta Earthquake in British India. Later, in 1941, the Society for the Protection of Hindu Children was established and it called for donations from people from all walks.

In spite of these initiatives, the fairly adverse perception of Indians remained in Singapore even more than a decade after the end of World War II. In the early 1960s, as a teacher, while marking papers for an essay competition, a Singaporean boy, in his description of the various ethnic groups living here, wrote about the Indians, "...and, of course, you cannot forget the Indians. Without them, who will wash our drains and sweep our roads?" The perception of the Indians then was that they just did menial work. However, it was discernible that changes were taking place.

The perception of Indians changed somewhat after the arrival of the Indian nationalist, Subhas Chandra Bose, to Singapore and the Indian National Army's support for the Japanese against the British. The independence struggle in India gave the Indians a certain degree of dignity in the eyes of non-Indians — they were no longer seen as supplicants. Another point I need to mention is that although a large number of Indians supported the Japanese in World War II, they openly condemned the latter's atrocities in China. This ensured that the relationship between the Chinese and Indians in Singapore did not become adversarial.

The changing political climate in Singapore also positively affected the perceptions of Indians among Singaporeans. As a student then, it appeared to me that the Indians were becoming more political than the other races. This was probably evident in Singapore's first general election for the legislative council in 1948 and, subsequently, in the municipal and assembly elections, which had proportionately more Indian candidates than those from the other races. In fact, my mother decided to contest in the first election. Voters were also mainly Indians. In contrast, only a minority of the Chinese were bothered about politics as many of them just wanted to earn a living and return to mainland China, which they considered their motherland. Mr Lee Kuan Yew saw some dangers in this and was able to persuade Mr Lim Yew Hock, Singapore's Chief Minister, to make voting compulsory. After this law was enacted in 1959, Mr Lee succeeded Mr Lim as Singapore's Prime Minister. I mention this event not just because it showed the political nature of Indians in Singapore, but also because it highlighted the contributions of a minority racial group to the democratic development of the country.

When was I was young, my father encouraged me to take up Mandarin at my Chinese-turned English school, Choon Guan English School. He strongly believed that Mandarin would become the language of the future and an Indian speaking Mandarin would certainly have an impact on the perception of Indians in Singapore. Sadly, I did it for a year before being asked to switch to Latin. My father also made me learn Hindi. He felt it would help if one day I was forced to return to India. The political situation in the region was volatile, and knowledge of languages and certain skills such as accountancy were useful for survival.

Fast forward, the relations between Singapore and India saw a significant change after Mr P V Narasimha Rao became India's Prime Minister in 1991. He pursued a 'Look East' policy and his counterpart in Singapore, Mr Goh Chok Tong, initiated what he called a 'mild India fever' in Singapore. Both leaders were sincere in wanting to achieve a positive relationship and close economic links. In January 2005, at the official launch of the Institute of South Asian Studies, Mr Goh reiterated:

> There will be many more two-steps forward and one-step backward to come. India will make it. India cannot turn back. Moving forward is a political and strategic imperative that no Indian government can ignore. Today, not just Singapore but the entire world is infected with 'India fever'.

In my view, we have not reached anywhere close to what our leaders had envisaged in terms of the India-Singapore relationship. Many a times, some stumbling block would appear in our way. Let me provide an example of an issue related to palm oil trading that occurred several years ago. Singapore, though not a producer, was a large trader of palm oil, mainly from Malaysia and partly from Indonesia. Suddenly, India decided to ban palm oil from Singapore because a few Singaporean traders had indulged in malpractices. I was involved in the discussions with the Indians to resolve the issue. I tried very hard to persuade the State Trading Corporation of India to punish the recalcitrant traders and not Singapore. After much discussion, the problem was eventually resolved. In my view, this episode was rather unnecessary and acted as an unnecessary blot in the relationship between our two countries.

Having said that, I must quickly add that the business relationship between Indians and non-Indian Singaporeans has been growing rapidly. An increasing number of Indians have invested in Singapore.

Joint ventures are also being established. However, these numbers are nowhere close to those between Singapore and the Association of Southeast Asian Nations-member countries.

From a position of abject poverty, Indians have moved up the socio-economic ladder not just in India, but also globally. The richest man in Asia is Mr Mukesh Ambani, an Indian. There are also several other Indians who are global leaders. They include Mr Sundar Pichai (Google), Mr Satya Nadella (Microsoft), Ms Padmasree Warrior (Fable Group), Mr Anshu Jain (Cantor Fitzgerald) and Mr Ajay Banga (Mastercard), just to name a few. In Singapore, the financial and banking sectors are well represented by Indians.

Now to my final point: the current perception of Indians by Singaporeans. People tend to forget that there is still polarity in the local Indian community, not only in terms of culture, but also in income levels. While the community has, in the past few decades, seen an increase in the number of people belonging to the high- and middle-income groups, as well as a reduction of numbers in the low-income segment, the stereotype that Indians are well off and generally misbehave is grossly incorrect. I am told that there are a few flies in the ointment, as would in any community. Recently, someone complained publicly that there were too many Indians in corporate leadership in Singapore. Social media also carried complaints that Indians are better dressed than others while also highlighting a whole list of corporate misbehaviour. While one can choose to dismiss these comments and viewpoints as nonsensical, one must remember that there is no smoke without fire. As a diversified small group that makes up less than 10 percent of the Singapore population, Indians need to learn to live in harmony with everyone else. The Chinese are very tolerant, who give a significant degree of weightage to what one can achieve in life. Many years ago, when Mr Lee was stepping down as Prime Minister, the Indian community presented a book titled *A Place in the Sun* to him. The message was clear that he assured this small community a place in the sun. We must always cherish it and work hard to enhance our role and contribution to Singapore.

As someone who is born here and has lived here for more than 80 years, I strongly believe all of us, including Indians, should give our best to Singapore in order to have the pleasure of seeing our children and grandchildren grow up here. Thus, the perceptions of us and our values will grow simultaneously.

And so we pray!

34

India-Singapore CECA

Leena Pinsler

The idea of a free trade agreement (FTA) between India and Singapore was first conceived in 2002 at a meeting in Singapore between Indian premier Atal Bihari Vajpayee and Singapore Prime Minister Goh Chok Tong. Following a high level Joint-Study and 13 rounds of negotiations, the Comprehensive Economic Cooperation Agreement (CECA) between India and Singapore was ultimately birthed in India on 29 July 2005 and was signed by the Prime Ministers of India and Singapore, Manmohan Singh and Lee Hsien Loong, respectively.

There were compelling attractions for both countries. From India's perspective, Singapore could serve as a gateway to trade with other countries in Asia and as a funnel for international investment in several priority areas. For Singapore, the removal or reduction of high Indian tariff barriers would enhance its traditional role as a trading centre. The rules of origin aligned with Singapore's plan to be involved in high-end value addition where materials originated from other countries.

The CECA also established a framework to promote investments, enhance trade in services, mutually recognise qualifications in key areas and facilitate movement of persons. Two reviews were subsequently concluded in 2008 and 2018 respectively.

Almost 15 years on, the highlights of the pact and its impact are considered.

Trade in Goods

The section on trade in goods confers a slew of tariff and non-tariff benefits. Currently, almost 82 percent of Singapore's exports to India enjoy preferential tariff treatment. Trade facilitation measures streamline areas of customs administration, standards and conformance requirements.

Originating goods from Singapore and India are given non-discriminatory 'national treatment' in the other country. The rules of origin require a minimum value of content from the relevant country. However, materials from the other (for example, India) would be deemed to be materials originating from Singapore and vice versa. This enhances the advantage of sourcing materials from the other party.

An item (which is not wholly obtained in either country) can still qualify for preferential tariff treatment if at least 35 percent of the content originates from Singapore or India. In addition, the goods must have undergone at least a change in the first six digits of the Harmonised System Code. Alternatively, the item would have to satisfy the Product Specific Rules in the CECA. The Singapore Customs determines whether goods to be exported to India satisfy these requirements before it issues a Preferential Certificate of Origin enabling the goods to enjoy the preferential tariff under the CECA. Severe penalties exist under the Regulation of Imports and Exports Act for offences such as making a false declaration, incorrect trade descriptions or failure to comply with the requirements for the issue of a Preferential Certificate of Origin. These have served as a deterrent to anyone tempted to take advantage of the preferential tariffs under the CECA.

There has certainly been an increase in bilateral trade in goods between Singapore and India since the CECA was signed. The High Commission of India in Singapore website states that:

> Bilateral trade expanded after the conclusion of [the] CECA from USD6.7 billion [S$9.6 billion] in FY2004–05 to USD27.85 billion [S$39.99 billion] in 2018–19.

However, comments in a 2008 paper by Dr Amitendu Palit from the Institute of South Asian Studies remain germane:

> It is not clear whether the changing pattern of trade between India and Singapore is a result of the CECA. It is difficult to establish a direct causality between the signing of the CECA and the emerging trade pattern ... At the same time, it is difficult to overlook the fact that [the] growth in Indian imports from Singapore has become much robust in the years following the CECA. There is a possibility due to the fact that Indian imports have increased with more items from Singapore being allowed duty-free access into India... It is also possible that the lowering of duties has encouraged Indian importers to procure more products that originate elsewhere via Singapore. And finally, there is also the possibility that more imports are taking place on account of higher demand from a rapidly expanding Indian industry and the process has simply been facilitated by the CECA.

Trade in Services

Services have for many years been a major driver of both the Indian and Singapore economies. The Indian services sector needed an infusion of investment, finance and new technologies. Singapore could serve a good base from which to expand their footprint and make available their services globally. Singapore, in turn, would have the opportunity to invest and access a market with vibrant domestic consumption and realise its own ambition to become a global services hub.

Liberalisation was based on the tenets of market access, national treatment, domestic regulations being fairly applied, transparency and recognition. Five service sectors were identified for recognition, namely, accounting and auditing, architecture, medical (doctors), dental and nursing.

The mutual recognition of certain Indian nursing degrees, pursuant to the second CECA review does not automatically confer any right on an Indian national, whose degree is recognised, to work in Singapore. It merely opens the door for Singapore-based employers to tap into another supply source for an occupation that is in high demand globally.

Financial services received specific treatment in the CECA. Three Singapore banks were allowed to establish a presence in India and open up to 15 branches over four years. DBS currently operates 33 branches in India across 22 cities. In 2016, it opened a technology hub for the group in Hyderabad. The hub employs more than 1,900 software engineers, coders and developers. DBS also launched Digibank. Although it was a mobile only service in India, it has acquired over 2.5 million customers.

Singapore, likewise, offered the Qualifying Full Bank (QBF) status to up to three Indian banks. The State Bank of India (SBI) and ICICI Bank have since acquired QFB status. SBI currently has five branches in Singapore besides a remittance centre. It also maintains 21 automated teller machines (ATMs) across Singapore. ICICI Bank has just one branch in Singapore. Its website states that: "[T]he bank is also a member of the special banking connection in Singapore which allows its customers to use the ATMs of different banks in the city."

Temasek and the Government of Singapore Investment Corporation (GIC) were treated as distinct investors. This means that their investments in any Indian company cannot be aggregated for the purposes of certain Indian securities' regulations.

Investments

Permitted investments by one country into the other are accorded national treatment. In addition, there are the usual bilateral investment treaty provisions. These include compensation in the case of expropriation, free repatriation and investment dispute mechanisms, which allow investor-to-state disputes to be adjudicated impartially.

Alongside the CECA, Singapore was accorded the 'Mauritius treatment' in 2005. This meant that long-term capital gains arising from the sale of shares in India by an investor from Singapore (meeting enhanced substance requirements) would not be subject to capital gains tax in India. Following a revision, capital gains on investments made after April 2017 will be subject to tax in India.

Nonetheless, Singapore emerged yet again as the top foreign direct investment source for India for the financial year ended 2019. It has been observed that a number of investments made from Singapore are actually not truly domestic. Just one example is the Singapore-based Walmart entity which invested US$16 billion (S$23 billion) to purchase 77 percent of Flipkart.

This should not obscure the fact that Singapore heavyweights such as DBS, Ascendas (now CapitaLand), Temasek, GIC and others have invested several billions over the past 15 years in diverse areas spanning the financial sector, telecommunications, development and operation of information-technology (IT) parks, healthcare, technology companies as well as start-ups.

From the Indian side, it is estimated that there are around 8,000 Indian companies in Singapore providing a range of services, including financial and software consultancy services.

Movement of Natural Persons

Just as trade in goods requires the facilitation of the movement of goods, trade in services and investment impetus similarly require the facilitation of movement of natural persons who perform those services or make investments. Evident as that might seem, these provisions have generated controversy.

In particular, does the CECA open the floodgates to Indian professionals and intra-corporate transferees? Was it a deliberate concession in the course of negotiating other benefits for Singapore? Does Singapore's Fair Consideration Framework, therefore, violate its commitments under the CECA? In my view, the answer to all three questions is 'no'.

Garbled interpretations of the CECA provisions surfaced which fuelled the controversy. Articles 9.3 and 9.6 and Annex 9A have been bandied to support the assertion that a 'loophole' was somehow created which allows unfettered entry to intra-corporate transfers of employees from 127 sectors. The relevant provisions of the CECA need to be examined to see what they actually do say:

1. Article 9.3.2 requires each Party to expeditiously 'process' applications for temporary entry and 'notify ...the outcome' of the application. The actual outcome is not guaranteed.
2. Article 9.3.3 restricts labour market testing, economic needs testing or other procedures but only in respect of 'natural persons upon whom the benefits of this Chapter are conferred.' The substantive benefits are conferred on business visitors, services suppliers and more significantly intra-corporate transferees (ICTs) and professionals who have met the criteria for immigration.
3. ICTs could potentially be given the right to stay for an initial period of two years with extensions for further periods of three years and up to a maximum of eight years. The ICT must be a person 'who otherwise meets [the Party's] criteria for grant of an immigration visa'. This means that an ICT aspirant from either Party is not entitled to benefit from the Chapter unless and until the employer is in a position to offer the ICT an offer of employment having complied with local hiring practices.
4. Professionals could potentially gain entry for an initial period of 'one year or the duration of the contract whichever is the lesser.' Once again, the professional must comply with 'applicable immigration measures.' It is the definition of 'professional' which alone alludes to a list of 127 occupations listed in Annex 9A. The provisions do **not**:

    - automatically guarantee entry to ICTs or persons from these 127 occupations;

- recognise the qualifications of people from these 127 occupations; nor
- provide a *carte blanche* to employ people in these occupations without regard to local hiring requirements.

5. Spouses and dependants of ICTs and professionals, who are able to find jobs in Singapore as managers, executives or specialists, are not subject to the usual work restrictions placed on accompanying spouses and dependants of foreign work-pass holders.

Indians can, like other foreign nationals, be hired by employers in Singapore completely apart from the limited CECA regime. With its vast pool of highly-educated, skilled English-speaking people, Indians have made an impact in many parts of the world, including Singapore.

Weighing in, Singapore veteran diplomat, Ambassador Tommy Koh, said:

> In 2016, India accused Singapore of not honouring its commitment under [the] CECA by blocking Indian IT professionals from securing the necessary work passes to work in Singapore. The issue was discussed during the second review of [the] CECA, which was concluded in June last year [2018]. The two governments decided not to make any changes to the chapter on the movement of people.

Dispute Settlement

All agreements should anticipate the possibility of differences in opinions and ensuing disputes. The CECA contains provisions for the resolution of state-to-state disputes. To date, neither party has thought it necessary to do so.

Where to for the CECA?

Some in India point at existing FTAs as the reason for India's growing trade imbalances. This might explain India's guarded approach to entry into new FTAs. As for the CECA, a third review was launched in

September 2018. This identified further trade facilitation and customs as areas of enhancement. E-commerce was also highlighted taking into account new technologies and processes. Relations between the two countries remain warm and cooperation continues apace in areas such as intellectual property rights, science and technology, education and media.

35

The Diaspora, India's Development and Foreign Policy Goals

Rajesh Rai

In March 1946, tens of thousands of Indians gathered at the Farrer Park, Singapore, to welcome Jawaharlal Nehru. In his address, the future Indian Prime Minister promised that "India cannot forget her sons and daughters overseas ... the time is soon coming when her arm will be long enough to protect them." While India's position towards her diaspora has fluctuated since independence — ranging from neglect and even contempt to concern and re-engagement — the diaspora has throughout remained steadfast in affirming its bonds with India, even as millions have settled as loyal citizens in new homelands.

This essay concentrates on two dimensions of the diaspora's connect with India in terms of contributing to her developmental and foreign policy goals. It argues that, through remittances, foreign investment, philanthropy and lobbying, the diaspora has left an impact even if this has sometimes been a double-edged sword. The essay suggests that, in time to come, as more Indians settle abroad, the diaspora's impact is unlikely to diminish.

International Migration and the Indian Diaspora

The last three decades have seen a 70-percent rise in the number of international migrants. More precisely, a 2017 United Nations report affirmed that 257.7 million people lived in a country other than where they were born. That number continues to increase, with some 50 million new migrants added each decade. In this context, scholars agree that diasporas will play an even more significant role in the economic development and foreign policy imperatives of their countries of origin in time to come. This has been the case for many diasporas — the most compelling being the role of the Chinese diaspora in propelling the Chinese economy from the 1980s and the Jewish diaspora's influence on the strategic partnership between the United States (US) and Israel.

India has remained the top source of migrants for over three decades. During that time, the size of the Indian diaspora increased considerably numbering approximately 30 million in 2020. Non-resident Indians (NRIs) — Indian citizens who reside abroad for employment or business — comprise about 40 percent of that figure while 60 percent constitute those for whom India is an ancestral 'homeland' even as they may have settled abroad for generations. Collectively, this large diaspora, second only to the Chinese overseas in numerical terms, is in its global spread, second to none.

The Indian diaspora is not homogenous. It is a microcosm of India's own ethnic, religious and linguistic multiplicity although certain regions are better represented — the peninsular states, Gujarat, Punjab, Uttar Pradesh and Bihar. Scholars have categorised the diaspora in myriad ways, the most utilised being divisions according to the 'old' and the 'new' diaspora. The 'old' refers to Indians who moved (or were forcibly moved) to British and, to a lesser extent, Dutch and French colonies during the period of European colonisation. Most were engaged in plantation labour — sugarcane, tea and rubber, amongst others — although in colonial port cities like Singapore, Rangoon, Penang and Hong Kong, and in South and East Africa, Indians were also involved in trade, commerce and entrepreneurship, and engaged as professionals and servicemen. Today, the largest 'old' diaspora Indian communities are settled in Malaysia, Myanmar, Sri Lanka, South Africa and Mauritius.

The 'new' diaspora refers to the movement of Indians after the Second World War, largely to the West as 'white only' settlement policies rescinded there. This diaspora comprises professionals, along with entrepreneurial groups and semi-skilled labour. The largest of the 'new' diaspora communities is based in the US, numbering approximately 4.5 million people, followed by the United Kingdom (UK) and Canada. Economically, the 'new' diaspora is well off, recognised in the US as the wealthiest ethnic community in terms of average household income.

Strictly speaking, the use of 'old' and 'new' is not meant to isolate communities. The 'old' has become part of the 'new' through re-migration or displacement, for example, Fiji-Indians moving to Australia, East African-Indians to the UK, and Surinamese-Indians to the Netherlands. They are sometimes referred to as the 'twice-displaced' diaspora.

To the categories 'old' and 'new', a third needs to be included, a more 'transient' diaspora of Indian workers but also professionals who are overwhelmingly based in the Gulf. Indian labourers, who, like those in the Gulf, have no or little possibility of permanent settlement, can also be found in Southeast Asia. Singapore holds a unique place vis-à-vis these differentiated segments, with nearly equal numbers of 'old' and 'new' diaspora, alongside a significant transient worker population. Collectively, these categories serve a strategic function in this analysis, with implications on the extent to which diverse diasporic groups have engaged in India's developmental and foreign policy goals.

Remittances

India is the largest remittance receiving country in the world. Since 1990, the increase has been startling — remittances have grown from less than US$2.4 billion (S$3.4 billion) to approximately US$80 billion (S$113.2 billion) annually. The key contributors of remittances to India have been migrants in the Gulf, followed by North America. Transient workers remit the largest amounts although the settled diaspora may also contribute, albeit less regularly. While the extent of remittances that India receives is considerable, questions arise over utilisation. For transient workers, the monies are used to alleviate debt, build homes and for family maintenance. The patterns of remittance distribution have a strong state-based characteristic, with Kerala, Tamil Nadu, Andhra Pradesh, Uttar Pradesh and Punjab accounting for over 70 percent of the total. In remittance-receiving households, studies suggest that developmental markers, especially in terms of children's education, health and nutrition, are clearly improved when compared to equivalent households without family members working abroad. That said, as most remittances are sent by the transient diaspora engaged in labour, this is usually insufficient for capital investment, an opportunity that becomes plausible only in the case of those who have been working abroad over long durations.

Foreign Direct Investment

Current statistical data make it difficult to discern the extent of diaspora foreign direct investment (FDI) as different from total FDI. It is evident, however, that countries with a significant Indian diaspora have been the main contributors to FDI in India. In 2016, when India gained US$46.4 billion (S$65.6 billion) in FDI, Singapore was the largest contributor, followed by Mauritius and the US. When compared to China, India has found it difficult to attract FDI — whether from the diaspora or other sources — because of limitations on the extent of foreign stake-holding, the gradual pace at which regulatory regimes have been lifted and continued opposition to FDI in certain sectors. That said, studies suggest significant diaspora involvement in Indian information technology (IT) industry and services, hotel and tourism and the education sector. As in the case of remittances, over 80 percent of FDI has centred on a few states, specifically, Delhi, Maharashtra, Karnataka, Tamil Nadu, Gujarat and Andhra Pradesh. In terms of FDI, the diaspora's contribution is not only a matter of total amounts, but also in encouraging business in their countries of residence to engage with India, knowledge transfer, enhancing trade and augmenting networks. In regard to the latter, the diaspora also becomes a facilitator of profitable Indian investments overseas, providing the wherewithal, the local knowledge and connections for ventures into new markets.

Philanthropy

Philanthropy is and has been a significant site of diaspora engagement. Historically, the classic cases were the Nattukottai Chettiars who demarcated part of their profits in Southeast Asia to establish educational institutions, hospitals and shrines in Tamil Nadu. Although precise studies on diaspora giving in the contemporary period are not available, there is consensus that the 21st century has seen a rise in diaspora philanthropic contributions with potentially even greater developmental impact than remittances. Some of these utilise formal channels although most act through informal channels through relatives and kinsmen to support local educational, social service, health and religious projects. That said, diaspora philanthropy, especially through informal channels, does tend to have a bias in terms of region, ethnicity, religion and caste. Two natural disasters in India at the turn of the new millennium exemplified this. The Orissa Cyclone in 1999 that saw approximately 30,000 deaths, received very little in the way of diaspora philanthropy, especially when compared to the considerable relief dispatched after the 2001 Gujarat earthquake. This clearly reveals that the differences in the size and wealth of a diaspora that roots from a particular region is a key determinant in the way in which charity is distributed.

Promoting India's Foreign Policy Interests

The value of the diaspora as a strategic asset became particularly evident in the late 1990s when sanctions were imposed on India following the Pokhran nuclear test. Diasporic groups in the West lobbied their host states for the removal of sanctions imposed on India which were quickly rescinded. The incident led to the recognition of the significant role that the diaspora could play as a lobby and the need to harness that potential, a position underscored in the 2002 Singhvi Committee Report. In this regard, the Indian diaspora lobby in the US has been especially successful and recognised for its role in the signing the Indo-US Civil Nuclear Cooperation agreement and in enhancing US-India ties. This strategic shift is clearly visible in terms of the heightened engagement of Indian diplomatic missions with resident Indian communities. While all prime ministers in the new millennium have reached out to the diaspora, the emphasis accorded by Prime Minister Narendra Modi has been qualitatively different and far more intense as evident from the numerous large-scale outreach events organised after the 2014 elections which have continued till date. Beyond traditional foreign policy concerns, the Indian diaspora has become an important medium for peddling India's 'soft power'. This may take the form of Indian cinema, cuisine and its spiritual traditions or yoga.

While efforts to utilise the diaspora as a strategic asset may yield positive outcomes, it also brings with it significant responsibilities. As C Raja Mohan posits: "[T]he diaspora expects that India will stand by them in their hour of need." Indeed, in numerous crises in the Middle East over the last 30 years, Delhi has had to expand considerable resources to evacuate Indians from war zones and very recently from sites affected by the spread of COVID-19 infections. The diaspora can also potentially damage India's relations with friendly countries, a case in point being Malaysia when, in late 2007, the Hindu Rights Action Force staged a massive rally to highlight the plight of the Indian minority living there. At that time, the Bharatiya Janata Party and the Dravida Munnetra Kazhagam expressed serious concerns but the then United Progressive Alliance-led government in India remained tight lipped, a position that was not viewed favourably in the diaspora.

Conclusion

The diaspora's long-standing contribution to India's development and its more recent role in lobbying 'home' governments underscore how central India has remained in the minds of its 'sons and daughters overseas'. In certain markers, for example remittances, that record is unparalleled. On the FDI front, however, there is room for expansion. While it is true that entrepreneurs and professionals from the diaspora have invested in certain sectors, the ability to augment this potential depends not only diaspora initiatives, but also on India 'getting its own house in order' in terms of consistent and fair regulatory frames, amongst others. Insofar as the strategic potential of the diaspora is concerned, this remains a double edged sword. While this has yielded dividends in strengthening US-India ties, there are limitations in younger nation states where lobbying on foreign policy issues may be viewed negatively, giving rise to anxieties of the minority being a fifth column whose loyalty is suspect and potentially even damaging ties. Indeed, even as India has adopted the extended family as metaphor of her relationship with the diaspora, there is a need to recognise that millions of India's daughters [and sons] overseas are members of new families whose sensitivities and sensibilities need to be handled delicately.

36

One Family, the Challenges Notwithstanding

Zainul Abidin Rasheed

Practically all my life, I have marvelled at India for being the largest democracy and a plural society with its overwhelming majority Hindus living in peace with its multiple minority communities, including the Muslims. Lately, however, reading about several troubling developments, I wonder what has gone wrong in the country.

Personally, I have strong views on the importance of multiracialism and inter-religious harmony. Three events have reinforced my commitment as such.

I was almost killed during the Chinese-Malay racial riots in Singapore in 1964. I was a secondary school student then. Surviving the ordeal, I am determined to ensure that such riots do not repeat themselves.

In 1973, I attended the Libyan President Muammar Ghadafy's International Youth Conference. The attendees opted for an inclusive approach of working with the non-Muslim world in overcoming challenges in inter-racial relations.

It was also in April 1973 immediately after the Libyan conference that I visited India for the first time. Rushing from the airport in Madras to catch the train to Tanjore district, I managed to jump onto the last coach as it pulled out of the station. Catching my breath, the ticket Inspector told me to move out as it was a First Class coach and I was holding a Third Class ticket. A man on the coach stood up and told the inspector that it was okay, I was family. It turned out that it was a Hindu family, embracing me, a Muslim, as family. Later, I came to know that the Hindu family was visiting the famous Catholic Velankanni Church in South India and the equally famous Muslim Saint Auliya Shahul Hamid Syed Shrine in Nagore. Coincidentally, I visited both these places during that visit.

Fifteen years later, as Editor of Singapore's *Berita Harian*, serving mostly the Malay/Muslim community, I covered Prime Minister Lee Kuan Yew's visit to New Delhi and Islamabad. I recall the flight between the two capitals. After meeting Prime Minister Rajiv Gandhi, Mr Lee flew to Pakistan to meet President Zia-ul-Haq. There was relative peace then. It appeared that there were no sensitivities at all for a visit between the two capitals when we knew of the history of the Partititon and the bloodshed that followed. The ruling Congres Party had taken, what a political commentator told me, a 'wide tent' approach towards politics, accepting all.

In the 1990s, I attended the Oxford University Centre for Islamic Studies' programme on Muslim minorities. I recall mentioning to its head then, well-known political scholar, Dr Farhan Nizami, that India should serve as a role model for multi-religious societies. Dr Nizami, till today at Oxford University, has contributed much towards a better understanding of inter-racial and inter-religious relations all over the world.

When I visited India again in 2004, then as Singapore's Minister of State for Foreign Affairs, accompanying Prime Minister Goh Chok Tong, I recall mentioning the conversation I had with Dr Nizami to Prime Minister Manmohan Singh who nodded very much in agreement.

During the course of writing this essay, I also benefitted from my conversations with several journalists, political observers and individuals from the corporate sector, emphasising the complex backdrop of understanding issues on inter-religious relations in India, especially after the Bharatiya Janata Party government came into office in 2014.

When I told a senior Indian journalist, Mr Rasheed Kidwai, my mentioning to Prime Minister Singh my thoughts of India being a model of inter-religious harmony, Mr Kidwai recalled how Prime Minister Singh, on a visit to the United States (US) in 2005, received a huge compliment from US President George W Bush. President Bush famously introduced Dr Singh to his wife Laura Bush as "the Prime Minister of India, a democracy which does not have a single Al-Qaida member in a population of 150 million Muslims."

At a time when the world collectively battles the scourge of terrorism in the guise of religious extremism, the Indian experience is worth a look. As a writer, journalist, diplomat and politician, I feel India too needs to look inwards on the rise of fundamentalism, incidents of mob lynching and cow vigilante.

Before dwelling upon specific instances to highlight India's syncretism, it is important to look at its glorious past that saw long spells of Hindu, Muslim and British rule which has made Indian experience an extraordinary socio-cultural phenomena. Muslims, for instance, have lived in India for over a millennium now. They first arrived in small pockets as traders. Cheramaan Juma Mosque in Kerala is said to have been built in 629 AD by Malik Deenar, a Persian companion of Prophet Muhammad. Muslims subsequently came to India in large numbers from Central Asia. Mughal dynasty alone ruled the country for 300 years. Emperors Akbar and Shah Jahan's contributions to Indian heritage are well documented. Even Emperor Aurangzeb, who was reported to have notoriously oppressed the Hindus, was said to have appointed a significant majority of his Prime Ministers from among the Hindus, wrote poetry praising the Hindu trinity of Brahma-Vishnu-Mahesh and gave donations to Hindu temples.

Then came the British rule in India spread over 190 years. It sowed seeds of Hindu-Muslim divide in a systematic and institutional manner to prevent a unified nationalist movement that could overthrow the British.

This resulted in the formation of Pakistan in 1947, created on the basis of a sectarian logic which saw millions killed and uprooted from their homes, and billions of rupees worth of property destroyed.

The spread of Islam in India was due to a strong Sufi movement and the influence of mystical teachings, including that of Sheikh Abdul Qadir Gilani and Hasan Al Basri. Many of their followers visited and settled in India. Some notable names were Khwāja Muīnuddīn Chishtī of Ajmer, and Nizāmuddīn Awliyā of Delhi. These Sufi saints did not use any coercive or aggressive means to propagate Islam. Rather, masses were attracted to their piety and spirituality, and their pantheistic doctrines appealed much to the Indian mind.

To my understanding, and as shared by Mr Kidwai, in addition to Sufi traditions, Islamic clergy in India stood by composite culture and pluralism. The strong ideological and theoretical foundations of organisations like Jamiat-e-Ulema, firmly rooted in Islam, acted as a bulwark against fissiparous tendencies. Several scholars have recorded Jamiat's contributions in propagating moderate Islam in India.

Jamiat owes its staunch nationalistic flavour to its mentor, Maulana Husain Ahmed Madani (1878–1957), who participated in the country's freedom struggle. One of his famous remarks in pre-independence India was: "All should endeavour jointly for such a democratic government in which Hindus, Muslims, Sikhs, Christians and Parsis are included. Such a freedom is in accordance with Islam."

Maulana Madani passionately advocated the idea of composite nationalism and joint struggle of all religious communities against the British and justified inter-communal unity and cooperation at a time when ideas of religion-based nationalism were advocated by the Hindu Mahasabha and the Muslim League. He advanced "the theory of territorial national hood", saying that it is "not necesarry that a nation, to be a nation, should share the same religion and culture."

It is due to men like Maulana Madani and Sufi influence that Islam in India has largely remained moderate and accommodative.

There are currently only 27 Muslim representatives in the 543-member Lower House of Parliament. It is inadequate and disproportionate to the Muslim population in the country.

Communalism is a causative factor responsible for the low representation of Muslims in parliament and state assemblies. Fewer Muslim candidates are being given tickets to contest elections by the major political parties. There is a growing sense of majoritarian worldview. Lynching incidents may have been sporadic but they have created panic and a degree of alienation. Widespread prevalence of false and fake news on social media, arrest of innocents on charges of sedition, selective use of the law, deteriorating socio-economic indicators, unemployment and a general sense of despondency among the Muslims are pointing to a situation that may trigger something undesirable.

In a vibrant and healthy democracy, participation and empowerment hold the key. Muslims in India have full citizenship rights protected by the rule of law and the constitution. Indian Muslims have taken a pledge to the Indian constitution. A multi-religious society, while providing diversity, may have elements of different faiths pulling in directions that may often not be conducive to cohesion.

Perhaps there is much we can share and learn from each other in terms of inter-religious and inter-ethnic relations.

I recall attending the Vibrant Gujarat Summit in January 2009 and made an official call on then Chief Minister Narendra Modi. On my return to Singapore, a Muslim friend asked me why the Singapore government sent a Muslim to shake the hands of a person who was Chief Minister of Gujarat during the riots of 1992 which saw hundreds of Muslims being killed. I shared this with a senior colleague at the foreign minstry who replied that Singapore did not send a Muslim but a Singaporean to meet Mr Modi.

In 2000, Indian President K R Narayanan visited Singapore. Among others, his visit also aimed to enhance cooperation in heritage and the arts. He presented three Hindu artefacts of a dancing Lord Shiva, elephant-faced deity Lord Ganesha and Yogini, a 10-armed mother goddess, to Singapore. Significantly, this was done for a multicultural, multi-religious Chinese majority Singapore, with a Muslim population almost doubled that of the Hindus.

Indian President A P J Abdul Kalam, a scientist and an aeronautical engineer by training, visited Singapore in February 2006. He enjoyed the Lion Dance presentation prepared for him before he engaged the Nanyang Technological University in several areas of cooperation. He also delivered the 27th Singapore Lecture on 'Evolution of Enlightened Societies on our Planet'. Inspiring no doubt, Dr Kalam symbolised to me the India I knew where Muslim minorities could excel and represent the country at its highest levels, without being hampered by narrow ultra communal interests. He also garlanded the statue of Mahatma Gandhi at the Global Indian International School as a reminder of the values of a secular inter-social, inter-religious India.

In 2019, I had the opportunity of meeting Mr Modi again, this time as Prime Minister, during his official visit to Singapore. While on a tour of Jamaek Mosque in Chinatown just before he visited the Hindu temple a few doors away, I mentioned my Gujarat visit to him and my wish to meet him again and to learn more about India, in particular its inter-religious relations and how we could learn from each other. He welcomed the idea and opportunity.

Issues are aplenty in India, from what I gather from my conversations and readings, and perhaps too complex to dwell at length here. Issues relating to the political void left by the Congress, emergence of right-wing Hindu nationalism, monopoly of small privileged groups, politics of religious fanaticism and minority bashing, corruption of democracy, instrumentalisation of religion and the Babri mosque dispute, among others, have been brought to the fore over time, and with that, some degree of chaos in the country. One must also not forget the recent issue of the Citizenship (Amendment) Act, 2019, which has weakened federalism and impacted the unity among the ruling coalition partners.

All the controversies notwithstanding, I personally believe that the return of a more united India will prevail with a strong leadership which believes in the strength of its unity rather than division.

India has always been on our minds, not only in terms of its ancient wisdom and civilisational linkages, but also the manner in which it has lived and showcased '*Vasudhaiva Kutumbakam*' (The World is One Family), ancient Sanskrit words I recently learnt from Mr Kidwai.

I am confident that in keeping with ancient Indian traditions of dialogue and engagement, India will peacefully and amicably resolve all the conflicts and continue to showcase a divergence of faiths through its state policies and social mores.

37

Hard Realities of India's Soft Power

Viswa Sadasivan

Soft Power — India's First-mover Advantage

The term 'soft power' was popularised by Harvard University's Professor Joseph Nye in his 1990 book, *Bound to Lead: The Changing Nature of American Power.* It is about the ability to persuade others to do something without using force or coercion. Unlike hard power, which refers to a state's military and economic resources, soft power works on persuasion aimed at furthering a country's 'attractiveness'. It has three main categories — culture, political ideals and values, and domestic and foreign policies. Soft power is based on "intangibles such as the power of example. It is, therefore, the ability to modify other states' preferences because of their perception of you." (Blarel, 2012) This means that states that possess soft power must score high on what I would term 'likeability quotient' where the values and actions of the perceiver and perceived must be aligned. This is why democracy-related values such as freedom, transparency and integrity are key to having and retaining soft power.

Soft power has little strength in itself. It gains potency only when it is projected successfully — with constancy and consistency. Public diplomacy is the process of connecting directly with the hearts and minds of the people in other states.

India projected immense soft power in the years immediately after independence in 1947. Mahatma Gandhi and Jawaharlal Nehru were respected and revered as freedom fighters, not only by members of the Indian diaspora, but also by people all over Asia and Africa who were on a similar journey. The world was in awe of how India 'defeated' the mighty British through peaceful means. Winston Churchill described the British defeat as a "shameful flight, by a premature hurried scuttle." The 1983 film by Richard Attenborough, *Gandhi*, won critical acclaim and was a box office hit very much because of the world's fascination with Gandhi. Prime Minister Nehru believed that India had a "tryst with destiny" and was determined to project it as a "new, softer kind of great power" that will lead a global shift in international relations which gives weight to equity and justice. The Non-Aligned Movement, founded in 1961, helped position India as the leader of small nations.

Losing the Soft Power Momentum

Prime Minister Indira Gandhi worked on a new hard power-centred equation which inadvertently destroyed the soft power arsenal built by the founding leaders. In December 1971, India allied with then-East Pakistan against West Pakistan forces, resulting in the creation of Bangladesh. This permanently altered relations between India and Pakistan, exacerbating Cold War tensions. The Indo-Soviet Treaty of Friendship and Cooperation was inked in August 1971. It signalled a clear departure from India's non-aligned stance. Possibly, in response, United States (US) President Richard Nixon visited Beijing in February 1972, resulting in rapprochement between the two countries. The US pivoted towards Pakistan. Then, in 1974, Indira Gandhi had her scientists conduct an explosive nuclear test, which irked not only the US, but also the other signatories to the Nuclear Non-Proliferation Treaty. A year later, she declared emergency rule in India, suspending democracy. All this happened when India had yet to build its hard power capability. It lost the goodwill gained from the strong soft power built in the early years of independence.

This is probably why and how India lost its massive first-mover advantage in soft power. In a 2006 seminal survey by the Chicago Council on Global Affairs, Americans gave a thumbs-down to India. Seventy-one percent opposed the highly-publicised agreement on nuclear cooperation between India and the US while 69 percent would not support a future militarily powerful India. Only 49 percent trusted India to act responsibly in world affairs.

In global governance, India has been accused of being a spoiler on issues as diverse as trade, nuclear non-proliferation and humanitarian intervention. On trade, India was held responsible to a great extent for blocking the efforts to rescue the Doha Round in 2009. (Bluestein, 2009) Western observers have frequently asked if India can be a 'responsible stakeholder' in the international system. (Dormandy, 2007)

These perceptions have a lasting residual effect. In a 2018 survey of top 30 countries with soft power, conducted by Portland Communications and the University of Southern California's Centre on Public Diplomacy, India fared abysmally. The United Kingdom ranked first with a score of 80.5, while India, with a score of 40.6, did not even make the shortlist.

Narendra Modi's Soft Power Ambition

It is under these circumstances that Narendra Modi came into power as India's prime minister in 2014. It was evident from the start that Modi wanted to project a new India that is audacious, means business and has lots of sex appeal! He was aware that he was starting from a low base, and that the rest of the world was not staying put. He is determined for India to have its seat at the roundtable of global powers.

Shashi Tharoor, a vociferous critic of Modi, said in 2019 that the ruling National Democratic Alliance built up the "most extraordinary personality cult in modern political history, buttressed by a larger-than-life imagery". Although it was meant to be a slur, what the opposition politician said is a compliment to Modi's vision and strategic prowess. This is what it takes for India to be noticed enough and taken seriously.

For the first time in decades, India has a strategic approach to project its greatness. Modi's plan is to revive national pride in residents as well as ethnic Indians living abroad. The promotion of soft power is aimed at meeting India's foreign policy objectives and showing its willingness to play a bigger role in global politics. (Pant, 2015)

Modi achieves this global soft power projection through several interconnected strategic moves.

First, he leverages on the power of association by being seen as having close and, more importantly, equal relationships with world leaders. Much of this has to do with India being a technology giant and Modi's 'cult personality'. These leaders desire to meet Modi as much as he wants to meet them.

Secondly, Modi not only makes it a point to personally attend major summits, conferences and events, but also often makes an impact. His speeches tend to be bold, rich in content and often inspirational. For example, in 2015 during COP21, Modi 'stole the show' when he pushed for 'climate justice' on behalf of the developing world. He also announced that India was spearheading a new International Solar Alliance.

Third, Modi has been systematically engaging the 25-million strong Indian diaspora as a force multiplier. No other Indian head of government has done it at this scale and made the members of the diaspora feel as valued. The diaspora is perhaps the most potent vehicle for projecting India's soft power. Modi prefers to see it not as 'brain drain' but as 'brain gain'. India leverages on the diaspora's immense influence to help achieve its foreign policy goals. In fact, the recent shift in Indo-US relations is credited to the lobbying, influence and reputation of the Indian American community. To millions of the non-resident Indians (NRIs), Modi is a 'rock star'. The famous 2019 'Howdy

Modi' event in Houston, Texas, had 50,000 people of Indian origin from across the US cheering Modi as he walked into the stadium with President Donald Trump.

Fourth, Modi wants to project India as an exciting place for business. This has made him a big hit, especially with young Indians many of whom stand shoulder-to-shoulder with the best of breed in the world of information technology and artificial intelligence. Pushing for a digitalisation culture, several iconic start-ups have become unicorns. Today, India has no less than 18 unicorns, worth billions of dollars. India ranks second in the Digital Adoption Growth index, far ahead of China, Germany and the US.

The final thrust is to have the world enthralled by India's rich culture and heritage, and be smitten by Bollywood. It is important that this endearing imagery gradually overrides the enduring image of an India that is unsanitary and poverty-stricken. Today, over 300 million people around the world are practicing yoga. Bollywood has a symbiotic relationship with the government where they are committed to mutually promoting each other. It is said that 'a thing of beauty is a joy forever' and Modi understands its potency.

The Modi government's strategy has helped raise India's profile internationally. According to the 2016 Soft Power 30 study India is a 'country to watch' as it is expected to make the top ranks in a few years. Modi's fan club goes beyond the diaspora and includes global leaders. Yet, India's ranking in the Soft Power Index has actually fallen since 2016.

Recognising the Hard Truth about Soft Power

An often-cited reason for this is that governments and the intelligentsia in several countries are not sure who Modi really is and what he stands for. Modi's aversion to addressing allegations, especially by India's mainstream media, is a big reason. In a survey, half of the countries in the Indo-Pacific region said that while they recognise Modi's rising popularity they are not sure if he is a 'morally right leader' when it comes to world politics.

Domestically, the albatross around Modi's neck is his perceived role as Gujarat's Chief Minister in 2002 during the Gujarat riots that killed 790 Muslims and 254 Hindus. Another issue seen as silence by the Prime Minister was when an eight-year old Muslim girl was abducted, raped for days and killed by eight Hindu men in January 2018. Then, there is the highly charged matter of the Citizenship Amendment Act in 2019. The amendment provides for citizenship specifically to non-Muslim persecuted minorities from Afghanistan, Pakistan and Bangladesh. This created fear that the Hindu nationalist government is seeking to disenfranchise and oppress the country's Muslim minority population. Students and professors from Jawaharlal Nehru University who protested the Act were attacked by masked goons and mobs. Dozens of protestors were killed in Delhi and other parts of India. Modi was again seen to be silent.

In an internet-driven globalised world, news spreads very fast. Bad news spreads at a raging speed. These issues cited are of interest not only to Indians or NRIs. They pertain to basic democratic liberties which are of interest to people and governments all over the world. By not engaging in these issues proactively, India's standing in the free world will diminish. Its immense effort in projecting soft power will be neutralised. It will be difficult for India to gain acceptance as a world leader.

Nye said, "[T]he values a government champions in its behaviour at home (for example, democracy) ... strongly affects the preferences of others." Similarly, India's multiple social and political identities continue to conflict with each other, both within Indian policy-making and the messages and images India portrays to the world. The end result is confusion at the receiving end and general distrust among India's interlocutors, neither of which is conducive to the effective exercise of soft power. (Mukherjee, 2013) This has to be addressed. The truth is Modi is often persuasive when he engages like how he convinced leaders in the 2019 France G7 Summit that Delhi's decision to revoke the special status of Jammu and Kashmir was a bilateral issue.

Unfortunately, India's struggle to effectively manage the COVID-19 pandemic and the huge impact it is expected to have on the economy and unemployment have thrown a spanner in the works, so as to speak. Yet, this is not reason enough to underestimate India's resilience and ability to get back on track to become a global power. India's soft power initiatives continue to give dividends, and are buttressed by a much stronger hard power base politically, militarily and economically. The irony is that as India enters the big league, these hard and soft power strengths become hygiene factors. What matter would be issues of integrity, transparency and trust. The higher your profile, the greater the scrutiny, especially if you are an emerging nation. In its ambition to be a world power, India is at a critical point of inflexion.

38

India and the Asia-Pacific

See Chak Mun

Non-alignment has been the hallmark of India's foreign policy since the time of its first Prime Minister Jawaharlal Nehru. It provided India the much-desired strategic space and enabled it to be far more influential in international affairs such as when it led the demand of the developing countries for a new international economic order in the 1970s in a leadership role more commensurate with that of a global power than that of a newly-independent state.

With the end of the Cold War and the collapse of the Soviet Union in December 1991, non-alignment suddenly lost its relevance. The P V Narasimha Rao government (1991–96) was confronted with a major change in the world strategic environment and an economic crisis at home. It was a watershed in Indian foreign policy as there was an urgent need to re-engage the United States (US) as the sole superpower. Addressing a joint US Congress session in May 1994, Prime Minister Rao spoke eloquently about the shared values between the Americans and Indians and the relationship between development and democracy. He gave assurances that India would change from being a closed protected economy to an open export-oriented economy.

To secure India's strategic flank, Prime Minister Rao visited several member countries of the Association of Southeast Asian Nations (ASEAN). During his Singapore Lecture on 8 September 1994, Prime Minister Rao said:

> The stakes in the Asia-Pacific region are indeed high. They involve rights of passage through crucial waterways, security of navigation from piracy, claims over disputed lands, maritime zones and resources, and hostilities through history that have been defused but not dispelled.

However, it was the Pokhran-II nuclear tests, a series of five nuclear bomb test explosions at the Indian army's Pokhran Test Range undertaken by the Bharatiya Janata Party (BJP)-led National Democratic Alliance in May 1998, which drew the world's attention to India's stature as a nuclear power. Prime Minister Atal Bihari Vajpayee (1998–2004) swiftly announced a new approach in India's foreign policy with diplomatic re-positioning, economic resurgence, military firmness and new links with democratic societies. India's security environment stretched from East Africa to the Persian Gulf and the Straits of Malacca, Central Asia and Afghanistan, China and Southeast Asia. The Indian navy was directed to develop the capability to project power beyond the Indian Ocean to demonstrate India's strategic reach. From 2000, the Indian navy began to project its power in the South China Sea. In the spring of 2007, there was even a bigger display of Indian naval prowess when an Indian flotilla launched a four-month expedition and operated deep into the Pacific Ocean.

This heightened sense of security threat was a reaction to the terrorist attacks on the Indian Parliament by two Pakistan-based terrorist organisations — Lashkar-e-Taiba (LeT) and Jaish-e-Mohammed — in December 2001. More significantly, there was a perceived threat of an Islamic Arc, stretching from the Gulf, Pakistan, Afghanistan and Bangladesh to Southeast Asia, as evidence pointed to jihadi links with terrorist groups in South Asia such as that between the Philippines-based

Abu Sayyaf group and Al-Qaeda, and between the Bangladesh-based Harkat-ul-Jehad-Islami and the LeT. These would further complicate India's relations with Pakistan, a long-time security threat.

India's other strategic preoccupation was China, which had been seeking closer ties with the ASEAN-member countries, particularly Myanmar. China had reportedly set up intelligence monitoring stations in the Coco Islands, and Chinese investment in Myanmar's infrastructure, including in deep-water ports, would provide China with direct overland access to the Bay of Bengal. India also closely monitored China's relations with Indonesia, Malaysia and Singapore. These three ASEAN-member states were littorals of the Straits of Malacca, which was China's gateway into the Indian Ocean. Hence, during its term, the Vajpayee government assiduously cultivated the ASEAN-member countries by offering an ASEAN-India Free Trade Agreement, open-skies to selected Indian cities and co-operation in counterterrorism.

The approach of the Manmohan Singh government (2004–14) to the ASEAN-member countries differed very little from that of the Vajpayee government, but a new emphasis was placed on developing transport and economic linkages between northeastern India and the ASEAN region. The aim was to provide an economic uplift to this relatively under-developed landlocked region where separatist groups continued to engage in armed struggle.

Spelling out the strategic perspectives of India's new 'Look East' policy, Defence Minister Pranab Mukherjee highlighted the need for an equitable strategic balance in the Asia-Pacific region. India welcomed the creation of the East Asia Summit in December 2005, which gave it a voice in a forum comprising the 10 ASEAN-member countries, China, Japan, South Korea, India, Australia and New Zealand, and a regional multilateral mechanism through which India could manage its relations with China.

Continuing the policy of Prime Minister Vajpayee, who considered the US a 'natural partner' and sought co-operation with the US, including in civilian nuclear activities, Prime Minister Singh's government made strategic partnership with the US a foreign policy priority and signed a New Framework for the India-US Defence Relationship with the George Bush Administration in June 2005.

When the BJP returned to power in May 2014, the Narendra Modi government (2014-to-date) served notice that India's immediate neighbourhood was its priority and invited the South Asian leaders to its swearing-in ceremony. The first country Prime Minister Modi visited was Bhutan (in June 2014) to signal India's close relations with and security commitments to its small Himalayan neighbour. This relationship was tested in June 2017 when India despatched its troops to stop Chinese soldiers from extending a road to Doklam, which was claimed by both Bhutan and China. It was a clear signal that India would not hesitate to use military force to protect its interests and its sphere of influence. It was also reminiscent of a similar situation in 1988 when the Rajiv Gandhi government sent 1,600 troops to the Maldives to help quell a coup attempt against President Maumoon Adbul Gayoom.

Prime Minister Modi visited Mauritius, the Seychelles and Sri Lanka in March 2015 as part of an outreach to India's maritime neighbours. It was also to counter China's growing activities in the Indian Ocean, including China's acquisition of an overseas military support base in Djibouti, and its financing of a military port at Gwadar in Pakistan and the Hambantota port in Sri Lanka. The message was that India would not countenance China's expansion at its expense, especially in a region traditionally regarded as India's sphere of influence.

India is keen to participate actively in the Indo-Pacific, a regional concept mooted by US President Barack Obama in his pivot to Asia policy as part of the US strategic plan to contain China's rise. However, Prime Minister Modi clarified that India did not see the new Indo-Pacific region as a concept for strategic containment directed against any country but as an open and inclusive arrangement. With this caveat, India agreed to participate in the Quadrilateral Security Dialogue (Quad), together with the US, Japan and Australia. To avoid being seen as actively adversarial towards China, India has declined to participate in Quad joint patrols in the South China Sea.

In redefining India's foreign policy, Prime Minister Modi was emphatic that India should cast off its past cautions and the ideological constraints of Nehruvian non-alignment. India would be ready to act as a leader to shape the trajectory and outcome of issue-based alliances, as opposed to simply being a balancer in an agenda set by others. The emphasis on issues-based alliances would keep India's options open and allow space for strategic flexibility. It would enable India to justify apparent divergences of interests such as being a participant in the Quad, while concurrently sharing membership with China in BRICS (Brazil, Russia, India, China and South Africa) and the Shanghai Cooperation Organisation.

In practice, there was no radical departure from the basic principles that have guided the foreign policy of successive Indian governments since Nehru. India's priorities have always been consistent: firstly, the preservation of India's strategic autonomy whether via a policy of non-alignment or keeping India's options open; and secondly, to protect India's status as *primus inter pares* within its immediate sphere of influence. However, India also aspires to be major player in a multi-polar world or at least within the emerging regional architecture in Asia. India recognises its current limits; it does not possess the capability to effectively project its power beyond its immediate region. Nevertheless, it has an expanding economy and grand strategic ambitions which include plans to acquire a blue-water navy.

Some have argued that India might find greater comfort in partnering the US as part of a grand alliance of democracies sharing similar values; and there is certainly some strategic convergence as far as China is concerned. Nevertheless, there has been visceral rejection of any suggestion that a big country like India should accept the role of a proxy or client state, or even as a balancer in someone else's game. The issues-alliance policy adopted by the Modi government maintains a strong streak of independence that has long characterised Indian foreign policy. It also creates space for India to manoeuvre in an evolving new world order, disrupted by technology and by the political and economic rivalry between an increasingly assertive China determined to rise and an increasingly unilateralist US equally set on preserving its status as the sole superpower.

39

India Loved and Unloved: Reflections from a Distance

Kirpal Singh

One of India's better-known poets writing in English was the late Nissim Ezekiel. I got to know him first through his poems and then met him a few times at various writers' conferences. He was always amiable, effable and sometimes even amusing, though for most of the time, he was serious and ironic. Whenever we met, we usually first talked about ourselves (bringing each other up to date) and then very quickly got into 'literary' politics. Nissim was a keen observer of literary politics, always cautioning me about not falling into any such group which was too closely identified with an 'idol'. I think he had someone like Purushottama Lal in mind. P Lal, as he was commonly called, was an Indian poet, essayist, translator, professor and publisher, who died in November 2010. Of course, many of us around the world were fond of P Lal and his writers' workshop in Calcutta (now Kolkata). Indeed my very first book of poems, *Twenty Poems*, was published by Lal in 1976. The book received good and not-so-good reviews but the one thing it did do was to kind of establish my name in Indian poetry circles.

When I finally met the well-known Indian literary critic, Meenakshi Mukerjee, at the residence of the man who 'mentored' so many of us,

C D Narasimhiah (fondly called CD) and who for years was the editor of the standard literary journal in which many of us first appeared either as creative writers or critics, or both. The *Literary Criterion*, as CD's journal was called, gave birth to hundreds of writers from around the globe. CD was always ready to read and give solemn advice to those of us who sought it. And many of us did because CD was always kind and generous. I recall a wonderful conference in Mysore (where CD lived) at the end of 1976 where we agreed that the conference should expand and include discussions of other Commonwealth nations. CD was a big name in the circles of what came to be established as Commonwealth Literature. As a founding father of this sub-genre, CD grew in eminence and became lauded globally as the champion of Literature from nations where the English language was not the native tongue. So from Africa and the West Indies to Singapore, Malaysia, Australia and the Pacific, Commonwealth Literature gained a sure and strong foothold.

The tri-annual Commonwealth Literature conference was acclaimed and, in 1980, we brought it to Singapore. The conference had a generous grant from the Commonwealth Foundation — a body set up by the nations of the Commonwealth to generate and promote and sustain interest in the broad issues and challenges associated with the use of English as a language of colonisation as well as a language of liberation. Though this was not the first time in world history that the same language underlined both dominance and independence, it was the first time that it was recognised as such on a huge scale. Every three years, we convened a literary gathering where writers from the entire Commonwealth were invited to read from their works as well as to share critical insights and observations. So, from as far away as Trinidad and Uganda to the more familiar landscapes of the United Kingdom and Canada, Commonwealth Literature provided us with an international forum to discuss, appraise and exchange ideas and views, ranging from good books to politics and personages. The starting point of all these was Mysore, India.

My first visit to India at the end of 1976 made me both 'love' and 'not love' India. From the time Dudley DeSouza, a fellow writer and critic from Singapore, and I got off the plane in Delhi to the time we got to the Mysore train station where CD had sent his ambassadors to receive us, we were both charmed and fascinated as well as anxious and flabbergasted. Frankly, both of us were exasperated and confounded at being constantly surrounded by beggars asking for *paisa* (money) and all the rough pushing and pulling we were subjected to. Once we were having a cup of coffee at a cafe, we heard a loud thud. We turned around and saw that a man had fallen face down and we immediately alerted our coffee attendant. He looked across, saw the fallen man and said to us: "Nothing to worry sir, every hour someone is falling and dying...not to worry." He was so nonchalant about the whole matter. To him, it was a common affair, seeing people fall, collapse and even die. So life was indeed cheap in India, as many had forewarned us prior to our leaving.

During the conference, there were various tours planned for us but many of us decided to take a tour to view the beautiful Mysore hills. Along the journey, we witnessed the rough treatment meted out to the poor and the meagre by our host. Years later, when I was older and had the temerity to raise this with some individuals whom I had witnessed treating their underlings unkindly, the immediate response was: "Kirpal, you do not live here. You do not know what we have to go through. The moment you try to be friendly with them, you are finished." The Polish-turned-Indian writer, Ruth Prawar Jhabvala, told me this as we had dinner one evening. So did Yasmine Gooneratne, the well-known writer and critic originally from Sri Lanka but then teaching at Australia's Macquarie University.

The young, robust and getting-revered Indian writer, S R Krishnamoorthy, author of the beautifully haunting and poignant novel, *Samkara*, had a different take. "Look", he began, "India is an ancient civilisation and all ancient civilisations go through traumatic transformations. I, for one, await a real transformation so badly needed and wanting here that if we do not achieve it, realise it, we are going to be in the doldrums for centuries to come." I inquired what it was and immediately the answer came:

> We need to get rid of our obsession with caste. This insidious system is so entrenched that those who know can tell simply from our names what our caste is and, having established our caste, they then move forward accordingly, either respecting us as if the Gods themselves owe us favours or despising us as if even the worst of humans do not have a kind word to say about us.

Those around the table were stunned. Here was a highly educated man, a creative writer of strong originality and well-regarded by readers and audiences alike, insisting that despite the fact that this was 1976, India was still stuck in ancient rituals and classifications of class, caste and gender. I recall a bright young female student asking our distinguished speaker: "Sir, are you, therefore, saying that we are not going to change for another hundred years?" The answer was immediate. "Yes, that is exactly what I am saying." The poor student was despondent, felt rebuffed and defeated in her attempt to receive a more enlightened response. I gleaned that had this been in Singapore, Krishnamoorthy would perhaps have had an earful from the lady. However, here in India, it was considered rude and ill-mannered for a female to question a male, especially one such as the guest and person of high distinction.

So my first impressions of India were (and remain) very mixed. While delighted to be there each and every time, I must confess that being there has always left me wondering and asking the eternal question: "Do I truly love the country of my origin?" My late paternal grandmother, who brought me up, used to sing praises of India, especially of Punjab and even more locally of Jalandhar, the province of my direct ancestors on my father's side. Indeed, we were *zamindars* (landlords). Sadly, I gave up ownership to my 40 acres of ancestral land to an uncle visiting from Jalandhar in the late 1980s.

In my more mature years, I tried to make up for 'lost time' by minimally trying to experience the charm and glory of India's great gift to humankind — Taj Mahal. Having resisted several times the opportunity to visit and see for myself what truly made the Taj Mahal so universally appealing, I finally visited this monument of a mausoleum in 2012. The splendour of this majestic marble tombstone, containing the tombs of the romantic and poetic Emperor Shah Jahan, who had built it in 1632 to house the remains of his beloved wife Mumtaz. I often wonder if Agra, the city where the Taj Mahal is sited, would be what it is if not for this grand testimony to royal romance. My visit to the Taj inspired me to compose the following poem:

Having visited your majestic reminder of love and passion
a million or more times I now finally arrive
and see you as you are and have been all these centuries.
The marble remains intact, mostly —
the cracks here and there testify time's ravages,
I realise that old truism, nothing remains forever.
Riding back to my hotel in the rickety cab
I keep thinking of love, passion and lovers —
how promises betray and faith crumbles.
Never say never I was told again and again;
it is clear now and I realise just how silly
love can be even in its proudest moments.

One other poignant reason for my love affair with India is my affinity with and for the great Indian writers who adopted their colonial language — English — to pen some of the most unforgettable lines in modern English poetry. Everyone will most readily think of the inimitable Rabindranath Tagore whose most eloquent poetry collection, *Gitanjali*, is still regarded as one of the best tributes to freedom. The haunting opening lines of this grandiloquent poem cannot be easily forgotten by anyone with the minutest of love for language:

Where the mind is without fear and the head is held high;
Where knowledge is free;
Where the world has not been broken up into fragments by narrow
domestic walls;

Where words come out from the depth of truth;
Where tireless striving stretches its arms towards perfection;
Where the clear stream of reason has not lost its way into the dreary desert sand of dead habit;
Where the mind is led forward by thee into ever-widening thought and action —
Into that heaven of freedom, my Father, let my country awake.

In the original Bengali, the words are set to entrance music and the paragraph above constitutes part of India's national anthem. The impact and meaningfulness of what Tagore is saying cannot, surely, escape anyone familiar with politics and particularly the politics of today where all that is really significant and good is all too frequently sacrificed for the instant gratification of individuals, communities and nations rather than in the pursuit of goodness and salvation for all of humanity. The ideal espoused in the verse quoted above bears a truly profound significance for our world today, fraught as it is with divisive forces, forces weighing in from all corners of the globe.

However, India is more than just history, romance and poetry. It is a nation that is one of the most powerful reminders of how civilisations change and fashion the destinies of millions. Its citizens are immensely proud and fiercely loyal. In today's technologically-driven ethos, people of Indian origin are making their presences felt everywhere. Several of the most powerful and prominent corporate leaders of today are Indians and, even if they may be nationals of nations like the United States or the United Kingdom, their loyalty and love for their motherland is unquesstionable. As India joins the great powers of our world to race to the further regions of outer space, I know its journey will be glorious, as glorious as is its witness to history lived and experienced till now.

40

India's Foreign Policy: New Directions

Sinderpal Singh

Independent India has both charmed and frustrated outsiders. This contradiction seems to extend to Indian foreign policy as well. This is unsurprising, given that domestic politics drive the manner in which leaders understand their national interests and India is no exception to this tendency. The terms 'non-alignment' and 'anti-imperialism' have long been associated with the practice of Indian foreign policy and there have been endless debates within India about what these exactly entail. While the term 'non-alignment' has increasingly been replaced by the notion of 'strategic autonomy' within India, there remains a deep aversion amongst Indian leaders to being dragged into great-power conflicts that do not appear to be in India's interests.

Indian foreign policy, despite this continuity, experienced a major shift from the early 1990s. A combination of both domestic and global factors drove this shift. Domestically, it experienced an acute balance of payments crisis driven by rising imported oil prices in the context of a predominantly centrally planned economy. Globally, the end of the Cold War and the demise of the Soviet Union as a superpower shrank India's strategic options considerably. This compelled the Indian government to do two things. Firstly, domestic economic reforms were initiated and the Indian economy was steadily liberalised with reduced obstacles to foreign investment in India. Secondly, the Indian political class began to re-evaluate its relationship with the United States (US), marked by mutual suspicion for large parts of the Cold War. Despite some misgivings from within sections of the ruling Congress Party in India, there was enough consensus in favour of a radical re-evaluation in India-US relations across the political class.

Indian perceptions of the US at this point were also shaped by increasing concerns about China's growing economic and military clout. The border war with China in 1962 is viewed within India as a singular instance of India's humiliation. This, many Indians believe, was also an instance of China's betrayal of Indian attempts at friendship with China. China's increasingly warm relations with Pakistan since 1962 have further reinforced Indian concerns about China's intentions. At the global level, the 1990s were also characterised by growing US concerns about China as a strategic competitor. These concerns about China led to a discernible convergence in strategic outlooks between India and the US and provided the impetus for both countries to fundamentally alter the nature of their bilateral relationship. The India-US Civil Nuclear Agreement (also known as the 123 Agreement), finally signed in 2008, was the culmination of this fundamental change in the India-US relationship. This agreement formally recognised India's nuclear arsenal after its nuclear tests in 1998 as well as granted the opportunity to India to import uranium for its civilian nuclear programme. In return, India agreed not to use imported uranium for its nuclear weapons programme. The significance of this agreement is difficult to understate. The 123 Agreement designated India as the first and thus far only non-signatory to the Nuclear Proliferation Treaty to be allowed to import uranium for its civilian nuclear programme while being allowed to retain its nuclear weapons.

The 1990s also marked another key shift in Indian foreign policy beyond solely a profound change in relations with the US. For large parts of the Cold War, India's relations with its neighbours to its east were either neglected or strained. At key points during the Cold War, India and the member states of the Association of Southeast Asian Nations (ASEAN) found themselves on opposite sides of the ideological divide. For the ASEAN-member states, India's decision to back the Vietnamese invasion and occupation of Kampuchea was a decisive moment in Southeast Asia's Cold War. It rendered India on the opposite side of the ideological divide and, for some time, fed deep suspicions about India within large parts of Southeast Asia. The end of the Cold War potentially removed a major impediment in India's relationship with most Southeast Asian states. India's Prime Minister, P V Narasimha Rao, took this opportunity to articulate India's 'Look East' policy in Singapore in 1994, signalling a new era in India's relations with countries to its east. Since the early 1990s, India's engagement with East and Southeast Asia has grown steadily, both bilaterally with individual countries as well as within the dense multilateral architecture in East Asia. There is widespread support within Southeast Asia for India to play a larger role in these multilateral forums and networks, with Singapore one of the strongest advocates of this position. Successive Indian governments have recognised Singapore's key role in advancing India's 'Act East' policy and it is thus not surprising that the bilateral relationship is one of India's most robust with any state, within and beyond Southeast Asia.

The sweeping victory of the Bharatiya Janata Party (BJP)-led coalition in India's general elections in 2014 signalled a potential transformation of the nature of the Indian state. For the first time since 1984, a single political party had managed to win a majority of seats in India's general elections with Narendra Modi emerging as the BJP's undisputed new leader. Bucking expectations, Prime Minister Modi made foreign policy a key agenda of his government's first term in office and extended overtures to Pakistan to repair bilateral ties. By the end of his first term, however, India's relations with Pakistan had deteriorated significantly with both countries poised on the brink of war. Against this background, Prime Minister Modi led the BJP to an even stronger victory in the 2019 Indian general elections. The BJP's ascension to power has had important ramifications for Indian foreign policy since 2014.

Firstly, the BJP has been able to unshackle itself from earlier deep-seated historical Indian concerns about closer relations with the US. While the Congress-led United Progressive Alliance government paved the way for the historic 123 Agreement with the US, Prime Minister Manmohan Singh endured significant political costs for this policy within his governing coalition as well as within his own Congress party. Prime Minister Modi's BJP does not suffer from this impediment and this has allowed India to develop a much deeper defence relationship with the US. The conclusion of the Logistics Exchange Memorandum of Agreement between the two countries in 2016 effectively designated India as one of the US' closest defence partners and crosses a key threshold in bilateral defence technology transfer and co-operation. Certain strategic divergences, however, still remain in specific areas such as policy towards Iran and the future of Afghanistan, which inadvertently relate to Pakistan's role in South Asia. Notwithstanding these specific differences, defence relations between India and the US have never been closer. For most countries in East Asia, this is a positive development as it demonstrates a confident Indian government willing to make pragmatic strategic choices in order to play a more effective security provider role both regionally and globally.

Secondly, relations with China have been significantly recast. India now acknowledges China as a strategic competitor within South Asia and the broader Indian Ocean and accepts that this will be a multi-dimensional competitive relationship across diplomatic, defence and economic realms. This competitive relationship, however, in the BJP's view, can be managed in a manner that does not lead to tensions beyond a specific threshold. The Indian response to the Doklam episode reveals, to a significant extent, this government's approach to China. It involves making Indian 'red lines' clear and demonstrating the will to defend them while moderating criticism of China publicly, demonstrating an appreciation of the Communist Party of China's domestic legitimacy imperatives. In the Indian Ocean region, since 2014, the Indian state has pushed back against perceived Chinese attempts to make strategic inroads via its various infrastructure building projects. This has involved diplomatic efforts directed towards specific Indian Ocean littorals and has implicated India in the domestic politics of these states. As domestic politics within smaller Indian Ocean littorals gets increasingly patterned along pro- and anti-China lines, India and China will increasingly be implicated in domestic political contests within Indian Ocean states. This attempt at managing strategic competition with China will obviously be tested in its formulation and implementation in future episodes. It remains to be seen the extent to which this Indian administration can avail potential benefits from increased US-China strategic rivalry while ensuring its own strategic options are not curtailed by its closer defence and diplomatic association with the US.

Thirdly, India's relations with East Asia have entered a new phase with mixed results. For many East Asian states, the nature of the BJP's victory raised hopes of a strong mandate for deeper Indian economic engagement of East Asia. The BJP, unlike the Congress party, seemed ideologically less hesitant to further liberalise India's economy. With Prime Minister Modi at the helm, the BJP, in fact, projected itself as the party of 'reform', both economically as well as in terms of domestic governance. India's eventual decision to not sign onto the Regional Comprehensive Economic Partnership (RCEP) in late 2019 was a major setback for many countries in East Asia. This raised serious doubts about the seeming trajectory of India's liberalisation agenda and assumptions about the BJP's ability to deliver these deep structural reforms. Currently, India and the other RCEP countries are looking for ways in which certain Indian misgivings can be addressed and agreed in the agreement. Both India and states in East Asia recognise the strategic importance of this economic agreement and India's position on the RCEP will be a key marker of India's strategic engagement with East Asia.

Beyond economic engagement, most states East Asia expected India to continue its deeper strategic engagement towards its east under the Modi government. India's more confident and pragmatic relationship with the US under Prime Minister Modi's government was viewed favourably. Indian requests to play a security provider role beyond its immediate South Asian region were also welcomed by several East Asian states such as Japan, Singapore and Thailand, to name three prominent examples. Indian requests to play a role in coordinated patrols in the Straits of Malacca to counter piracy was one such initiative by the Modi government and while certain littoral states had historical anxieties about the role of non-littorals in the Straits of Malacca, this was perceived as a sign of increasing Indian confidence and capability to play a security provider role in East Asia. However, the Modi government's strong push for the 'Indo-Pacific' as a replacement for the 'Asia-Pacific' when it came to diplomatic and strategic language in East Asia made several states uncomfortable. To a large extent, this discomfort also stemmed from the manner in which the US, under President Donald Trump, had increasingly been using the 'Indo-Pacific' as a strategy, rather than a description of a new strategic space, meant to push back against China's perceived belligerence in East Asia. ASEAN, accustomed to being both the initiator and lead conductor of the growing number of Asia-Pacific institutions, was faced with a quandary. While the Indo-Pacific legitimised further India's place within the East Asian strategic landscape, it was also largely driven by a small group of states which were also members of the Quadrilateral Security Dialogue (or the Quad). India's desire to play a larger role was welcomed by most East Asian states but the manner in which it chose to do so via the discourse of the Indo-Pacific seemed exclusionary. For the first time since the end of the Cold War, Indian strategic ambitions in East Asia were too audacious for the ASEAN-member states.

Indian foreign policy has undergone fundamental transformation in the last 20 years. Over the tenure of this transformation, the bilateral relationship between Singapore and India has deepened significantly. This robust bilateral relationship has aided India in negotiating a larger role within East Asia as it increasingly looks to its East to define the future of India itself.

41

The Indian Economy: Improving Competitiveness, Reducing Debt and Enhancing Productivity

Tan Khee Giap

India's Economic Competitiveness since 2014

The year 2019 turned out to be quite tumultuous for the Indian economy. With the novel Coronavirus pandemic affecting the globe, India is now faced with the twin challenge of handling a health crisis and an ongoing economic slowdown. The tourism, hospitality, transportation and aviation industries will be the worst impacted by COVID-19. With a lockdown in the entire country from 25 March 2020 onwards, the economic slowdown is most likely to exacerbate in the coming months. Due to supply chain disruptions in China, the Indian chemical, textiles and apparel and automotive industries will be affected. However, e-commerce, logistics and communications have seen a surge in demand.

Indian Prime Minister Narendra Modi secured another five-year term with a historic mandate in May 2019. However, since that victory, India has been faced with a slowdown in consumption, increasing number of bad loans in public sector banks, stress and asset-liability mismatch in non-banking financial companies, lagging exports, increasing losses in the central public sector enterprises and distress in the agriculture sector.

India's gross domestic product (GDP) growth rate has been decreasing after reaching a peak of over eight percent in 2015. India's growth rate has declined to about six percent in 2019. This could impact the government's vision of creating a US$5 trillion (S$7.1 trillion) economy by 2024–25.

India's manufacturing contribution increased significantly till the first quarter of 2018–19. However, it plummeted from a high of around 10 percent in the first quarter of 2018–19 to just about 1.7 percent in the first quarter of 2019–20. The shrinking share of agriculture is equally worrisome. The agriculture sector has been hit hard by falling crop prices and wages, and stressed rural credit. The share of services, on the other hand, has remained somewhat constant on average in the corresponding period.

An examination of the demand side components of GDP growth reveals that the proportion of contribution of various components has remained roughly consistent from 2012–13 to 2018–19, with private consumption expenditure contributing to nearly 60 percent of the GDP growth, followed by gross fixed capital formation hovering at 30 percent and government consumption expenditure around 10–11 percent over the last seven years.

Despite a slowdown of the economy, the Indian government has managed to tame inflation. It has been falling steadily from the high of more than 12 percent in 2009. Since the Modi government first took to office in 2014, inflation reduction is one of its biggest economic achievements as the Reserve Bank of India has steadily brought down inflation to below the targetted four percent since 2017. The Modi government has also succeeded in improving the country's fiscal balance.

India's performance in each of the 10 environments, comprising the World Bank Doing Business Index between 2019 and 2020, has shown significant improvement. The overall ranking for India improved from the

77th position in 2019 to the 63rd position in 2020. The most significant improvements shown by the country are in resolving bankruptcy (improvement by 52 positions) and dealing with construction permits (improvement by 25 positions).

India's Precarious Debt Situation and Labour Productivity Enhancement

India's total national debt has followed a somewhat exponential trend since 1980. The debt-to-GDP ratio has fluctuated significantly between 1980 and 2015. India's expected increase in its debt-to-GDP ratio is a source of concern for India's national debt sustainability as it exposes the economy to external shocks and can worsen its fiscal stability, thereby raising the probability of a future fiscal crisis.

In India, governments at the national and state levels have borrowed extensively to fund their growing fiscal deficits as it is a more straightforward and politically favourable substitute to increasing taxes or curbing spending. Compared to other G-20 countries, India ranks at the lower end in terms of tax collection, one of the reasons for this large fiscal deficit. Predictably, this increasing fiscal deficit trend is a major threat to India's debt sustainability and its long-term economic stability as it suggests a growing national debt in the future as well.

Some Indian states have already displayed debt unsustainability due to excessive borrowing to finance their growing fiscal deficits. The fact that states like Kerala, Punjab and West Bengal have been declared "fiscally unsound" by the central government indicates the magnitude of the issue in the states. As a result, India should continue to actively pursue policies to maintain its fiscal sustainability in order to ensure macroeconomic stability.

It is important to understand the cyclical nature of government expenditures and its relation to debt sustainability, as it informs future attempts for fiscal consolidation. Given the concern for India's state economies to maintain their solvent position, increased welfare spending may not be possible in the long run. Coupled with unsustainable debts, continued increases in welfare spending can jeopardise the states' debt sustainability. The government should also show a committed approach to fighting corruption at the national and state levels.

Given the current protectionist sentiment and nationalism fervour, the world economy is shifting from synchronised global growth to synchronised global slowdown which has implications for the new growth economies, especially India. There is a pressing need to create new sources of growth by moving into higher value-added services in e-commerce to cater to the increasingly sophisticated needs of a rising middle class, including consumer-driven food and beverages, tourism-related activities, modern lifestyle and enhanced professional services. Governments must promote and host (but not invest in) manufacturing clusters and manufacturing related services under Industrial Revolution 4.0 involving digital economies, artificial intelligence and technological game changers such as electronic cars, e-logistics, financial technology and new business start-ups.

Enhancing productivity as a competitiveness factor would be crucial in reviving economies in the difficult global environment we live in. Governments can do so by (i) promoting and identifying urgent needs in specific digital capability and providing subsidized funding for training micro, small and medium enterprises (MSMEs) so as to enhance firm level management efficiency and labour productivity; (ii) empowering on-line technology to the public, including e-government to facilitate public policy resilience and quality of public services; (iii) productivity upgrading through updated life-long learning in tertiary and technical education curricula to acquire future skills and entrepreneurship drive on new technology-related start-ups; (iv) persisting to participate in regional free trade agreements (FTAs) for continued specialisation and strengthening in global production value chains; and (v) ensuring inclusive growth.

Challenges Facing India and Tentative Policy Suggestions

In September 2014, Prime Minister Modi launched the 'Make in India' initiative with an aim of making India a global manufacturing hub.

A total of 25 sectors were targetted to facilitate job creation, enhance skill development, foster innovation and protect intellectual property. The government announced it would allow 100 percent foreign direct investment (FDI) in sectors such as railway, defence and pharmaceuticals. With this initiative, the government laid down the target of increasing the contribution of the manufacturing sector from 16 percent of the GDP in 2014 to 25 percent in 2025.

India still struggles to win over the confidence of foreign investors. The main reason for the slow development in India's manufacturing industry may be due to its late opening in 1991 compared to China which opened up in 1978, inadequacy of physical and financial infrastructure to support the manufacturing industry, lack of urgency to urbanise, significant brain drain, lack of a skilled labour force and strict labour laws which prevent the free flow of labour.

There are at least six areas where policies can be adopted by India to attain its vision of becoming a global manufacturing hub.

Firstly, it should simplify the process of starting a business. The central government has reduced the effective corporate tax rate for domestic companies to around 25 percent and proposed an effective tax rate of around 17 percent tax rate for manufacturing companies set up after 1 October 2019. Simplifying land acquisition laws and devising a partial compensation scheme for capital expenditure incurred by certain key industries would not only reduce the time and cost incurred in bureaucratic processes, but also act as a major selling point to attract more businesses and industries to the country.

Secondly, it is vital to ensure the availability of skilled labour. The government has taken the initiative to address the mismatch between the demand and supply of skilled manpower in India by establishing the Ministry of Skill Development and Entrepreneurship in 2014 and launching a series of skill development schemes. However, there is still a long way to go. Given the demographic dividend the country enjoys, focus should also be laid on upskilling the labour force by providing grants to companies to train their employees on new technological, digital and industrial skills.

Thirdly, in the present big data-driven world, with so many new technological disruptions changing the pace of the world so quickly, promoting greater research by way of increased funding and intellectual properties through a synergistic industry eco-system will make the economy a preferred FDI destination. This will also incentivise talented Indians working outside the country to return to do businesses and pursue research, thereby also retaining some of the best talent within the country and reversing the brain drain.

Fourthly, India needs to enhance its market access in the international arena. To do so, it needs to reduce the tariff and the non-tariff barriers by strengthening its existing bilateral arrangements and FTAs and by being a part of the mega trade agreements like the Regional Comprehensive Economic Partnership from which it has withdrawn. It is not in the interest of the country to resort to protectionism if it aims to increase its share in global exports.

Fifthly, the immigration policies for foreign talent need to be relaxed. Currently, there are two types of work visas offered — the Business Visa designated as 'B' Visa and the Employment Visa designated as 'E' Visa. To be eligible for the 'E' visa, a foreign employee must draw a salary higher than US$25,000 (S$35,500) per annum and must also register with the foreign regional registration office if he/she intends to stay in India for more than 180 days. In addition, the duration of the visa is contingent on whether India has a bilateral agreement with the employee's country of origin and whether the employee is being employed in the information technology sector.

Lastly, digital banks, which are online-only banks, should be set up in the country to facilitate easier loans for lower income households and MSMEs to set up their businesses. These banks offer lower interest rates on loans since they do not incur infrastructure and overhead costs like physical banks. Through these banks, the government can further its mission of financial inclusion and assist in the upliftment of those who are economically vulnerable.

42

Understanding Politics in India

Ravi Velloor

How does one take the measure of politics in a nation that is unlike any other in its complexities — its social stratification, its plenitude of languages and its multiple religions — and influenced by cultural traits from modern-day nations as varied as Britain and Portugal in Europe to Central Asia and the Gulf states, China in the northeast corner of Asia and Java to the southeast?

A discussion on understanding Indian politics, therefore, needs to start by stating the obvious. First, with an estimated 1.4 billion people, India is probably already the world's largest nation by population. It also is the world's largest democracy; its constitution commits it to be a "socialist, secular democratic republic". And it practices a multiparty system within the framework of a periodically elected national parliament and state assemblies within a broadly federal structure.

No one seriously ever considered this ambitious experiment in democracy — or nation-building for that matter — to be perfect, either when free India held its first election in 1951 or now. At Independence from colonial rule in 1947, there were even questions raised on whether the country would survive and thinkers such as Milovan Djilas predicted its imminent collapse. The national literacy level was a mere 12 percent and, even today, one in seven Indians cannot even write his or her name.

The dominant Hindu society was divided along four orders, each with hundreds of castes within its fold, and below them were people so low in the social order that they were considered 'outcaste'. Additionally, the Indian constitution provided for 'reservations' in legislatures and in government employment for the most socially-disadvantaged castes and tribes for a period of 10 years — something that has since been regularly renewed and even expanded, thus turning these communities into significant vote banks. This contributed to the well-worn cliché that while people cast their votes in the rest of the world, in India, people vote their caste. Even class-based parties such as the Communist Party of India (CPI)-Marxist do not completely ignore the caste orientation of candidates when allotting tickets, whether in municipal, state or national elections.

As the party that led the Independence fight — Indians, raised on the non-violent ethos of Mahatma Gandhi, like to characterise it as a 'struggle' — the Indian National Congress dominated for the first three post-Independence decades. While socialist streams of this movement found a separate voice as early as 1925 — the birth year of the CPI — freedom provided the space for other groups such as the Hindu nationalists to emerge and assert separate identities.

Under Jawaharlal Nehru's dominating shadow, India gained three broad influences; secularism, socialism and dynasty. Nehru himself was a dynast — his father, the barrister Motilal Nehru, twice served as Congress president and Jawaharlal had succeeded his father to the position in 1929. Nehru's daughter, Indira Nehru Gandhi, and her son, Rajiv, would go to become Prime Ministers and party chiefs. Rajiv's widow, Sonia, is currently Congress president, having taken back the position from her son, Rahul. Her daughter, Priyanka Gandhi Vadra, is a Congress general secretary. While endemic in the Congress, several other parties are prone to this phenomenon.

After the Nehru-Gandhi family and the Congress' hold on the nation loosened after Indira Gandhi's unpopular Emergency Rule between 1975 and 1977, which saw the first non-Congress government in India, a ramshackle coalition that lasted for barely two-and-a-half years before Indira Gandhi swept back to power. Upon her assassination in 1984, she was succeeded by her son, Rajiv, who ruled for five years, the Congress yielding to another coalition at the federal level.

Since then, India has been run by coalition governments. Although this era effectively ended with the Bharatiya Janata Party's (BJP) Narendra Modi wave in 2014, and the Prime Minister's resounding re-election in 2019, India is nominally run by the National Democratic Alliance (NDA). While dominant BJP fielded candidates for 437 of the 543 seats contested for the powerful Lower House of Parliament, Lok Sabha, another 18 parties gathered under the NDA fought the rest. The BJP won 303 of these seats — a success rate of nearly 70 percent — the rest, put together, accounted for 50 seats for an NDA total of 353.

Post-Emergency politics centred around three broad themes.

The first and most visibly successful is embodied in the rise of the BJP as the dominant national party. While retaining and even enhancing some of the socialist policies of the Congress, the BJP has positioned itself as an anti-dynasty grouping that stands vehemently in contrast to the unevenly applied secularism of the Congress and its supposed pandering of minorities, chiefly Muslims.

The second wellspring was from the splintering of the Congress' political compact, KHAM, or Kshatriya dominant castes, Harijans — former Untouchables also known as Dalits — Adivasi aboriginals and Muslims. This led to the rise of the Dalit-oriented Bahujan Samaj Party and Samajwadi Party, a collection of backward castes that rank above the Dalits but low in the Hindu social order, nevertheless. These castes, according to a government report of 1980, constitute 52 percent of India.

A third feature was the emergence of powerful regional groups of proven durability, a phenomenon that manifested early in provinces such as Tamil Nadu and the now-splintered Jammu and Kashmir state. Today, Tamil Nadu and several other populous states, including West Bengal, Maharashtra, Orissa, as well as Andhra Pradesh and its rump state, Telangana, are controlled by regional parties, while in Kerala to the southwest, the ruling CPI-Marxist is a regional outfit for all practical purposes after it was decimated in its longtime bastion, West Bengal.

In a perverse way, Prime Minister Modi's overwhelming dominance of the BJP and the nation has left his party without powerful regional leaders who could, say, take on a Mamata Banerjee (current Chief Minister) in West Bengal. And even when Modi brings his powerful oratory to West Bengal, he cannot live down the perception of being a 'Hindi wallah' addressing an intensely culturally proud Bengali populace. In Punjab, Chief Minister Amarinder Singh of the Congress embodies in himself a Punjabi personality rather than being a mere satrap of the Gandhi-led party. Try as it might, the BJP's communalism has not fully succeeded in blunting regionalism.

Since the turn of the century, the rise of the Hindu as an ethnic category, based on majoritarian logic, is the big change that has settled over the Indian political landscape. Today, many Indians vote as 'Hindus' and the BJP appears to be able to count a third of the electorate as a secure vote bank. While the BJP's muscular Hinduism is borne equally from its roots in the Hindu nationalist Rashtriya Swayamsevak Sangh movement, it also denotes a calculated ploy to paper over the multiple fissures in Hindu society.

To do this successfully, however requires an identification and vilification of the 'other', and the BJP has profitably found this 'other' in the country's substantial Muslim minority, estimated to number more than 180 million.

The Muslims are easy targets because at Independence, Pakistan, whose eastern wing broke away in 1971 to become the new nation of Bangladesh, was carved out of India as a homeland for the Muslims. Mohmmed Ali Jinnah, who led the fight for a Pakistan, saw the two communities as being so dissimilar in religion, thought and social customs as to warrant a new life as separate nations. This 'two-nation theory', robustly rejected by Nehru, Mahatma Gandhi and their political legatees, has increasingly found fertile ground among the Hindu majority in India. While dog whistling at Muslims is commonplace in BJP political campaigns, including that of Modi, it is notable that even the Congress, moulded by Nehru's fierce secularism and currently led by the Italian-born Sonia Gandhi, has not been able to avoid, or unable to resist, projecting its 'Hindu' credentials. During the 2019 campaign for parliamentary elections, her first-born Rahul, son of a Roman Catholic mother and a half-Zoroastrian father, projected himself as a temple-going worshipper of the Hindu God Siva and as one who habitually wears the sacred thread of the twice-born Hindu. This was a tactic clearly meant to blunt the BJP's attacks on the Gandhi family's 'foreign' orientations although it is unclear whether it paid political dividends, given the dismal showing of Congress in the national poll. Still, the political scientist Pradeep Chhibber, Director of the Institute of International Studies at the University of California-Berkeley and Chair of India Studies, says that while there are no good studies showing how much religion affects Indian politics, Indians tend to be pious and "in a ritualistic society, rituals matter."

As India's democracy matured over the last seven decades, so too did the voters. Increasingly, Indians seem to distinguish between who they want to see govern them at the provincial level and who they want to place in the federal government. After giving the BJP a clean sweep of all seven parliamentary seats from Delhi in 2019, voters there did an about-face to give a second, resounding endorsement of the Aam Aadmi Party for the Delhi state assembly in the elections held in February 2020. Such examples are numerous. For instance, in Madhya Pradesh, India's largest state by territory, the BJP-led alliance improved its parliamentary tally to all but one of the 29 seats from the state, five months after yielding power to a Congress-led state government.

Especially viewed from the Singapore perspective, a big question about India is why a country with such notable talent in science and corporate management does not throw up politicians of matching quality. One palpably visible weakness in India's democracy is the high entry barriers, particularly the large amounts of money required to fight a credible campaign at any level and the use of muscle by parties, factors leading to the criminalisation of politics. This perception of politics as a 'dirty' game has prevented top professionals and many idealistic and qualified youth from considering careers in politics. Many who are inclined to serve, therefore, are more comfortable going the non-government organisation route.

An analysis by *India Today* magazine showed that, of 539 winners in the 2019 parliamentary poll, 233 members of parliament had declared criminal cases against themselves when filing papers. This, the magazine said, denoted a 44-percent increase from a decade earlier. While candidates with clean records had a 4.7 percent chance of victory, those with cases against them were assessed at having a 15.5-percent chance.

The true costs of fighting elections can be multiples of that permitted by the Election Commission of India. For instance, in 2019, it was estimated that a credible campaign for a state seat cost a candidate ₹50 million (S$935,000), and for a national seat, ₹200 million (S$3.74 million) — this in a nation where monthly per capita income was estimated at ₹11,254 (S$210) in 2019–20. Since most parties expect their candidates to substantially self-fund their campaigns, this elicits obligations and tradeoffs that subsequently manifest in governance distortions and stops professional classes from considering careers in politics even if they have independent means.

Given the increased voter participation in polls, suggesting Indians see value in the democratic process, this is indeed a pity.

43

Business Ties between India and Singapore

Benjamin Yap

Many accounts of business relations between India and Singapore begin the narrative with the early 1970s when Singapore was building new townships domestically while actively pursuing foreign investments to help industrialise the country post-independence.

My formative years thus were surrounded by services and products which bore marks of India. This included individuals like Mr Raju, a migrant from Tamil Nadu, who cut my hair and completed it with a sturdy massage of the neck and shoulders, or Ms Nadesan, who taught me English Literature with the textbook in one hand and a wooden ruler in the other. I also recall the 'smart city' technologies of the day such as Godrej door locks and Usha ceiling fans which featured vividly in my memory. Beyond the confines of my childhood encounters, Indian companies like the Tata Group had, by then, already established a strong presence in Singapore. Today, its services encompass steel manufacturing, communications and consulting, among others, and it has made Singapore the nodal office for its international operations.

India-Singapore Connect

Singapore's efforts to reach out to the world during that time took off with the formation of Singapore Airlines (SIA) in 1972. Soon after its inception, cities in the Indian sub-continent were added to SIA's destination list. Some accounts say that SIA modelled its flight operations and in-flight services after Air India, the leading airline in the region at the time.

This connectivity led to a jump in visitor arrivals from India to Singapore. Within a decade from 1979 when Singapore reportedly welcomed over 70,000 annual visitors from India to Singapore, the numbers quickly tripled to nearly 200,000. By 2019, arrivals from India had multiplied 20 times over to 1.4 million visitors.

Today, Singapore is home to over 350,000 Indian expatriates. It reportedly also counts the highest number of Indian Institutes of Technology and Indian Institutes of Management alumni in any city outside India.

At the outset, our business ties with India were driven along two parallels of social and economic development which have been closely intertwined. Arguably, the two parallels have created a unique value proposition between Singapore and India, based on relevance and complementarity that spans three fronts. The three fronts are trade, investment and finance, and digital, the third being a loose proxy for technology and innovation. While the first two fronts are well developed and continue to grow and evolve, the digital front is somewhat nascent and exciting, offering great opportunities for both countries.

Trade

India and Singapore entered into a free trade agreement (FTA) under the Comprehensive Economic Cooperation Agreement (CECA) in 2005, marking a significant milestone in bilateral relations. This paved the way for increased market access and clarity on a broad range of tariff lines, accelerating trade growth between the two countries.

Between 2005 and 2019, bilateral trade between India and Singapore more than quadrupled from US$6.7 billion (S$9.6 billion) to US$27.9 billion (S$39.8 billion). On the heels of the CECA, the ASEAN-India FTA, signed in 2009, further extended the benefit for Singapore-based companies exporting out of countries such as Malaysia, Indonesia, Thailand and Vietnam. The CECA was subsequently enhanced in 2018 to include expanded tariff concessions for additional 30 products and improved rules of origin to provide more flexibility for Singapore exports into India to qualify for preferential tariffs under the agreement.

At the infrastructure level, expansion in container handling capacity has also grown with trade. For example, PSA International's Bharat Mumbai Container Terminals at Jawaharlal Nehru Port Trust in Mumbai was opened in 2018 with an annual capacity of 2.4 million twenty-foot equivalent units (TEUs) in India's busiest container terminal. A further 2.4 million TEUs are slated for completion by 2023. This would significantly increase container handling capacity by 4.8 million TEUs for Western India to 17.5 million TEUs, enabling India to handle its growth in trade with the world.

In 2018, India and Singapore also launched a third review of the CECA to take discussions beyond tariff lines. The ongoing third review will look deeper into areas of trade facilitation, e-commerce, customs and movement of professional workers. What is notably exciting in the third review is that trade facilitation and e-commerce are largely technological and innovation intensive areas of cooperation that come under a digital front.

Investment and Finance

Every now and then, Singapore is mentioned in connection with business-related activities across India in the media. For example, Bengaluru-based real estate developer Prestige Group received an infusion of equity funds from Singapore's sovereign wealth fund, Government of Singapore Investment Corporation (GIC), to enable the former to pursue new real estate developments across India. GIC was also reportedly interested to venture further with investments into the infrastructure sector, in partnership with other players.

Earlier, in 2013, SIA and Tata Sons entered into a joint venture for the formation of a full-service carrier under the Vistara brand. The venture made entry into the challenging and competitive aviation sector. Starting off in the red, it required both investors to plan for the long haul. The SIA-Tata partnership, however, has allowed Vistara to tap not only into investments, but also SIA's expertise in aviation. Vistara has since gone beyond domestic flights to offer International destinations as well.

These examples are perhaps the more prominent of many partnerships and investment flows between India and Singapore, reflecting the relevance of Singapore as a place for enterprise and infrastructure financing for India. In FY2018/19, Singapore became India's largest source of foreign direct investment (FDI), registering over US$16 billion (S$22.8 billion) in FDI flows, overtaking Mauritius (US$8 billion [S$11.4 billion]), the Netherlands (US$3.9 billion [S$5.6 billion]), the United States (US$3.1 billion [S$4.4 billion]) and Japan (US$2.9 billion [S$4.1 billion]).

Other flows relate to asset management, trade finance, and foreign exchange and derivatives which reflect the multi-dimensional nature of India-Singapore financial ties. Looking ahead, I anticipate new areas such as sustainable finance will further deepen linkages between India and Singapore.

Digital

I use the term 'digital' as a loose proxy for the talent and innovation connect between India and Singapore. This third front is a confluence of a new generation of entrepreneurs, companies (start-ups) and, more vitally, a transnational and global business front that transcends nationality and traditional ideas of marketplaces. In my view, it is an area which has the potential to flourish as Indians and Singaporeans work together to create value in India, Singapore and globally.

Singapore and India entered into an agreement to work together on start-ups, financial technology, innovation, and science and technology as new areas of bilateral engagement during the visit of Indian Prime Minister Narendra Modi to Singapore in September 2018.

Prime Minister Modi's visit also coincided with India's first international launch of the Bharat Interface for Money-Unified Payments Interface (BHIM-UPI) app developed by the Indian government for money transfer between different banks to enable payments. Ideas about connecting India with Singapore in the area of payment were discussed during Prime Minister Modi's visit.

The discussions led to the BHIM-UPI app's first international linkage developed with the Network for Electronic Transfers of Singapore and the BHIM-UPI app was later pilot-launched in Singapore in 2019. Payments via the app are expected to be accepted by merchants across Singapore from 2020.

At the entrepreneurs' level, Singapore launched the Singapore Global Innovation Alliance (GIA), a network that aims to foster entrepreneurs coming together in the innovation space. To start, the GIA brought global players to host immersion programmes for Singapore start-ups entering India (for example, Anthill Ventures). Other efforts include tapping on networks to connect Singapore start-ups to mentors and venture capitalists (for example, The IndUS Entrepreneurs) or by providing flexible workspaces that serve as a launch pad for Singapore start-ups setting up their business in India (for example, Bridge + by CapitaLand located in the International Tech Park Bangalore).

These are early efforts which I believe will multiply in the days ahead as a new generation of knowledge workers from India and Singapore collaborates to create new enterprises with applications that span across a broad range of domains such as finance, medicine, artificial intelligence, blockchain, smart cities, internet-of-things, social media, agri-technology and more.

Looking Ahead

India and Singapore have successfully established strong ties in trade, and investment and finance in the first 50 years of bilateral relations. While we continue to strengthen bilateral trade flows and deepen investment and financial linkages, the future value of the digital front has the potential to exceed that of trade, and investment and finance. Growing this front will vitally depend on how each country develops its talent and technologies that will foster the connection between entrepreneurs and start-ups across India and Singapore.

Section III

THINKING ABOUT THE FUTURE

44

The India of My Dreams

Tommy Koh

My political awakening happened when I was in secondary school in the 1950s. I became aware that there was a worldwide movement of people living under colonial rule, and these people were rising up against their colonial masters. They wanted self-determination and independence.

The struggle by India against the British rule caught my imagination and support. There were two heroic figures in that struggle. They were Mahatma Gandhi and Pandit Jawaharlal Nehru. Gandhi's rejection of violence and his use of civil disobedience as a weapon against the British were contrarian and astonishing to a young student. Gandhi's victory in gaining independence for India in 1947 seemed like a miracle.

When Gandhi was assassinated on 30 January 1948, many of us cried. I am, therefore, shocked that there is a movement in India to glorify Gandhi's assassin, Nathuram Vinayak Godse. Something must be seriously wrong in India if the assassin of its national hero is being glorified instead of being vilified.

What is the India of my dreams?

First, I dream of an India which is secular. By this, I mean that the Indian state has no religion and all Indians have the constitutional right to choose their own religions. Hindus, Sikhs, Jains, Buddhists, Muslims, Christians, Zoroastrians, Jews, Bahais and atheists would live harmoniously with one another. The Hindus, who form the majority, would respect the other faiths and would not persecute any religious minority. India could be an example to the world of religious diversity and religious harmony.

Second, I dream of an India which is a strong and vibrant democracy. India has a population of 1.339 billion people. It will soon be the most populous country in the world. Some people say that China cannot become a democracy because it is too big. Those who make this argument have obviously forgotten the case of India. The success of the Indian democracy is particularly impressive as the country is culturally and linguistically diverse. It is, of course, true that the Indian democracy is not without its flaws. But it is impressive that a country with such a big population could go regularly to the polls to elect a government of its choice. Transitions of power take place peacefully. I dream of a day when vote-buying, corrupt politicians and criminal politicians and other irregularities will be a thing of the past.

Third, I dream of an India which is admired for its strong adherence to the rule of the law. The rule of law is one of humankind's most precious achievements. What it means is that no one is above the law and everyone is subject to the law. It means that the policeman, the prosecutor and the judge cannot be bought. In other words, justice is not for sale. It also means that the judiciary is independent of the executive. In the World Justice Project's Rule of Law Index 2019, India ranked 68 out of 126 countries. One of the reasons for India's low ranking is judicial delay. In India, it can take years for an aggrieved person to obtain justice through its courts. There are 4.3 million cases pending in the country's high courts, with 800,000 being over 10 years old. Another problem is the abuse of the legal system by unscrupulous persons as a means to extort money from persons they have sued. I dream of the day when India will be ranked among the top 10 countries of the world for the rule of law.

Fourth, I dream of an India in which girls and women will enjoy equal rights with boys and men. In the World Economic Forum's Global Gender Gap Index, India is ranked 112 out of 153 countries. In the UNDP's Gender Inequality Index, India is ranked 135 out of 187 countries. The female literacy rate in India is 60.6 percent compared to 81.3 percent for men. The rates of malnutrition are exceptionally high for adolescent girls and pregnant and lactating women. Violence against women, especially sexual violence, has been on the rise. I dream of an India in which no person, no matter what caste he or she belongs to, will be discriminated against. I dream of a day in which the rights enshrined in the Universal Declaration of Human Rights and in the two covenants will be enjoyed by all Indians, irrespective of race, religion, gender and caste.

Fifth, I dream of an India in which the abject poverty we see today will no longer exist. According to the Indian government, 29.8 percent of the population lives below the poverty line. This means about 360 million people. This is based upon a poverty line fixed at US$0.65 a day. The World Bank draws the poverty line at US$2 a day. Whatever the figure, the number of poor people in India is shockingly high. Who are the poor people? They are farm workers in villages, casual workers in cities, the tribal people, the Dalits or Untouchables and the Muslims. To reduce poverty in India, we need the Indian economy to grow at a much faster rate than the present. We also need a fairer distribution of the fruits of economic progress. We need Indian leaders who will make the reduction of poverty, a national priority, not in words but in deeds.

Sixth, I dream of an India whose economy is on par with that of China. The two countries have populations of approximately the same size. However, in 2019, the Chinese economy was 4.78 times bigger than that of India. India has been grossly under-performing. In order to catch up with China, India has to raise its annual rate of growth to between 8 and 10 percent and maintain it at that level for two to three decades. Can it be done? The answer is yes if the government and people of India have a shared political will to accomplish that ambition.

Seventh, I dream of an India which is high for good governance and low for corruption. In Transparency International's Corruption Perception Index for 2019, India was ranked 80 out of 179 countries. Corruption is a serious problem in India. At present, India is ranked high for corruption and low for good governance. I would like to see that reversed.

Eighth, I dream of an India which is admired for its soft power. India has a rich and ancient civilisation. Hinduism, Buddhism, Sikhism and Jainism are four of the world's great religions. India is renowned for its Bollywood movies and its cricket stars. Gandhi, Nehru, Rabindranath Tagore and Amartya Sen are world icons. However, in spite of these assets, India's soft power today is weak. In the 2019 Soft Power 30, India is not included in the top 30 countries for soft power. I have asked the author of the index why India is not included. He said that there were too many negatives about India, for example, poverty and inequality, oppression of women and other minorities, polluted cities, poor state of education and public health, etc.

Conclusion

The India of my dreams is a secular India and a model of religious diversity and harmony. It is a vibrant democracy with a strong adherence to the rule of law. It protects the rights of girls, women, Dalits, the tribal people and other minorities. India will have caught up with China economically. Poverty will be reduced to below 10 percent. India's soft power will be admired by the world. I hope that the India of my dreams will, one day, become a reality.

45

India: A Brave and Imaginative Superpower?

Kishore Mahbubani

Fortune favours the brave, the Ancient Romans said.

This is equally true for individuals as it is for nations. India is now about to enter a geopolitical sweet spot. It will have a once-in-a-millennia opportunity to emerge as the world's most respected superpower. The only question is whether it will be able to muster the courage and the imagination needed to seize this opportunity.

So, where does this opportunity come from? It comes from many sources. First, we are entering a new historical era. The artificial era of Western domination of world history is coming to an end. Second, we are seeing the natural return of China and India as the world's largest economies. This is perfectly natural as China and India were the largest economies of the world from 1 to 1820 AD, as documented by Angus Maddison. Third, the world has shrunk. As Kofi Annan said, we live in a global village. In the 20th century, the American century, the United States (US) naturally provided leadership of this global village. Post-Donald Trump, the US has lost its shine. The world is, therefore, looking for a new guiding light. India can provide a festival of lights.

However, to emerge and be globally acknowledged as a leading superpower, India has to develop a unique combination of three strengths: economic heft, geopolitical shrewdness and moral courage. All three are within reach of India.

Take economic heft. In theory, India should have the most competitive economy in the world. Empirical evidence backs this claim. The most competitive human laboratory in the world is the US. The best minds from all over the world come to compete in the world's best universities and companies in the US. Guess which ethnic group has the highest per capita income in the most competitive human laboratory? It is the Indian community. Indeed, it is even more striking that if we add up the market capitalisation of the American companies that have been run by Indians born in India, including Google, Adobe, Microsoft, MasterCard, PepsiCo and Micron, this sum could add up to around US$2 trillion (S$2.85 trillion). By comparison, the gross domestic product of India, with a population of 1.3 billion, is US$2.7 trillion (S$3.85 trillion).

Curiously, even though overseas Indians thrive in competition, India, as a country, is still wary of economic competition. This explains, in part, India's reluctance to join free trade agreements like the Regional Comprehensive Economic Partnership. The reluctance could have also been due to opposition from vested interests. The corollary of the concept of economic competition is creative destruction. The sad reality is that if India tries to protect its current industries (some of which are globally uncompetitive), it is preventing the emergence of dynamic new industries which could be as globally competitive as the American companies run by Indians. Surely, if Indians can run the most competitive companies in the world, they can also develop the most competitive companies in India. This is why India needs to make a courageous leap into the future with its economic policies. If any Indian government official opens up and liberalises the Indian economy, it will be rewarded by years of rapid growth a decade later, as proven by the bold liberalisation moves made by Manmohan Singh and Montek Singh

Ahluwalia in the early 1990s. Jeffrey Sachs of Columbia University and a leading expert on the fight against poverty states this in his book, *The End of Poverty: Economic Possibilities of Our Time*. Before the reforms, "India remained trapped with low and erratic growth… Enter Manmohan Singh, who understood clearly that it was time to end the License Raj. From mid-1991 onwards, India became part of the global wave of market reforms…" These reforms were met with a lot of scepticism. Sachs writes:

> My protestations that trade liberalization works — that India's exports were bound to grow — were met with repeated warnings that 'India was different'… To nearly worldwide astonishment, India became the hub of large-scale service-sector exports in the new information technologies.

Just as courage paid off in the 1990s, it can also pay off in the 2020s.

Similarly, geopolitical shrewdness is clearly within reach of India. There is now no question that the biggest geopolitical contest in the next few decades will be between China and the US, as I document in great detail in my book, *Has China Won*? The luckiest country in this geopolitical contest is India. Both the US and China are courting India assiduously as they know that the only country that has the heft to tilt the geopolitical balance one way or another is India. It doesn't take a geopolitical genius to figure out the best place for India to be in this geopolitical context. If an Indian Henry Kissinger or George Kennan were advising India, he would say: just imagine China and the US as two elephants balancing each other on the two ends of a see-saw. The best place for the third elephant to take would be to stand in the middle of the see-saw. Whichever way the third elephant leans will significantly affect the geopolitical balance between the US and China.

This is geopolitical common sense. Yet, it is equally true that a strong head of steam has built up in the Indian body politic against China. Some of it is understandable. China's support of Pakistan against Indian interests has jeopardised Indian security. Yet, this is also where geopolitical shrewdness comes in. During the Cold War, the US supported Taiwan strongly. China claimed Taiwan. The Chinese and American positions were irreconcilable. Mao Zedong and Chou Enlai could have insisted that Nixon and Kissinger abandon Taiwan completely before China could cooperate with the US. China pragmatically ignored the Taiwan issue and instead used the US to increase its geopolitical leverage. China's rapid emergence as an economic power could not have happened if it had not cleverly taken advantage of all the opportunities provided by the US (big markets, access to science and technology and university education for China's youth). Clearly China took advantage of its potential future adversary, the US, to enhance the social and economic transformation of its society. Today, India could take advantage of the economic opportunities provided by China, for example, the Belt and Road Initiative (BRI). Right now, joining the BRI is an unthinkable option in India. Geopolitical shrewdness would recommend that no option be deemed unthinkable.

Finally, moral courage. The country that has produced the most morally courageous leader in the world is India. Mahatma Gandhi epitomises this moral courage. He didn't just care for India. He cared for humanity as a whole. As Prime Minister Narendra Modi said:

> Whether it's climate change or terrorism, corruption or selfishness in public life, Gandhiji's ideals are the guiding light for us when it comes to protecting humanity. I believe that the path shown by Gandhiji will lead to a better world.

What would Gandhi say if he were alive today? He was a great admirer of the US. In 1931, he said: "When real Peace and Disarmament come, they will be initiated by a strong nation like America..." Gandhi would, therefore, be deeply troubled by the rallying cry of President Trump: "Make America Great Again". He would expect America, the richest and most powerful country in the world, to make the world great again.

Yet, it is equally true that there is a great sense of exhaustion in the American body politic about providing leadership to the world.

Domestically, America is a deeply troubled society. It is the only major developed society where the average income of the bottom 50 percent has gone down over a 30-year period. As Anne Case and Angus Deaton, two Princeton University economists, say, the White working classes of America used to carry the American dream of getting a better life in their hearts and souls. Today, however, there is a 'sea of despair' among them. In view of this, the US can no longer be the 'Shining City on the Hill'. Neither can China take this role. The Chinese believe that their civilisation is one of the best in the world. However, it is a civilisation that can primarily be enjoyed by the Chinese. The Chinese, unlike the Americans, have no universalising mission.

This provides India a unique opportunity. As we move away from a mono-civilisational world dominated by the West to a multi-civilisational world where Asian civilisations are coming back strongly, the world is looking for leaders to provide bridges between the East and the West. India is in a unique position to provide such bridges. It is trusted by both the East and the West.

The world is, therefore, longing for a moral leader like Gandhi who will point out the follies of the many wars that the West had engaged in. Indian voices do speak out. For example, Shyam Saran, a leading Indian official, has written eloquently about the folly of Western interventions:

> In most cases, the post-intervention situation has been rendered much worse, the violence more lethal and the suffering of the people who were supposed to be protected much more severe than before. Iraq is an earlier instance; Libya and Syria are the more recent ones. A similar story is playing itself out in Ukraine. In each case, no careful thought was given to the possible consequences of the intervention.

Likewise Shivshankar Menon, former National Security Advisor to the Indian government stated:

> Unilateral (sometimes covert) interventions, as in Libya or Syria, have led to unexpected and dangerous outcomes... We clearly need

> to improve, strengthen and use the processes and institutions of multilateral consultation and action available to the international community.

Menon is right. Multilateralism is the solution. India is a natural leader in the multilateral arena.

In 1941, Henry Luce exhorted Americans to realise an American century through an imaginative vision:

> No narrow definition can be given to the American internationalism of the 20th Century. It will take shape, as all civilisations take shape, by the living of it, by work and effort, by trial and error, by enterprise and adventure and experience.
>
> And by imagination!

Luce was right. The American century was brilliant and inspiring because it was driven by imagination. Today, India has that opportunity to be equally imaginative. It should seize the moment.

46

India's Aspiration of Growing into a Manufacturing Power

Dipinder S. Randhawa

India's development path in recent decades has traversed a distinct trajectory. In contrast to the experience of developed economies where growth was led by industrialisation, India's development was spearheaded by the growth of services.

Industrial development forms the bulwark for employment, growth and the emergence of a middle class. India, however, may well be deindustrialising before developing a mass industrial base. Industrial growth in India plateaued at a much lower share of gross domestic product than in countries at comparable stages of development. Why has India grown along such a different path? Despite starting from a diversified, if modest, industrial base, why did industry stagnate? Can India realise its ambition of becoming an industrial power? Will the COVID-19 pandemic impair prospects for industrialisation?

The Legacy

The reasons underlying the services-led growth experience have a bearing on India's aspiration to grow into a global manufacturing power. The policy framework articulated in 1956 with the onset of economic planning defined India's strategy for transformation into a modern industrialised economy. The belief was that a large, newly-independent developing economy, impoverished over an extended colonial period and by the depredations of World War II, needed to establish a foundation of basic industries, including steel, cement, power generation and heavy machinery, which would form the bedrock for development. The nascent industrial sector was sheltered behind tariff walls that planners hoped would give the economy time and the space to grow, while the private sector would be subject to controls and quotas to deter the emergence of monopolies. Foreign investment, though welcome, was limited to industries deemed to be of national interest. Once an industrial base was established, the economy would open up to trade and foreign investment.

By the end of the 1960s, India had developed an industrial base with a network of steel plants, a growing power generation sector and a network of institutions of research and higher learning. The fruits of the green revolution in agriculture were evident in the rapid growth of agricultural output. Many observers suggested the time was right to open up the economy to increased trade and investment, encourage investment by the private sector, introduce competition and efficiency in the public sector, and draw much-needed capital to boost investment. However, an increasingly inclement domestic environment and later an unfavourable external environment, and a focus on 'self sufficiency' only served to steer the economy towards an increasing regulatory grip on economic activity.

This import substitution strategy of industrialisation continued until the 1980s. Rigid labour laws shielded workers from layoffs, rendering labour markets inflexible and, ironically, discouraging labour-intensive manufacturing. Banks were nationalised in 1971, and the market for land for use for industry limited. Thus, all factors of production — land, labour and capital — were heavily regulated, impairing the flexibility firms need to operate in competitive markets. As growth in size would attract stringent regulations, firms chose to remain small, and facing little competition, had minimal incentives to innovate and grow.

The consequences of decades of protectionist barriers was a diverse, albeit, sheltered, high cost and inefficient industrial sector, uncompetitive in international markets. In most industries, the average size of firms was smaller than that needed to realise economies of scale. Furthermore, restrictions in labour markets induced modernising enterprises to adopt capital-intensive production techniques. Investments were further hobbled by the poor quality of infrastructure. An unintended but predictable consequence of the approach was widening income inequality and increasing disparities across states, as high-value investments gravitated towards states with better infrastructure and a skills base. Over time, the high demand for energy imports, coupled with low exports and a fixed exchange rate, resulted in a steadily increasing trade deficit. By 1991, India was faced with a severe balance of payments crisis and forced to turn to the International Monetary Fund for an emergency loan.

Post-1991

The reforms of 1991, resulting in the opening of the domestic and external economies, were a watershed. Trade, investment and consumption boomed, leading to annual growth rates reaching well over eight percent by 2005–06 and a near tripling of per capita incomes in 20 years. Investment flowed into high-technology skill-intensive sectors, such as information, communications and technology and finance, and into states with proactive business policies, skilled labour force and sound infrastructure — accentuating disparities within and across states. By contrast, manufacturing attracted a modest volume of investment with industry continuing to bear a heavy regulatory burden. Despite prospects of a demographic dividend, and producing outstanding engineers and technical experts, poor standards in primary and secondary education and at skill development institutions resulted in low levels of skill acquisition for the majority of youth, leading to a conundrum — a labour surplus economy faced with perennial shortages of skilled labour.

Looking Ahead

India's biggest challenge today is to create jobs for the millions of youth entering the labour force every month, a tiny fraction of whom are absorbed in formal employment. The remainder find work in the vast amorphous informal sector. History shows that no economy has developed without industrialising and opening up to trade and investment. It is difficult to envision an alternative path to development. Can India expand its industrial base and absorb the millions of youth seeking work with decent wages and prospects for economic mobility? Can the economy cope with the devastation wreaked by the COVID-19 pandemic and get back on track?

The answer is yes and it may well lie in the Fourth Industrial Revolution (4IR). This revolution encompasses new technologies such as robotics, artificial intelligence, smart manufacturing and additive manufacturing. A transition to the 4IR, though challenging, is feasible and would require sweeping reforms exceeding the scale of those carried out in 1991. Contrary to the belief that manufacturing across the world is shrinking, it is actually increasingly concentrated in a smaller number of countries. Few countries have the capabilities to enter the 4IR. High technological barriers, increasing levels of skill requirements and the challenge and capabilities required to integrate with the global economy — through value chains and trade — limit prospects for most countries. The pandemic will pose serious challenges, aside from triggering nationalist and protectionist instincts around the world. India has not been immune to these trends.

Public and private debt are already stretched to the limits. The deep recession that is likely to follow will further inhibit efforts to take on the challenge of reforms. However, closed doors and inward looking policies will further margnialise the economy and risk a vicious cycle of falling productivity and competitiveness and a return to low growth rates.

On a positive note, segments of Indian industry are already enmeshed in the 4IR. The use of robots in manufacturing (Maruti, Hyundai), smart firms (Mahindra & Mahindra), artificial intelligence (Amazon, Flipkart) additive manufacturing (Maruti, Hindustand Aeronautics) and the emergence of a small cohort of 'smart' firms (Mahindra & Mahindra, Bharat Forge) are indicative of India's potential to bypass mass manufacturing into the 4IR. Rather than a binary view, the transition to the 4IR from traditional manufacturing should be viewed on a continuum, a growing cohort of firms are at various stages of deploying elements of new technologies. However, as in many other countries, high technology manufacturing in India is confined to 'technology islands' where a few digital leaders coexist with a vast majority of firms using outdated technologies.

India undoubtedly has the potential to stake a claim and make a name for itself as a global centre of high-technology manufacturing excellence. The globalisation of manufacturing continues to be the main driver of job creation and the rise of a middle class in developing economies. However, certain preconditions have to be met first. The question is what does India need to do develop cutting-edge 4IR firms such as Tesla? Three areas merit particular attention.

1) The most critical need is to invest in its citizens and equip them with the wherewithal to participate in the evolving knowledge economy. The 4IR demands high levels of cognitive and non-cognitive skills — areas where a large part of the population falls short. While India produces outstanding information technology professionals, they are a tiny proportion of the cohort entering the labour force every year. School and college graduates fall substantially short of international requirements on virtually every measure. The problem starts at a very young age. Despite near universal enrolment, evaluation tests reveal learning levels are far below what they should be at every level of schooling. These learning deficits carry on through the education life cycle. To reap

the 'demographic dividend', public authorities should endeavour to raise learning standards from the primary school or even earlier and start nurturing digital skills soon. A massive increase in investment in education, starting with early childhood education to address deeply embedded socio-economic inequities, and skill development as well as the use of digital technologies and interactive pedagogic techniques are imperative for India's aspirations as a 4IR power. Investment in secondary and tertiary education needs to be ramped up substantially. As the Knowledge Commission pointed out in 2016, skills and innovation can be boosted only if there is close collaboration between academia, research and industry. This is particularly true for skill development institutions.

2) While India's rise in the Ease of Doing Business rankings is evident, much remains to be done to attract and nurture domestic as well as foreign investors, including rationalising and streamlining the regulatory permissions required for projects, enhancing the flexibility of labour markets and digitising regulatory compliance and clear tax planning and administration that would do away with oddities such as retrospective taxation. The development of a digital infrastructure, ranging from broadband access to cloud computing, is essential. Policy-makers should streamline and accelerate efforts to create a conducive environment for start-ups.

   India must commit to greater multilateral engagement. In a period of growing economic nationalism, there is a pressing need to rethink the stand on the Regional Comprehensive Economic Partnership (RCEP) and engage with its member economies. The appeal runs both ways. The member states of the RCEP remain keen and committed to bringing India on board. Trade liberalisation has unequivocal benefits, but to attract capital and investment, trade in services also needs to be liberalised. Streamlining trade facilitation will help lower costs of trade.

3) Policy design should keep the objective — the firm — in view. The Indian government has launched programmes to invigorate

industrial growth, including the 'Make in India', 'Digital India', 'Start-up India' and 'Skill India' programmes. The challenge for policy-makers is to create an ecosystem with incentives for firms to adopt 4IR technologies. The state acts as a catalyst providing information and access, through conduits such as international partnerships, incentives for research and development, sharing of expertise, technology transfers, knowledge banks, boosting connectivity and easing access to finance. To enhance access for small and medium enterprises (SME), India needs to deregulate further and streamline regulatory processes. The experiences of Germany, Singapore and the United States (US) offer useful insights into policies and institutions, including the benefits of clusters that help the SME sector move up the value ladder.

The effects of the COVID-19 pandemic have been devastating for public health and the economy. Uncertainty about the multilateral trading system, the consequences of the disputes between the US and China and steady hardening of attitudes cloud prospects for the global economy, and, of course, for India. However, aside from the stated risks, there may be opportunities for India to work towards attracting investment and capital. A steady, concerted shift towards removing domestic obstacles and streamlining processes to facilitate domestic and foreign trade and investment could provide the much-needed boost India needs to propel it on the path to the 4IR. At the very least, this would call for reforms in labour laws, a proactive policy nurturing active collaboration between skilling institutions and industry to equip labour with skills needed in the marketplace, reforms in the judicial system to expedite resolution of disputes, or ceding to arbitration tribunals in India and overseas, urgent reforms in logistics — some of which are already underway, and raising the efficiency of ports to internationally competitive levels.

For inclusive sustainable growth, it is imperative that India works diligently and relentlessly towards social cohesion by stamping out divisive forces and offering its vast, diverse and talented citizenry an opportunity to grow and realise its potential. The bilateral dispute with China, the uncertainties permeating supply chains opening up opportunities for India, and the availability of capital — if reforms are executed — offers India a distinct opportunity to chart a path to a new environment-friendly path to growth.

India's strength as a rising digital power places it in a favourable position to capitalise on the opportunities offered by the 4IR. It needs to develop an ecosystem that offers socio-economic stability and attracts investment in this growing sector, drawing upon the capabilities of its vast and accomplished diaspora. Singapore and the rest of Southeast Asia are keen on seeing India on board as a major 4IR power — a prospect that will be of immense benefit to all of South and Southeast Asia.

47

Achieving Inclusive Prosperity in India: Tackling the Fundamentals

Tharman Shanmugaratnam

India has the largest unfulfilled social and economic potential of any country today. I say this as a friend, and from a country that wants India to succeed and play a full and positive role in the world.[1]

There have been impressive strides in recent years, especially in India's social infrastructure. The results speak for themselves — electrification, sanitation, bank accounts and a basic health safety net have been brought to the villages and the vast majority of the population. India is achieving this in a nation of unparalleled scale and diversity. It provides the world with many lessons in development.

However, India's challenges remain immense. The central problem is a lack of jobs for the mass of young people. Failure to address this gap and meet their aspirations will have more than economic consequences. However, it can only be achieved through a bold effort to erase long-standing legacies.

[1] This essay draws on two lectures delivered by Senior Minister Tharman Shanmugaratnam in India: the Suresh Tendulkar Memorial Lecture delivered at the Reserve Bank of India on 7 January 2020 and the Inaugural NITI Lecture on Transforming India in New Delhi on 26 August 2016.

In its first seven decades, government in India has over-intervened in the economy, while under-investing in human and social development. The legacy of the 'Licence Raj', beginning with Nehruvian state planning and import-substitution from the time of independence, and compounded over many years, still weighs heavily on the economy. The legacy of social neglect goes much further back in history, but has also persisted in independent India, including an education system that is an injustice on most young people.

Overcoming these legacies is complex, but a fundamental and pressing task. The next phase of India's development must involve a major step-up in both social and economic transformation. The two go together. India needs stronger economic growth to create enough jobs and achieve inclusive prosperity. But without social transformation, it will not be possible to achieve economic vibrance and realise India's potential.

It needs a greater sense of urgency in politics, society and the business community. India faces a race against demography. Its labour force is growing by 12 million young people each year, the largest in the world. But job creation is less than three million a year. Youth unemployment and underemployment is already very large, and growing.

India also faces a race against technology. The next five years are critical. If we look at what is happening globally in supply chains, and the increasingly intelligent machines and software being introduced in every sector, time is not on India's side. It has to regear quickly to reskill and upskill people, and get them into jobs which offer a ladder of future improvement and wage increases.

India needs growth of 8 to 10 percent per year over the next 20 years, to prevent significant increases in unemployment and to get closer to realising its potential. It is much higher than the six-plus percent average over the last 20 years, but a vital goal. And even with 8 to 10 percent growth, India would in 20 years reach little more than today's level of per capita income in China.

It will require bold strokes in economic and social policy to achieve this. But we should avoid the misconception that the task is simply about reducing the role of government and growing the role of markets. We cannot get an inclusive society and vibrant economy anywhere without good government and state capacity. What this really involves in India is a reorientation in the role of government.

India needs much stronger and more effective interventions in the social foundations for prosperity, especially in education and healthcare. It also needs to move away from a long-standing statist tradition in running and regulating the economy, towards investing in public goods and enabling enterprises and workers to build up capabilities and compete globally.

The social foundations are where the gaps are most critical. There have been improvements in primary school enrolment and the transition to secondary school, but the quality of learning is still India's biggest crisis. More than half of India's children fail to reach the basic reading proficiency expected by the later years of primary school; many fall well below. Yet, the country also has exceptional talent. Those who go to the Indian Institutes of Technology and Indian Institutes of Management are first rate by international standards. India has the biggest gap I know of, between the talent at the top and the unfulfilled potential of the vast majority.

But it is the state of education for girls that expresses most profoundly India's social challenges, and is rightly receiving greater attention now. It is at the heart of a vicious cycle of poverty, girls shouldering the burden of housework, their high drop-out rates from school, early marriage and poor maternal and child nutrition. These gender inequalities limit girls' ability to live a life of their choosing, but also perpetuate broader social inequalities in the next generation. Deep-set social attitudes make this a complex challenge, but there are essential, practical steps that will enable progress. The proportion of schools with usable toilets for girls doubled between 2010 and 2018, although a third of schools were still without.

There is cause for optimism in NITI Aayog's state-level School Education Quality Index. It ranks states and puts information in the public eye. The results show large variation in standards across states, highlighting the gaps that can potentially be closed. The fact that some states — both small and large — have made major improvements in the space of a few years shows how long-standing legacies of mismanagement and neglect can be overcome. It comes down to the current policy focus on the governance of education, especially in the recruitment of teachers and selection of school leaders. This is the biggest decider of quality in schools, in districts and states. Transparency and incentives for local authorities, and for educationists themselves, matter greatly in education.

In healthcare too, there are pilot projects where good results are being achieved, and which only need to be scaled up. *Poshan Abhiyaan* is now the world's largest nutrition programme, aimed at expectant mothers and the first thousand days of a child's life. It was started in Maharashtra more than a decade ago, and began showing very significant reductions in childhood stunting. State Nutrition Missions were then introduced in several other states — Madhya Pradesh, Uttar Pradesh, Gujarat and Karnataka. India now has a national Nutrition Mission.

The problems in human development are hence not insoluble. Improvements are being seeded locally, including in India's 'Aspirational Districts' that have long lagged in human development, and scaled up across the country. There is a gathering momentum.

India is also rightly focused on skills development. Like many countries — but more than most — it faces a serious mismatch between the skills that young people are equipped with and the needs of the market. It requires a reorientation of tertiary education, away from an overly academic focus, towards applied, skills-oriented curricula that give the majority of young people greater confidence as they enter the workforce and seek to build a future. Here too, progress is being made. Singapore, as a much smaller nation, is contributing where it can by collaborating with the Indian government and a few state governments to develop technical training institutions that borrow from our own experience.

However, India also has to move more decisively to transform its economy. It will not solve the jobs shortage, and raise productivity and incomes significantly, without major reforms.

The solution to joblessness cannot be to keep people trapped in low-income, subsistence living in the rural heartlands. There is huge potential to lift productivity in Indian agriculture, as international comparisons make clear. Putting digital technologies in the hands of farmers will help them cut out middlemen and directly access seeds, fertilisers, credit and markets. Increased farm productivity will also help free up labour for jobs that offer better livelihoods elsewhere. Compared to East Asia, India has seen a much smaller shift of labour from low-productivity agriculture into manufacturing, infrastructural work and services in both rural hubs and the cities.

India should set its sights high in manufacturing and move quickly. It can be a major global producer in four to six industries. But to achieve this, India has to be more open to the world. No large developing country has achieved strong economic and jobs growth without strong export growth and progressive liberalisation of imports. The reason has to do with learning. Playing in the global competition, and being part of global value chains, brings a discipline of constant learning — and a whole ethos of wanting to meet the latest standards or even exceed them.

This essential lesson of the last four decades remains true even in today's less favourable global trade climate. There is still a huge world market. India also has the opportunity today to attract global producers as they seek to avoid over-reliance on existing bases. 'Make in India' has to be about making for the world.

However, to achieve global competitiveness, India also needs domestic reforms to enable firms to grow larger and to develop stronger supply-side capabilities.

India's labour market laws and rules, amongst the world's most rigid, have led to the bulk of its manpower being stuck in an informal urban sector and very small enterprises, besides the rural economy. Bolder reforms are needed to encourage small players to grow, and enable more manpower to be employed in medium- and large-sized firms and on long-term rather than short-term contracts so that firms have incentive to invest in their capabilities. Scale economies and investments in the workforce are critical for India to sustain higher productivity and wage growth.

Secondly, central and state governments can work actively with the private sector to develop the benefits of industrial clustering — or what economists call agglomeration economies — in specific industries. Clusters of firms and R&D and training institutions can create a growth dynamic by spurring innovation and skills upgrading, creating deeper supply networks, and reducing logistics costs. Andhra Pradesh's pharmaceutical cluster, one of the largest in the world, shows what is possible.

Finally, India has committed itself to a more sustainable economy, the critical 21st century goal. Together with a stronger system of basic healthcare and education, the transition towards clean energy and the green economy will be the most important externality that the state has to address in the years ahead. It is also integral to tackling the crisis of urban pollution and waste in Indian cities, and to any future conception of an inclusive society.

Cities have an important role to play in this. The rapid growth that India needs to create jobs and uplift incomes cannot rest on migration into ever larger and more congested cities. India will need new and more compact cities, including those close to the rural heartlands, which are cleaner, smarter and more inclusive. Implementation of the 'Smart Cities' programme, focused on water, sanitation and efficient urban mobility, will help achieve this. Indian cities can also benefit from governance changes to give urban local bodies more autonomy and hold them accountable.

I believe in India's potential. The weight of history constrains its progress. More than half a century of over-regulation, a many-layered bureaucracy, an inward-looking orientation and protection of inefficient businesses, cannot be quickly overcome, even with promising reforms. Nor will deeply-rooted social prejudices be easily erased. However, tackling these economic and social legacies requires much greater urgency now to meet the needs and aspirations of a young population, the scale of which no country has seen before.

The reforms require a long view, and are politically challenging. They are additionally complex in a federal structure with multiple states and rolling electoral contests, which make taking the long view more difficult. But India can, and will I hope, persevere in these reforms so as to achieve its immense potential, build socially-inclusive prosperity and provide lessons to the world in sustainable development.

48

India and Southeast Asia: The Unfinished Agenda

Pushpanathan Sundram

India and Southeast Asia share an economic, political and cultural history that can be traced back several centuries. There are close similarities in their languages, food, dressing habits, and cultures. However, their shared histories and commonalities have not resulted in a deeper modern-day relationship.

The basis of India's relationship with the erstwhile kingdoms of Southeast Asia was trade and commerce. Maritime trade flourished between the two regions, resulting in deeper political ties and exchanges of cultural influences. There was substantial migration too. Many traders and businessmen left the shores of India for better business prospects in the region and, of late, have been joined in no small measure by Indian professionals who have found employment here. Owing to these factors, the member states of the Association of Southeast Asian Nations (ASEAN) now account for a fifth of the 31 million overseas Indians comprising Indian citizens and persons of Indian origin.

Given these historical ties, stronger strategic and geopolitical ties between India and Southeast Asia should be a given but this has not fully materialised. While trade and investment numbers have increased steadily, the two entities have not been able to realise the full potential of deeper economic, political, diplomatic and strategic ties.

Together, India and Southeast Asia are home to two billion people and it is in their strategic interest to successfully forge closer relations with each other. One of the key factors that could (and should) drive the next phase of the relationship between ASEAN and India is the ambivalence of the United States (US) administration towards the region, which is being seen in tandem with the growing strategic and economic influence of China.

Strengthening Cooperation across Multiple Fronts

ASEAN-India bilateral trade has registered a substantial increase from just US$2.9 billion (S$4.14 billion) in 1993 to a hefty US$81.3 billion (S$116.1 billion) in 2017–18, owing largely to the ASEAN-India Free Trade Area (AIFTA), which came into effect at the beginning of 2010. Foreign direct investment inflows from India also saw a recovery in 2018 amounting to US$1.7 billion (S$2.32 billion). Both sides are now working towards achieving a total trade target of US$200 billion (S$273.6 billion) by 2022. The AIFTA came on the back of years of work behind the scenes which saw ASEAN and India come closer along several areas of mutual cooperation.

India became a Sectoral Partner of ASEAN in 1992, Dialogue Partner in 1996 and Summit-level Partner in 2002. It established a separate permanent mission to ASEAN in Jakarta, Indonesia, in April 2015 with a dedicated ambassador to strengthen engagement with ASEAN and ASEAN-centric processes. India is also member of the East Asia Summit comprising ASEAN, Australia, China, India, Japan, New Zealand, South Korea, the US and Russia.

Since 2014, India has in place an 'Act East' policy, which emerged from its earlier 'Look East' policy. The 'Act East' policy seeks to push for closer economic, strategic and diplomatic relations with the Asia-Pacific region, including ASEAN. The policy also takes into account security spheres, and it now involves the entire Indo-Pacific region. In its earlier version, it was limited to only Northeast and Southeast Asia. In recent years, there has also been a concerted effort by ASEAN and India to cooperate more closely across different areas.

ASEAN and India are deepening connectivity linkages, in keeping with the Master Plan on ASEAN Connectivity 2025, in the areas of land, air and maritime connectivity. India is pushing for the completion of the extension of the India-Myanmar-Thailand Trilateral Highway Project and the creation of an accompanying economic corridor and its possible subsequent extension to Cambodia, Laos and Vietnam. India has also earmarked a US$1 billion (S$1.43 billion) line of credit to boost infrastructure development and connectivity in the ASEAN region. There are also the ASEAN-India Air Transport Agreement and ASEAN-India Maritime Transport Agreement, which are currently awaiting conclusion.

Security is going to be an important area of cooperation going forward. In November 2018, ASEAN and India agreed to "deepen cooperation in countering terrorism, extremism and radicalisation through the sharing of best practices and information", law enforcement, and capacity-building under existing ASEAN-led mechanisms. They also agreed to strengthen cooperation on cyber-security capacity-building to address a growing, cross-border risk.

Besides, the softer element of cooperation in the form of deeper people-to-people ties is a key area of focus for the future. There are education- and youth-focused initiatives such as the ASEAN-India Youth Summit, the ASEAN-India Students Exchange Programmes, a media exchange programme and scholarship programmes, among others. These will allow the youth of the two regions to better understand one another, which in turn will help forge closer bonds in the future.

Cooperation on all these fronts and others such as agriculture, humanitarian relief, maritime affairs, science and technology, nuclear safety, governance, corruption, renewable energy and energy security, natural resources management, tourism and disaster management will be as important as economic cooperation in the deepening of the India-ASEAN partnership.

An Opportunity Missed?

India's pull-out of the Regional Comprehensive Economic Partnership (RCEP), while not a surprise given domestic political constraints, is an opportunity missed for deeper economic and strategic ties. It has also been referred to as a 'historic blunder'. Indian Prime Minister Narendra Modi's decision to withdraw from the RCEP is seen as a big setback in forging closer ties between India and Southeast Asia, particularly given that the RCEP is driven by ASEAN and has all 10 ASEAN-member states as signatories.

Joining the pact would have intertwined India's economic and strategic future with that of the ASEAN economies even more closely. India decided to not join the RCEP in late 2019, citing domestic economic reasons.

The RCEP is a partnership that goes beyond economics. It is a signal to the world that the countries of the Asia-Pacific region can put their differences aside to come together for the greater good. Through the RCEP, the region can build on trade and make its mark on the global rules-based order.

India has, however, not shut its doors on the RCEP yet and it is hoped that in the near future, once it is more comfortable with the terms of the RCEP, it will join the agreement that is likely to shape the economic and strategic future of the Indo-Pacific.

The Strategic Imperative

At a time when key members of the developed world are choosing to look inward — a trend that may continue in the wake of the COVID-19 pandemic — the mantle for supporting globalisation has fallen upon Asia.

In this context, apart from the obvious economic benefits of closer ties, Southeast Asia and India have much to gain strategically. While not always openly articulated, a key reason for the two regions wanting to engage more closely with each other is to balance the growing influence of China in Southeast Asia. China has become a critical economic partner for most Southeast Asian countries in the past two decades, resulting in greater geo-strategic influence — this is something that ASEAN would want to address as a grouping.

The territorial disputes in the South China Sea show that China is willing to adopt a more aggressive diplomatic stance over its territorial claims. In such a context, the presence of India as a counterweight is important for ASEAN. Moderating China's influence in the region is also important for India. In fact, in 2018, Prime Minister Modi wrote that India's relations with ASEAN are "free from contests and claims" and also that both India and ASEAN believe in "sovereign equality of all nations irrespective of size".

However, India's response to recent protests in the country relating to its passing of a Citizenship Amendment Act that is widely believed to discriminate against Muslims in the granting of citizenship to migrants has drawn the ire of prominent Southeast Asian countries such as Malaysia and Indonesia, important ASEAN members. This is an unanticipated development.

That said, there are far more commonalities than differences that must be emphasised. Even the problems faced by the two parties are largely similar — those of poverty, urbanisation-related challenges, the effects of climate change and the lack of adequate infrastructure, among others. ASEAN and India must collaborate to find solutions to these issues that will define the wider region's future, and which lend themselves to enhanced mutual cooperation and deeper ties.

Prospering Together

With globalisation fraying at its seams, Asia stands out as a champion for greater economic integration. It also stands at the forefront of addressing transboundary challenges such as climate change and transnational crimes, in particular, terrorism and cybercrime. The current global uncertainty should provide an impetus for ASEAN to enhance its strategic ties with key dialogue partners such as India to contribute to the maintenance of Asia's open regionalism.

ASEAN and India are natural allies with deep cultural, political, social and economic ties. By 2030, ASEAN and India are expected to be among the five largest economies in the world. Both will have a sizeable demographic dividend, which will present opportunities for the two to prosper together. These opportunities must be grasped.

The deeper trade and economic cooperation and enhanced strategic, diplomatic and people-to-people ties between ASEAN and India will contribute to a redefining of the global international order, and will leave a lasting imprint on the wider Asia region and its people.

49

India, Higher Education and Opportunities of Development

Tan Eng Chye

The linkages between India and Southeast Asia reach far back into recorded history, and probably even earlier. Over the course of many centuries, India has profoundly influenced the cultural, religious, political and even architectural development of the region. For its part, Southeast Asia has shown a remarkable ability to absorb and syncretise powerful influences, not just from India, but also China and the West and, in the process, create new and unique expressions and perspectives.

India is now ramping up ambitiously for the 21st century. Deutsche Bank projects that India's economy could reach US$7 trillion (S$10 trillion) by 2030 and the Japan Center for Economic Research forecasts that China and India will account for 35 percent of global gross domestic product by 2060. China and India will be the two key engines of growth in the coming Asian century.

Along with growth, India's global networks will expand. The Association of Southeast Asian Nations (ASEAN) has been highlighted as among the key regional groupings India will seek to interact with extensively. The engagement approach has been described as multi-dimensional, encompassing commerce, connectivity and culture — a 21st century envisioning of ancient models of exchange and trade.

The Indian government reported in 2018 that ASEAN is India's fourth largest trading partner, with trade valued at US$81.33 billion (S$116.78 billion), amounting to 10.6 percent of India's overall trade. Exports to ASEAN stand at 11.28 percent of India's total exports.

ASEAN is also on the move. By 2050, the combined regional grouping may be the fourth largest economy in the world, worth US$10 trillion (S$14.4 trillion). ASEAN's middle class could grow to 334 million people by 2030 and emerge as one of the most significant consumer markets globally.

Two great regions, connected by long historical associations, are poised to usher in an exciting and vibrant new era of exchange and interactions in the decades ahead.

As India's economy develops, knowledge creation, innovation, entrepreneurship and talent development will become leading drivers of growth and opportunity. The National University of Singapore (NUS) is well suited as a synergistic and collaborative partner to India's leading universities and companies, and help play a role in driving scientific advances, bringing ideas and solutions to markets, and enhancing human potential.

NUS has long placed great importance in our engagement with India. We established the Institute of South Asian Studies (ISAS) in 2004, and it has taken a leading role in developing knowledge and communicating insights about contemporary South Asia to policy-makers, the business community, academia and civil society. To enhance deeper understanding, we also established the South Asian Studies Programme at the Faculty of Arts and Social Sciences. It offers bachelor's, master's and doctorate qualifications and it is the only such programme in ASEAN.

Indian nationals have been attracted to the wide range of programmes we offer at NUS, particularly at the post-graduate level, ranging from executive training programmes to master's and PhD programmes. For example, our Lee Kuan Yew School of Public Policy (LKYSPP), which has an Executive Education arm, has trained 3,000 leaders from South Asia in government and public policy. In addition, five of the 18 official chapters of the LKYSPP are in South Asian countries, namely, India, Pakistan, Bangladesh, Sri Lanka and Bhutan.

We have an active and growing base of alumni who are Indian nationals, the vast majority of whom are of prime working age. This augurs well for increasing the diversity and density of linkages among India, Singapore and Southeast Asia in the years ahead. We also have an official alumni chapter in New Delhi which is actively promoting engagements and interactions.

Entrepreneurship education and exposure is one of NUS' globally recognised strengths. In recent years, we have expanded our efforts internationally and recently launched the NUS Enterprise Summer Programme on Entrepreneurship. The intake has grown steadily and, in 2019, some 200 students from 50 universities across 20 countries participated in the programme. Seeding and promoting entrepreneurial creativity among an emerging generation of young people across the world will be critical to tackling some of the most pressing challenges now confronting us.

With its immense size, and pace of change, India is a nation at the forefront of navigating the complexities of rapid development. These challenges encompass a wide spectrum of issues, including urbanisation, health education and resource management, amongst many others. To achieve maximum impact, solutions will have to be effective, integrated, sustainable and widely deployable. In time, India will also be well placed to share its successful solutions and insights with other nations and communities, opening the way for further adaptations or innovations.

In considering these challenges and solutions, higher education can play a transformative role, as universities can uniquely offer an integrated and holistic approach in the development of human talent, application of science and technology, and creation of new markets. Here, India's leading institutions of higher learning have gained growing recognition, with global ranking agencies such as Quacquarelli Symonds publishing a ranking of Indian universities. The Indian Institutes of Technology lead the way, with their renowned focus on technology and engineering.

India has articulated bold future visions in three distinct areas of development, and their successful implementation will require close linkages between education, research and solutioning. These three areas are in close alignment with NUS' own strategic priorities, based upon our assessment of the most important future challenges where universities can make an impact. We have dedicated substantial resources in recent years building up human talent and research capabilities in these areas.

The first is urbanisation and digital cities. A 2019 United Nations (UN) report stated that the Asia-Pacific region had become majority urban for the first time in human history, with more than 2.3 billion people living in cities. India is among the leading nations experiencing unprecedented, rapid urban growth: by 2050, it is projected that India will have added 416 million urban dwellers. Cities in India are projected to be major drivers of innovation and employment, with 70 percent of future employment occurring in cities.

In response, India has unveiled a vision for 100 'Smart Cities' that will utilise the latest technologies, particularly digital technologies, as an enabler to design and create better infrastructure and services, and create environments that reduce inefficiencies while raising the quality of life. Singapore has also embarked on its version of smart cities, with its 'Smart Nation' initiative. It calls for a whole-of-nation approach in the use and integration of next-generation technologies to create a better life for all citizens. NUS has dedicated an entire research cluster with an interdisciplinary focus in key smart city domains such as data science, analytics and optimisation, artificial intelligence, and cybersecurity.

The second area would be resource management and climate change mitigation. Every country's sustainable development journey will be unique. Unlike Singapore, which is equatorial, India's geographic and climatic conditions vary enormously, ranging from deserts and forests to snow-capped mountain ranges.

Nonetheless, responsible resource management and climate change mitigation are important components of sustainable development, and to that end, India has ratified the UN Paris Agreement on climate change. These issues will also take on increasing importance in discussions and exchanges between nations regarding trade, community, technology and natural resources. The countries most able to adapt, innovate and manage resources efficiently and sustainably will gain considerable advantage.

India has pledged ambitious goals, such as deriving 40 percent of installed electric power capacity by 2030 from non-fossil-based energy resources, as well as creating an additional carbon sink of 2.5 to 3 billion tonnes of carbon dioxide equivalent through additional forests and tree cover, also by 2030. Singapore's target is to cap greenhouse gas (GHG) emissions by 2030, and then halve its 2030 peak GHG by 2050, and to achieve net zero emissions as soon as conditions and technology allow.

To support Singapore's objectives, NUS has created the sustainability research cluster, which seeks to explore integrated solutions for tropical, urban and Asian settings. Some key technologies we are looking at include environmental surveillance, waste-to-energy conversion, seawater desalination and sustainable urban transport systems.

Given the complexities and scale of these challenges, there will be many opportunities and, indeed, a need for collaborations among universities, companies and governmental bodies to explore and implement solutions.

The final vision that India has articulated relates to talent training and development. India has entered its 'dividend boom', a period when it will have not only one of the largest workforces in the world, but also the youngest, with a low average age (29 years in 2020), and a correspondingly lower ratio of dependents. Fully capturing the potential of the dividend boom will super-charge India's economic development, but this will require a labour force that is dynamic, adaptable and well-trained to take advantage of market opportunities.

To gear up its manpower, India has unveiled ambitious programmes, such as the Skill India Mission, which aims to impart skills training to 400 million people by 2022, and Start-Up India, which envisages entrepreneurship as a key driver of progress and employment with 50,000 new start-ups, 100 innovation zones, and 500 new incubators and accelerators by 2024.

However, India and the world are also entering an era where disruption to industries and employment has become the norm. Technologies, particularly of the 4th Industrial Revolution, as well as new market entrants, are reshaping entire industries at an accelerated pace. To remain viable, companies and workers will have to embrace lifelong learning and training.

Singapore is seeking to establish lifelong learning as a national movement and as one of the core strengths of its economy. Through the SkillsFuture initiative, the government, employers, individuals and training providers are brought together to map industry training requirements, benchmark qualifications and create flexible pathways for individuals to upgrade continuously and, if need be, transition to new opportunities. In 2019, 500,000 individuals and 14,000 enterprises benefitted from various SkillsFuture programmes.

At NUS, we launched the NUS Lifelong Learners or L^3 programme, which automatically enrolls present and future students for 20 years. This is a transformational initiative that allows our alumni to seamlessly access a diverse catalogue of short courses, modular programmes and post-graduate certifications across our 17 schools and faculties.

The continuous upskilling and re-skilling of an entire adult labour force, while simultaneously allowing for flexible, individualised training pathways, is an exciting and pivotal turning point in how countries envisage education going forward. Much pedagogical innovation will be required, and countries and institutions can gain greatly through sharing insights and experiences.

India's rapid ascent into one of the leading economies of the world will inject tremendous new dynamism into its exchanges and linkages with ASEAN and Singapore. The challenges of sustainable development are formidable but higher education institutions can play an important role in tackling these challenges through an integrated approach in nurturing human talent, advancing science and research, and bringing solutions to market. There is also ample scope for trans-national and trans-regional collaboration between institutions, as this will accelerate learning, spark fresh innovation and amplify positive impact by improving lives and communities across a greater domain.

50

India and the RCEP: Time to Reconsider

Tham Siew Yean

The 10-member states of the Association of Southeast Asian Nations (ASEAN) and six other countries — India, China, Japan, South Korea, Australia and New Zealand — started negotiating for the Regional Comprehensive Economic Partnership (RCEP) in 2013. The agreement would create a free trade area covering half the world's population and just over a third of global gross domestic product. On 4 November 2019, at the Third RCEP Summit, it was announced that 15 out of the 16 participating countries have concluded their negotiations for all 20 chapters of the agreement, which is scheduled for signing in 2020. India withdrew from this mega free trade agreement (FTA) at the last minute as it felt that its concerns were not adequately addressed.

The agreement is considered to be relatively modest, compared to the Comprehensive and Progressive Agreement for Trans-Pacific Partnership (CPTPP) (or Trans-Pacific Partnership [TPP-11]), which is a trade agreement comprising Australia, Brunei, Canada, Chile, Japan, Malaysia, Mexico, New Zealand, Peru, Singapore and Vietnam, as the latter has 30 chapters and deeper provisions. Nevertheless, the RCEP is still a landmark agreement in the current era of increasing protectionism.

There are several reasons for India's retreat from the RCEP. Its past experience with FTAs may have contributed towards its cautious and defensive approach towards the RCEP. India's trade deficit with its previous bilateral FTA partners such as ASEAN, South Korea and Japan has widened after concluding the agreements with them. This is partly because the agreements were not well utilised due to the lack of information and awareness on the part of Indian domestic producers and the complex rules of origins. FTA utilisation is generally dependent on wide dissemination and ease in using the rules of origin to reduce the compliance costs. Current empirical evidence indicates that FTA utilisation tends to increase over time as the business community becomes more aware of the opportunities and learns to navigate the rules of origin requirements.

Based on its less favourable experience, India feared that its participation in the RCEP would further widen its trade deficit due to a potential influx of imports as it has the highest average tariff rates on all imports, compared to the other participating countries. Domestic protests and lobbying from the protected industries, which were afraid of the impending competition, especially from China, further compounded India's difficulties in the trade negotiations for the RCEP.

Two possible solutions were suggested by India and both were hotly debated by the participating countries. The first was the rules of origin requirements in the agreement. India preferred requiring a value-add of more than 25 percent for an exporter to a country as the country of origin for any product. The RCEP's rules allowed for value addition to take place in any of the member countries. Second, India pitched for an auto-trigger mechanism in the RCEP as a remedy against a sudden and significant surge in imports to protect its domestic players but this did not garner the support of the other participating countries.

India also did not favour the idea of free market access for digitally-traded goods since it did not support the free flow of data and sharing of source codes. However, the RCEP includes a chapter on e-commerce which would be problematic for India even if the problems on the trade in goods could be resolved.

However, taking a step back also implies missed opportunities. In not taking an offensive approach, some of India's manufacturing exports such as automobiles, pharmaceutical products and cotton have lost the market access gains accorded by the agreement. Services exports are another beneficiary which would have contributed towards a better trade balance for India. Should these be penalised for some inefficient domestic producers?

There is also the need for a deeper understanding of trade beyond the mere trade of final goods. Imported intermediate inputs can help to lower the costs of production for domestic industries that are allowed to import these goods, thereby enhancing their competitiveness in the domestic and export markets.

The RCEP would have reduced the complexities that Indian businesses would have to deal with in trading with the RCEP partners. The agreement would have reduced the transaction costs for businesses by removing the famously spaghetti-bowl effect of different rules of origin in the bilateral FTAs between the RCEP partners into a single, consistent and cohesive set of trade rules. Indian businesses that plan and or wish to export to the participating RCEP countries will definitely suffer from the lost prospects of an easier access to the partner countries.

The RCEP would also have provided India with a presence in the regional economic architecture since it is not a member of the Asia-Pacific Economic Cooperation or the ASEAN-Plus Three.

However, the ongoing Coronavirus pandemic is providing India with another opportunity to reconsider its decision. The pandemic has ravaged the economy, as in other countries, with an estimated loss of US$2.1 billion (S$2.97 billion) for 2020 for the tourism and hospitality sector alone. Services, including tourism and hospitality, contribute to as much as 55 percent to the economy. A survey conducted by the Center for Monitoring Indian Economy suggested that the unemployment rate was about 23.4 percent for the week ended 5 April 2020. The International Monetary Fund, in April 2020, has further cut down India's growth estimate to 4.2 percent and 1.9 percent for 2020 and 2021 respectively from its earlier January 2020 estimate of 4.8 percent for 2020 and 5.8 percent for 2021.

Hence, India, as is the case with many other countries, needs new investments that can create more jobs. Inward foreign direct investment (FDI) in India has gone more into services than manufacturing. An analysis of the FDI data from 2000 to 2019 indicates that the services sector, such as financial services, software, telecommunication, construction and trading, attracted the lion's share (65.4 percent) while only 34 percent went into manufacturing. Critically, more than half of the FDI (55 percent) in manufacturing from 2004 to 2014 was in the form of mergers and acquisitions rather than greenfield investments which are needed for the creation of new manufacturing capacities and employment. FDI in manufacturing is important as it typically creates more employment than services and can potentially bring in more capital especially for capital-intensive manufacturing that is expensive to establish. More importantly, it enables manufacturing production in the host economy to connect with the global value chains that are governed by multinational production.

On the global front, the pandemic has escalated the pressures for export-oriented companies in China, especially multinationals, to again consider relocating their manufacturing plants. This pressure first emerged towards the end of the 2000s with the increase in the costs of production as demand especially for labour outstripped supply, thereby reducing China's low-wage advantage. The shift out of China was subsequently reinforced by the 2018 trade war between the United States and China. Global value chains are increasingly considering reducing their dependence on China and multinationals will be assessing shifts to home or third countries. Some FDI source countries are actively facilitating this shift. The Japanese government, for example, has earmarked US$2.2 billion (S$3.1 billion) of its stimulus package to enable Japanese manufacturers to shift their production lines out of China and back to Japan.

The earlier relocation, especially for export-oriented, labour-intensive manufacturing, prior to the current pandemic, has benefitted several member countries of ASEAN, especially Vietnam, which has used this opportunity to expand its manufacturing capacity as well as upgrade its position in the region's global value chains. Samsung, which has invested considerably in Vietnam, has also moved into research and development there as well as in complementary investments in services such as transportation that will facilitate the exports of goods produced by Samsung in Vietnam.

India can offer competitive, if not better, locational advantages to host the impending relocation of manufacturing investments with the realignment of global value chains as a result of the pandemic. It has a strategic and central location in the Indian Ocean, a large human resource base, demographic advantages, knowledge clusters and a growing large domestic market.

What India lacks, however, is a credible commitment towards trade and investment liberalisation. FTAs are the most credible form of trade and investment liberalisation as they are irreversible as compared to unilateral reforms which may change with changing governments. Certainly, for the remaining participating countries in the RCEP, any new investment considerations will definitely prioritise the member countries over non-member countries, given the market access commitments and reductions in transaction costs as explained earlier.

Moreover, the World Trade Organization has projected that world trade will fall steeply in every region in the world and in every sector of the economy in 2020. Now, more than ever before, the RCEP is crucial to keep markets open to trade and investment that will in turn help economies recover from the economic crisis as a result of the pandemic.

India should seize the chance to use the RCEP to facilitate its own economic recovery. The only other current trade agreement that can promote trade and investment is the TPP-11, of which India is not a member and even less likely to join since it was not a party to the negotiations and the terms of the agreement may be even more difficult for India to accept compared to the RCEP.

India still has the opportunity to join the RCEP as the door has been kept open for it. Nonetheless, although invited, India did not attend the subsequent RCEP meetings in 2020. However, the current pandemic has changed the global and domestic landscapes to such an extent that the decision to be or not to be a part of the RCEP may now need to consider other areas, such as services, investment and the employment potential of the agreement. India should take advantage of these opportunities to renegotiate and resolve the outstanding issues it has with the agreement rather than miss the boat completely.

About the Authors

Goh Chok Tong was Singapore's Prime Minister from 1990 to 2004. Between 1979 and 1990, he served as Minister for Trade and Industry, Health and Defence, and was Deputy Prime Minister from 1985 to 1990. After relinquishing the premiership in 2004, Mr Goh remained in the Cabinet as Senior Minister and was Chairman of the Monetary Authority of Singapore (MAS). Upon leaving Cabinet in 2011, he was given the honorary title of Emeritus Senior Minister, and appointed Senior Advisor to MAS. In 2017, Mr Goh was appointed Chairman of the Governing Board of the Lee Kuan Yew School of Public Policy at the National University of Singapore.

Section I: Thinking About The Past

A. Mani, PhD, is Professor Emeritus at the Ritsumeikan Asia Pacific University, Japan. His academic career spans the ISEAS-Yusof Ishak Institute, University of Brunei Darussalam and the National University of Singapore. His research, published as journal articles, book chapters and books, cover migration, education and ethnicity in Southeast Asia.

Eirliani Abdul Rahman FRSA published *Survivors: Breaking the Silence on Child Sexual Abuse* in 2017. She works with Nobel laureate Kailash Satyarthi and won the 2015 BMW Foundation Responsible Leaders Award. Ms Eirliani holds a Master of Science in Public

Administration and Public Policy from the London School of Economics, United Kingdom.

Umej Bhatia studied at Cambridge University and Harvard University. A career diplomat and historian, he has written on Crusades and violent extremism. His latest book, *Our Name is Mutiny*, (Landmark Books 2019), uncovers the true story of revolt against the British Empire and the hidden history of the Singapore Mutiny.

Meira Chand's multi-cultural heritage is reflected in her nine novels. Her book, *A Different Sky*, was long-listed for the Impac Dublin award 2012, and on Oprah Winfrey's reading list. She has a PhD in Creative Writing and is involved in promoting literature in Singapore.

Nalina Gopal is Curator at the Indian Heritage Centre and oversees its curatorial team. Her recent publications include *Sojourners to Settlers: Tamils in Southeast Asia and Singapore* (co-edited with Arun Mahizhnan) and *Singapore Indian Heritage* (2017). Apart from the permanent galleries, she recently curated exhibitions at the Centre on the lesser known aspects of Singapore's Indian heritage.

Arun Mahizhnan is Special Research Advisor at the Institute of Policy Studies, Lee Kuan Yew School of Public Policy, National University of Singapore. He is also Director, Centre for Singapore Tamil Culture, a voluntary organisation to promote interculturalism. His edited publications include *Sojourners to Settlers: Tamils in Southeast Asia and Singapore* and *Singapore Chronicles*, a 50-volume book series commemorating Singapore's 50th anniversary.

Mustafa Izzuddin, a Dawoodi Bohra Muslim, is an Adjunct Senior Lecturer with the University Scholars Programme at the National University of Singapore. He was formerly a Research Fellow with the Institute of South Asian Studies and ISEAS-Yusof Ishak Institute. He received his PhD in International Relations from the London School of Economics and Political Science.

K. Kesavapany was Director of the Institute of Southeast Asian Studies from 2002 to 2012. He is currently a Board member of the Puan Noor Aishah Intercultural Institute. He holds several civic and community appointments. He recently published his biography, *From Estate to Embassy: Memories of an Ambassador.*

Sat Pal Khattar studied Law and served as Deputy Public Prosecutor and State Counsel. Later, he started a law practice. He has served on numerous public institutions, including the Public Service Commission, the Presidential Council of Minority Rights and the Securities Industries Council. In 2011, he was conferred the Padma Shri award by the India government for his efforts to promote India-Singapore relations.

Gauri Parimoo Krishnan has dedicated 27 years of her life to the arts and heritage sector in Singapore. She is an art historian, independent curator and museum consultant. She developed the Indian Heritage Centre and the South Asian galleries of the Asian Civilisations Museum at their inception and curated major exhibitions.

M. Rajaram is a lawyer and currently the Chairman of KL Gates Straits Law Practice, a firm co-founded by him. He was actively involved in the Singapore Indian Chamber of Commerce and Industry (SICCI) during the period that India was liberalising its economic policies and was Chairman of SICCI when the historic India-Singapore Comprehensive Economic Cooperation Agreement was signed.

Ma Swan Hoo is a medical professional in the cosmetics industry. She volunteers as a weekend docent at Singapore's museums. Married to an Indian, the late Balaji Sadasivan, a neurosurgeon turned politician, she helped to bring his book, *The Dancing Girl, A History of Early India*, to publication. She serves on the Advisory Board of the Indian Heritage Centre and Apsaras Arts.

Sureshkumar Muthukumaran is a postdoctoral fellow in the Humanities at Yale-NUS College. He specialises in the history of connectivity in ancient Eurasia, with a particular focus on its eco-biological aspects.

Uma Rajan has received national and community awards during her career in healthcare, arts and community service. Her books include *A Life For Others*, a Buddhist nun's biography and *Spice Potpourri*, which received the World Gourmand Award for the Best Indian Cuisine Book in Singapore and Best Fund Raising, Charity and Community Cookbook in Asia in 2012.

Hernaikh Singh is a Senior Associate Director at the Institute of South Asian Studies in the National University of Singapore (NUS). He has over 20 years of experience in government and non-government organisations, the business sector and the academia. Mr Hernaikh holds a MA (Southeast Asian Studies) and BA (Honours) degrees from NUS.

Vineeta Sinha is Professor and Head, Department of Sociology, National University of Singapore (NUS). She holds a Master in Social Science degree from NUS and Master of Art and PhD from the Johns Hopkins University. Her publications include *A New God in the Diaspora? Muneeswaran Worship in Contemporary Singapore* (2005, NUS Press and NIAS); and *Religion and Commodification: Merchandising Diasporic Hinduism* (2010, Routledge).

Karen Tan is Senior Advisor, International Affairs, at the Ministry of Communications and Information and Singapore's Non-Resident Ambassador to the Caribbean Community. Prior to her retirement from the Foreign Service in 2016, Ms Tan served as Permanent Representative to the United Nations (New York) and the World Trade Organization (Geneva), High Commissioner to India and Ambassador to Laos.

Tan Tai Yong is Professor of Humanities (History) and President of Yale-NUS College. He is Deputy Chairman of the Institute of South Asian Studies in the National University of Singapore. He has written on the partition of India, the Sikh Diaspora and the contemporary history of Singapore. His recent publications include *700 Years. A History of Singapore* (co-authored, 2019) and *The Idea of Singapore. Smallness Unconstrained* (2019).

Jonathan Tow covered Singapore-India relations in the Ministry of Foreign Affairs from 2011 to 2018 as Deputy High Commissioner to India and Director General for South Asia and Sub-Saharan Africa. During this period, he oversaw negotiations for the India-Singapore Strategic Partnership. He was appointed Singapore's Ambassador to Turkey in 2019.

Walter Woon is a David Marshall Professor, National University of Singapore; and Dean, Singapore Institute of Legal Education. He is the author of The Advocate's Devil Quartet of novels (*The Advocate's Devil*; *The Devil to Pay*; *The Devil and the Deep Blue Sea*; and *The Devil's Circle*), set during World War II and dealing in part with the Indian National Army's activities.

Section II: Thinking About The Present

Zulkifli Baharudin is Executive Chairman of Indo-Trans Logistics Corporation, a logistics and supply chain company across Indochina. He is also an independent director of several companies in Singapore, China, the United Kingdom and the United States. He is also currently Singapore's Non-Resident Ambassador to Kazakhstan and Uzbekistan.

Gautam Banerjee is a senior managing director and Chairman of Blackstone Singapore. He was previously Executive Chairman of PricewaterhouseCoopers Singapore. Mr Banerjee serves as a non-executive director of several companies, including Singapore Airlines Limited and Singapore Telecommunications Limited. He served as a nominated member of the Singapore Parliament from 2007 to 2009.

Manu Bhaskaran is a Partner of the Centennial Group, a strategic advisory firm headquartered in Washington DC. As Founding Chief Executive Officer of its Singapore subsidiary, Centennial Asia Advisors, he coordinates the Asian business of the Group which provides independent economic research on Asian political and macro-economic trends.

Lawrence Boo is an international arbitrator. He has sat in more than 300 international commercial and investment disputes. He was the founding Chief Executive Officer and Registrar of the Singapore International Arbitration Centre and, later, its Deputy Chairman. He has been teaching international arbitration at the Law Faculty at the National University of Singapore since 1994.

Chan Jia Hao was a Research Analyst at the Institute of South Asian Studies in the National University of Singapore from January 2018 to September 2020. His research focused on international technology developments and policies across South and Southeast Asia. On youth engagement, Mr Chan represented Singapore in the United States-Young Southeast Asian Leaders Initiative TechCamp in 2017.

Francis Chong leads the Ministry of Trade and Industry's (MTI) Emerging Markets Division to grow Singapore's trade with the countries of Africa, Central Asia, Latin America, the Middle East and South Asia. He also leads MTI's Singapore-India Partnership Office on a mission to draw the two countries closer through public-, private- and people-sector partnerships.

Rosa Daniel is Deputy Secretary (Culture) in the Singapore Ministry of Culture, Community and Youth and Chief Executive Officer of the National Arts Council. She was Chief Executive of the National Heritage Board from February 2013 to May 2017. Prior to joining the culture sector, Mrs Daniel held senior appointments in the economic and social sectors.

Piyush Gupta is Chief Executive Officer and Director of DBS Group. He is Vice-Chairman of the Institute of International Finance, Washington, and a member of the United Nations Secretary-General's Task Force on Digital Financing of the Sustainable Development Goals, and Singapore's Advisory Council on the Ethical Use of AI and Data.

Vikram Khanna is Associate Editor and economic affairs commentator at *The Straits Times*, where he has worked since 1993. Earlier, he served at the International Monetary Fund in Washington DC. He has Bachelor of Arts, Master of Arts and Master of Philosophy degrees in economics from the University of Cambridge, United Kingdom.

Asad Latif is a former journalist with *The Straits Times*. He graduated with Honours in English from Presidency College, Calcutta. He was a Chevening Scholar in History at Cambridge and a Fulbright Visiting Scholar at Harvard. Among his books is *Celebrating Europe: An Asian Journey* (Institute of Southeast Asian Studies, 2012).

Lim Thuan Kuan is currently Singapore's High Commissioner to the United Kingdom. He was High Commissioner to India, with concurrent accreditation as Singapore's Ambassador to Bhutan and Nepal (resident in New Delhi), from 2013 to 2020. Prior to that, he was Singapore's Ambassador to Vietnam from 2005 to 2008 before becoming the first Singapore Permanent Representative to the Association of Southeast Asian Nations in 2009.

N. Varaprasad was Principal/Chief Executive Officer of Temasek Polytechnic, Deputy President of National University of Singapore and Chief Executive of the National Library Board. He is now a partner in an international education consultancy, Singapore Education Consulting Group LLP, and has provided advisory services in Southeast Asia, the Middle East and Africa.

Ong Keng Yong is the Executive Deputy Chairman of S. Rajaratnam School of International Studies in Nanyang Technological University, Singapore. He was previously High Commissioner of Singapore to India and later Secretary-General of the Association of Southeast Asian Nations. He co-chairs the India-Singapore Strategic Dialogue with his Indian counterpart.

Gopinath Pillai is Chairman of the Management Board of the Institute of South Asian Studies in the National University of Singapore; Ambassador-at-Large in the Ministry of Foreign Affairs; and Chairman of the Indian Heritage Centre. For his efforts to advance Singapore-India relations, the Indian government conferred upon him the Padma Shri Award in 2012. He has also received several awards from the Singapore government.

Leena Pinsler is a senior Singapore lawyer and consultant with Drew & Napier LLC. Following the signing of the India-Singapore Comprehensive Economic Cooperation Agreement in 2005, she co-authored a book on the treaty. She was also an adjunct professor at the National University of Singapore where she taught a course on Indian business law.

Rajesh Rai is Head of the South Asian Studies Programme in the National University of Singapore. His research interests include diaspora studies and South Asian nationalism, postcolonial history and politics. He is the author of *Indians in Singapore, 1819–1945: Diaspora in the Colonial Port City* (Oxford University Press, 2014). He has also edited and co-edited several books on the South Asian/Indian diaspora.

Zainul Abidin Rasheed last served as Singapore's Senior Minister of State for Foreign Affairs. He is now Non-Resident Ambassador to Kuwait. He is also a member of the Nanyang Technological University Board of Trustees and Board of Directors of Mediacorp. He has had a fulfilling career in news media, government and community service.

Viswa Sadasivan is the Chief Executive Officer of Strategic Moves, a leading corporate strategy consulting practice. He is a sought-after speaker and has interviewed several world leaders and moderated over 300 policy forums. He is an accomplished international mediator. Mr Sadasivan served a term as Nominated Member of Parliament in Singapore. He has a Master of Public Administration degree from Harvard University.

See Chak Mun has served as Singapore's Ambassador to Australia, the Federal Republic of Germany and India, and as Permanent Representative to the United Nations and General Agreement on Tariffs and Trade/World Trade Organization in Geneva. He has written a monograph on *India's Strategic Interests in Southeast Asia and Singapore* (2009).

Kirpal Singh retired after 45 years of university teaching in 2017. He was last Director of the Wee Kim Wee Centre at Singapore Management University. He has more than 150 publications to his name and is a highly sought-after speaker at global conferences and seminars. He is currently Director of the Centre for Educational Leadership, Training Vision Institute.

Sinderpal Singh is Senior Fellow and Coordinator of the South Asia Programme and the Regional Security Architecture Programme at the S. Rajaratnam School of International Studies, Nanyang Technological University, Singapore. He received his PhD from the University of Wales, Aberystwyth. He received his earlier degrees from the Australian National University and the National University of Singapore.

Tan Khee Giap is Co-Director of the Asia Competitiveness Institute at the Lee Kuan Yew School of Public Policy, National University of Singapore. He is also the Chairman of the Singapore National Committee for Pacific Economic Cooperation. He has consulted extensively with Singapore ministries, statutory boards and government linked companies, as well as international agencies.

Ravi Velloor is Associate Editor and Asia columnist with *The Straits Times*. His four-decade career in journalism has included stints with *Bloomberg News*, *Time Warner Inc.* and *Agence France-Presse*. A Jefferson Fellow, he is a frequent panelist and moderator on international fora. His book, *India Rising: Fresh Hope, New Fears*, was released in May 2016.

Benjamin Yap is Senior Vice-President at CapitaLand where, till recently, he headed the Amaravati Project. Prior to that, he was Group Director (South Asia) at International Enterprise Singapore where he actively promoted trade and investment between Singapore and India. In his spare time, Mr Yap enjoys sharing a hearty Indian meal with close friends and family.

Section III: Thinking About The Future

Tommy Koh is a Professor of Law at the National University of Singapore and an Ambassador-at-Large at the Ministry of Foreign Affairs. He is the Co-Chairman of the China-Singapore Forum and the Japan-Singapore Symposium. He served as the founding Co-Chairman of the India-Singapore Strategic Dialogue for 10 years.

Kishore Mahbubani is a veteran diplomat, student of philosophy and author of eight books. He is currently a Distinguished Fellow at the Asia Research Institute, National University of Singapore (NUS). He is also a former Permanent Secretary of the Ministry of Foreign Affairs and the Founding Dean of the Lee Kuan Yew School of Public Policy, NUS.

Dipinder S. Randhawa is an Adjunct Senior Fellow at the S. Rajaratnam School of International Studies in the Nanyang Technological University. He was earlier at the National University of Singapore Business School and the Institute of South Asian Studies. His research interests are in the area of Development Economics and Finance. Dr Randhawa received his PhD from Syracuse University.

Tharman Shanmugaratnam is Senior Minister in Singapore. He served as Deputy Prime Minister for nine years, and as Minister for Finance and Minister for Education earlier. Internationally, he chairs the Group of Thirty, and was chair of the G20 Eminent Persons Group on Global Financial Governance. He also co-chairs the Global Education Forum and the advisory board for the United Nations' Human Development Report.

Pushpanathan Sundram was the Deputy Secretary General of the Association of Southeast Asian Nations (ASEAN) from 2009 to 2011. He held various senior positions as a professional staff with the ASEAN Secretariat from 1997 to 2008. He is currently the Chief Executive Officer of PublicPolicyAsia Advisors, a business advisory firm in Singapore.

Tan Eng Chye was appointed President of National University of Singapore on 1 January 2018. He is the University's fifth president and the 23rd leader to head Singapore's oldest higher education institution. As President, Professor Tan is the chief academic and administrative officer of the university.

Tham Siew Yean is a Visiting Senior Fellow at the ISEAS-Yusof Ishak Institute, Singapore, and Professor Emeritus, Universiti Kebangsaan Malaysia. Her latest publication includes a monograph, *China in Malaysia: State-Business Relations and the New Order of Investment Flows*, co-authored with Edmund Terence Gomez, Ran Li and Kee Cheok Cheong (Springer Singapore, forthcoming, 2020).

Index

A

B

J

M

O

P

Q

R

S

T

U

V